AF352543

LEGISLATION AND REQUIREMENTS FOR PERMISSIBLE COHABITATION IN INVALID MARRIAGES

THE CATHOLIC UNIVERSITY OF AMERICA

CANON LAW STUDIES

No. 356

LEGISLATION AND REQUIREMENTS FOR PERMISSIBLE COHABITATION IN INVALID MARRIAGES

A Historical Synopsis and a Commentary

A DISSERTATION

SUBMITTED TO THE FACULTY OF THE SCHOOL OF CANON LAW OF THE CATHOLIC UNIVERSITY OF AMERICA IN PARTIAL FULFILLMENT OF THE REQUIREMENTS FOR THE DEGREE OF DOCTOR OF CANON LAW

BY

REV. BERNARD O. SULLIVAN, J.C.L.

A PRIEST OF THE DIOCESE OF BELLEVILLE, ILLINOIS

THE CATHOLIC UNIVERSITY OF AMERICA PRESS

WASHINGTON, D. C.

1954

Respectfully Dedicated

With

Reverence and Gratitude

To

His Excellency

The Most Reverend Albert R. Zurowste, D. D.

Bishop of Belleville

Family life is the very basis or foundation of our social structure. Because a sound, Christian home-life has a tremendous bearing on the salvation of immortal souls, the Divine Founder of the Church elevated the institution of marriage to the exalted dignity of a sacrament. More than once He emphasized the indissolubility of the marriage bond. The Church, from its very inception in a world blighted by the laxity of Jewish and Pagan-Roman divorce practices, has incessantly fought for the sacredness of the marriage bond, the sanctity of the home and the integrity of family life. In the course of history the Church has more and more integrated its doctrines, consolidated its traditions and reinforced its laws and regulations regarding marriage.

Despite the generosity of God and the constant effort of the Church for these nineteen centuries, one finds that the Christian civilization is Christian in name rather than in fact in many instances. There has been inherited a culture strongly molded by secularism, and in its secular outlook society places the stamp of approval on the ever increasing practice of divorce. In the United States alone, with its many pagan influences, approximately twenty-five percent of the marriages end in divorce. Over 4½ millions of divorces were reported for the years 1940 to 1951 inclusively. It is not surprising that some Catholics are included in the thousands and even millions of divorces in the United States, and that all too many of them subsequently become involved in canonically bigamous unions which do not admit of convalidation.

Many non-Catholics feel no need of trying to justify such invalid and bigamous unions, and there are Catholics who endeavor to justify themselves by means of specious arguments. After taking on new obligations and begetting children, the baptized non-Catholics upon their conversion to the Catholic Faith, and the Catholics upon their sincere repentance and desire again to receive the saving graces of the sacraments of Penance and Holy Communion, are faced with the problem of complete separation. Frequently these people become discouraged. Their longing to enter the Church or again to partake of the benefits of sacramental life is hindered, since they do not feel free, and in fact are not free, to cast off the obligations incurred through their invalid union . . . obligations which bind in justice and which, in some instances, are enforceable at civil law.

It is because the Church like a good shepherd desires the salvation of the entire flock that it seeks to take care not only of the faithful sheep within the fold, but also goes out after the sheep lost along the way. To accomplish this the Church uses all known remedies for the convalidation of such marriages. When all else has failed and the marriage cannot be convalidated, the Church, in certain cases and under very strict conditions, grants to the couple the permission of living together as brother and sister.

Because of the delicate and serious nature of such permission, it must be immediately added that canonists and theologians uniformly warn that the sanctioned cohabitation in the brother-sister arrange-ment is a *"res plena periculis"* and is seldom to be recommended; some say *"raro"* (Vermeersch-Creusen, Merkelbach, Sporer-Bier-baum); others say *"rarissime"* (De Smet, Genicot, Coronata, Chrétien, Payen); others say *"fere numquan"* (Gasparri, Vlaming-Bender, Cap-pello). It is evident that all apparantly mean to say as Chelodi and Wernz-Vidal put it: "Cohabitation on the brother-sister basis is per-missible only in extraordinary circumstances and when no other remedy is possible."

However, because of the current flood of divorces and remarriages, the number of requests for such permission has increased consider-ably and will undoubtedly increase in a greater degree in a relatively short time. In fact, it does not seem unreasonable to think that every pastor and confessor has encountered or soon will encounter some cases in which cohabitation of this kind (frater-soror), if permissible, may become the only happy and Christian solution of a tragic situation. But, since the Code of Canon Law is completely silent in the matter; since theological and canonical authors say little about this drastic remedy, and then only in general terms; and finally, since there are practically no published decisions of the Holy See except in the case involving a priest,[1] the normal pastor or confessor remains uncertain as to what can be done. Because of the meager literature on the practical principles and procedure that attend the handling of this *"res plena periculis,"* [2]some chancery offices seem to refuse all cases as a matter of course. As a result there is a tendency among those in the active ministry to regard this remedy for invalid marriages as highly impractical and therefore never, or at best most rarely, to be used. This is indeed, a safe point of view, but as Bishop Krol pointed out, "it can be carried to unwarranted extremes."[3]

It is a fact, as Doctor Joseph Donovan, J.C.D· pointed out, that an act wrongly done is not the same as if it were not done at all. Working with this principle as coupled with extenuating circumstance, one finds that the "brother-sister" permission is available and can be employed as a practical solution in some cases—which cases are constantly increasing. Those who have dedicated their lives to the cause of saving souls must employ, according to right reason, every lawful and practical means of promoting this cause. Canon law and moral theology are practical sciences. The principles of these sciences must be rigidly applied to all the practical problems which confront the Church today.

It is the purpose of the present work to give a brief historical synopsis and a canonical commentary on the legislation and requirements for permissible cohabitation in invalid marriages, otherwise known as the *"brother-sister arrangement"* or *"fraternal cohabitation."* In the historical portion it is shown that during the early cen-

---

[1] The Sacred Penitentiary decreed on April 18, 1936, that absolution from the censure incurred by a priest who has attempted marriage, where separation is impossible, is reserved exclusively to the Sacred Penitentiary. (S. Poenit., April 18, 1936) · *Acta Apostolicae Sedis Commentarium Officiale* (Romae, 1909-1929; Civitate Vaticana, 1929—) XXVIII (1936), 242-243 (hereafter cited as AAS). To eliminate any remaining misunderstanding the S. Poenit. issued a "Declaratio" on the decree *"Lex Sacri Coelibatus"* in May, 1937. *AAS,* XXIX (1937), 283.

[2] Bishop John Krol, D. D., now an Auxiliary in the Cleveland Diocese, in a paper delivered on October 11, 1950, to the Canon Law Society of America, pointed out the practicality of using the brother-sister arrangement. He also outlined the procedure followed in the Diocese of Cleveland. Cf. *The Jurist,* XI (1951), 7-32.

[3] Cf. John Krol, "Permission to Parties Invalidly Married to Live as Brother and Sister," *The Jurist,* XI (1951), 10.

turies of the Church's history this arrangement was definitely permitted by the the Church as a method of attaining greater spiritual
perfection. Attention is given to the origin of this "brother-sister"
arrangement as a canonical remedy for invalid marriages and to its
jurisprudential development after the Council of Trent.

By way of canonical commentary, it is the main purpose of this
work to expose the nature and rôle of the brother-sister arrangement
as a practical and salutary remedy for invalid marriges and at the
same time to emphasize the careful consideration that must be given
the five main elements involved, viz., the absence of any other solution: the forestalling of scandal; the avoidance of the occasion of
sin; the presence of proportionate reason; the concession of the proper
permission. Special attention is given to the application of this
canoncial remedy with reference to marriages invalid by reason of
the impediments of prior bond, impotence, consanguinity, Holy
Orders, and specific criminality (crimen). The objective requirements for the use of the brother-sister arrangement as well as the
subjective requirements on the part of the parties concerned are
treated. Important also is the rôle of the confessor, the pastor and
the local ordinary in the granting of the permission.

It is hoped that the present work will prove beneficial not only
to the repentant souls who find themselves intimately involved in this
dilemna, but also to the priest and the local ordinary who are faced
with the rapidly increasing problem of incurably invalid marriages
in which a complete separation is morally impossible.

Grateful acknowledgement is due and is humbly offered to
the Most Reverend Albert R. Zuroweste, D. D., Bishop of Belleville,
Illinois, for the opportunity to pursue graduate studies in Canon Law
at the Catholic University of America; to the Director of this dissertation, Dr. Clement V. Bastnagel, J.U.D.; to the Faculty of the
School of Canon Law for their devoted encouragement and assista-
ance; to my classmates and friends for the many helpful services
they afforded in the preparation of this dissertation; and finally to
Joseph N. Buechler, Fr. Carl Pimeskern and my beloved parents for
their generous efforts in the final preparation of this work.

TABLE OF CONTENTS

Table of Contents

CHAPTER

LEGISLATION AND REQUIREMENTS FOR PERMISSIBLE COHABITATION IN INVALID MARRIAGES

PART ONE

HISTORICAL SYNOPSIS

INTRODUCTION

Actually the subject of the *"frater-soror"* arrangement is not a novel idea, although the use of the phrase *"cohabitatio fraterna"* to indicate one of the four possible solutions suggested by modern authors for marriages which cannot be convalidated may be very recent.[1] Explicit use of the brother-sister arrangement as a remedy for hopelessly invalid marriages is not found until the Middle Ages. As such it did not emerge as a definite canonical entity until the Decretals of Gregory IX were published as the official law of the Church.

The brother-sister arrangement and the phrase *"cohabitatio fraterna"* were used in the earliest days of the Church not however as a remedy for invalid marriages. The Fathers of the early Church used the phrase *"cohabitatio fraterna"* to indicate that the brother-sister arrangement which both married and unmarried people entered solely out of a motive of greater spiritual perfection or for a higher way of life. The early councils and the popes pointed to the use of this arrangement in the discipline of the clergy. Its early use, therefore, seems to have been limited to cases in which a valid marriage or no marriage at all was involved. There seems to have been a complete

---

[1] Of the various authors consulted, only one uses the phrase *"cohabitatio fraterna."* Cf. Coronata, *Institutiones Iuris Canonici, De Sacramentis,* III (Taurini, Romae: Marietti, 1946) p. 929, (hereafter cited *De Sacramentis*). The common way of expressing this canonical entity is: *"cohabitatio uti frater et soror."*

unawareness of this brother-sister arrangement as a remedy or "last resort" solution for incurably invalid marriages.

It was possibly in the tenth century, but certainly so in the twelfth, that this arrangement was definitely used as a solution for invalid marriages ... and then only for marriages invalid by reason of impotence. There is no evidence that this arrangement was employed as a solution for marriages invalid by reason of any other diriment impediment until almost modern times. The eminent canonist and moralist Reiffenstuel (1642-1703) played a major rôle in the integration and expression of earlier canonical and theological principles, which probably prepared the way for more recent canonists and moralists to formulate and extend the requirements and legislation for the brother-sister arrangement. Only after Reiffenstuel had prepared the way did the later authors see fit to apply this canonical remedy to marriages invalid, not only by reason of impotence, but also by reason of any diriment impediment of the divine or ecclesiastical dispensation.

From a spiritual point of view, therefore, it must be admitted that the "cohabitatio fraterna" spoken of by the Fathers is entirely different from the "cohabitatio fraterna" spoken of by modern authors. But it must also be admitted that in its physical structure the very same thing is meant in both cases, i. e., a total abstinence from any and all sexual or marital relations.[2]

It is felt that the brother-sister arrangement as found in the Fathers and early church writers may have had some bearing on its more recent use as a solution of "last resort" for invalid marriages. Some of the principles, conditions and mandates involved are the same in both. For this reason and also inasmuch as it may help to clarify the legal mind of the Church regarding the brother-sister arrangement, the historical section of this work points not only to the origin of the brother-sister arrangement as a canonical remedy or solution for invalid marriages, but also to its origin and use in earlier Church legislation as a means of spiritual perfection and disciplinary measures. Consequently, the "cohabitatio fraterna" or "cohabitation on a brother-

---

[2] Cf. Cappello, *Tractatus Canonico-Moralis de Sacramentis* (5 vols., Vol. V, *De Matrimonio*, 5. ed., Romae: Marietti, 1947), Vol. V, p. 374, n. 370 (hereafter cited *De Matrimonio*).

sister basis" in the historical section of this work is to be understood simply in a physical sense (total abstinence), in abstraction from any and all motivation, unless the contrary be indicated. In the second part of this work (Commentary) the same phrases are to be understood as referring exclusively to that canonical solution that is offered as a last resort for marriages which cannot be convalidated.

The brother-sister arrangement as such is not treated in any particular place in the history of canon law, but the idea is treated either explicitly or implicitly under several topics such as: Continency; Clerics; Divorce; Separation; Impotence; Adultry, etc.

The first and indeed most outstanding case in which the brother-sister arrangement was recognized and even held in highest esteem by the Church, was that of the Blessed Virgin Mary and St. Joseph.

Since there is no longer any essential disagreement regarding the essence of the marriage contract (whether it be consent alone or consent together with consummation), there is likewise no longer any corresponding reason for disagreement as to the reality of the marriage bond that existed between Mary and Joseph. For centuries, however, those who supported the "Copula Theory" denied that the union between Joseph and Mary was a real marriage, precisely because the union was not physically consummated. Consequently, as will be seen later, it is true that many authors sanctioned the use of the brother-sister arrangement in what they considered to be invalid marriages.

When clerical celibacy came into effect, the brother-sister arrangement served as a convenient method for circumventing the problem created in the lives of clerics who were already married and who wished to receive the Order of Priesthood, or, already being priests, desired to continue serving at the altar as priests. This arrangement could apparently lend itself to serve as a form of separation.[3]

For the better understanding of precisely what is meant when it is said that "cohabitatio fraterna" is a form of divorce or separation, it should be noted that a threefold distinction is made by the authors.

---

[3] Canonically taken, the abstaining from conjugal intercourse and its related elements is not strictly called separation. Cf. Bouscaren-Ellis, *Canon Law, A Text and Commentary* (Milwaukee: Bruce, 1946; Reprint 1948), n. 570. (hereafter cited *Canon Law*).

This distinction serves to clarify the nature of the brother-sister arrangement. The first is "*divortium quoad vinculum, seu plenum,*" in which it is understood that the marriage bond is broken and a new marriage may be entered. The second is "*divortium quoad cohabitationem, seu semi-plenum,*" in which the parties are separated from bed, board and cohabitation, but the marriage bond remains. The third type of divorce or separation, the one under consideration here, is "*divortium quoad torum,*" in which the couple continue to cohabit (live together under the same roof), not however as husband and wife, but simply as adult brother and sister. The latter type is, for the validly married couple, a separation from those sexual relations to which they have a fundamental right. For the invalidly married couple it is a separation from that to which they have no right whatsoever.[4]

It is, then, this way of life, the "*cohabitatio fraterna*" (living under the same roof without enjoying the marital rights), about which the discussion will turn. It is the purpose of the historical section of this work to determine, first, that the Church officially recognized and granted such permission to persons validly or invalidly married, or perhaps to persons not married at all, and secondly, to point out under what circumstances such permission may have been granted by law. Historically there is a canonical foundation for the use of this brother-sister arrangement as a solution for invalid marriages.

---

[4] Cf. cans. 1081; 1082; 1128-1131; Cappello, *De Matrimonio*, pp. 791-802, nn. 793-805.

CHAPTER I

A METHOD OF GREATER SPIRITUAL PERFECTION

Article 1.   A Unique Case

The first case of cohabitation on a brother-sister basis recognized by the Church is that of the Blessed Virgin Mary and St. Joseph as recorded in the Sacred Scriptures.[1] The marriage of Joseph and Mary is, without question a unique case by reason of the parties involved, its qualities, purpose and fruits.   As such, it seems appropriate to treat this case individually and in the first place.

The union of Joseph and Mary was indeed a valid marriage, but one in which the marital rights were left unexercised by both Mary and Joseph. They cohabited (lived under the same roof), but maintained a strict *separatio a toro*, for the Church teaches that Mary retained her vow or purpose of virginity in body and soul before, during and after the birth of Christ.[2]

---

[1] Some say that there are two such cases in the Scriptures, since they also consider the marriage of Adam and Eve not to have been consummated in the Garden of Paradise. But it seems that they base their reasons simply on the fact that they had no children while in the Garden. Such a conclusion is, at most, only probable. Cf. Prümmer, *Manuale Theologiae Moralis* 3 vols., Vol. III, ed. E. M. Münch, 10 ed., Barcelona: Herder, 1946, III, p. 447, n. 631.

[2] "Beata Maria semper virgo fuit ante partum, in partu et post partum." (St. Thomas, *Summa Theologica*, III, q. 28). This is "*de fide*" from the ordinary and universal "magisterium" of the Church. Canon 3 of the Lateran Council (649) stated: "Si quis secundum sanctos Patres non confitetur proprie et secundum veritatem Dei Genitricem sanctam semperque Virginem et immaculatam Mariam utpote ipsum Deum Verbum specialiter et veraciter .... absque semine concepisse ex Spiritu Sancto et incorruptibiliter eam [eum?] genuisse, indissolubili permanente et post partum eiusdem virginitate, condemnatus sit ..." cf. Denzinger-Bannwart-Umberg-Rahner, *Enchiridion Symbolorum* (ed. 28 *Augmentata*, Friburgi Brisgoviae: Herder, 1952,) nn. 256, 218, (hereafter cited as Denzinger-Rahner, *Enchiridion Symbolorum*.)

The fact that between Mary and Joseph there existed a true marriage in the proper sense of the word and that, therefore, Joseph was the husband of the virginal Mother of God is unmistakably related in the Gospels. For according to the Jewish mind regarding marital propriety and chastity, two mature persons of different sex and families could not dwell under the same roof or live a common life unless they were married. That Mary and Joseph, from a certain date, had been living together was common knowledge. Joseph had taken Mary "to him" (Math., 1:25), into his home, and was thereafter faithfully attending to his duties as a husband, and Mary doing the same as a wife. Together they went to Bethlehem to be enrolled; together they journeyed to Jerusalem on legal feast days; together they fled to Egypt to escape the persecution of Herod (Math., 2:13-15), and upon their return lived together at Nazareth (Math., 2:23). Jesus was considered by all, even by the Scribes and Pharisees, as the legal son of Mary and Joseph.[3]

Tradition also furnishes full endorsement of the Catholic teaching. Julian the Pelagian had denied that there was a true marriage, and based his argument on the false premise that sexual union was an essential element of marriage. St. Augustine (+430) effectively refuted him in his *Adversus Julianum Pelagianum* cited above. However, apart from this work, one does not find, in general, a clear and uniform teaching of the Fathers and ecclesiastical writers regarding the true marriage between Joseph and Mary. Some seemed even to oppose this teaching. But this is understandable, since they had not as yet a completely clarified notion of the essence of marriage. They did not advert specifically to the "*matrimonium ratum sed non consummatum*", and consequently did not have any concepts regarding virginal marriage.[4]

---

[3] Math., 1:16; 1:19; 1:20; 1:24; Luke, 2:5. St. Augustine, in his *Adversus Julianum*, Lib. V, n. 47, pointed out that the expressions "husband" and "wife" were not mere accommodations to the way of speaking on the part of the Jews of that time. Cf. Migne, *Patrologiae Cursus Completus, Series Latina* (221 vols., Parisiis, 1844-1855) XLIV, 811 (hereafter cited as *MPL*).

[4] Cf. canon 1015.

The early writers in the Church[5] definitely precluded the notion of any marital intercourse between Mary and Joseph, but became ambiguous regarding the marriage itself, since they probably made no formal study of Roman Law, and since they evidently did not consider or fully understand the essential difference between simple betrothal in the Christian sense and betrothal in the Jewish law, which was practically a giving in marriage and therefore a true marriage.[6]

From the earlier confused notions of marriage, a change began to appear with St. Ambrose (+397). The clarity of St. Ambrose was bypassed, however, and authors up to and including Gratian (ca. 1140) used the same confused language, and employed the same in-exact ideas as those who had gone before them.[7] St. Ambrose, before his conversion, had held high positions in the Roman Government. One may assume that accordingly he had a thorough knowledge of Roman law. This may well have led him to investigate fully the question of whether or not a true marriage ex-isted between Mary and Joseph. He became convinced that such a marriage, valid according to the principles of law,[8] existed, and he

---

[5] E. g., Tertullian, Origen, Basil, Chrysostom, Epiphanius, Ephraem, Cyril of Jerusalem, Hilary, Peter Chlrysologus, etc.

[6] Cf. C. F. Wrzaszczak, *The Betrothal Contract in the Code of Canon Law, A Historical Synopsis* (Typewritten Licentiate Dissertation, School of Canon Law, The Catholic University of America: Washington, D. C., un-published) p. 19.

[7] The notion of the essence of marriage remained obscure and confused until the time of Gratian and Gregory IX in the 12th and 13th centuries. At that time the problem of the relationship of marital consent to consummation was at the zenith of discussion and debate. The ideas of the ancient writers, such as Ambrose, had become obscured, and it became imperative to state with finality whether or not "consent" alone effected marriage, or whether "consummation" was likewise necessary. The marriage of Mary and Joseph was a main point of the discussion. But the canonists at Bologna held to the *Copula* theory, and even the eminent Gratian was led somewhat astray in this problem. Some Catholic authors maintained, even as late as 1892, that by *carnal copula* a marriage became true and perfect. Cf. Prümmer, *op. cit.,* III n. 630.

[8] "... non enim coitus matrimonium facit, sed maritalis affectio (i. e. consent). " D. (24.1) (32.13).

defended it in classic language that was afterwards adopted in part by canon law.[9]

All the Fathers writing against the Ebionites and the Cerinthians taught that Christ was born of a virgin. Such Fathers were Aristides, Justin, Iranaeus, Hippolytus, Jerome, etc. They were unanimous in teaching that Mary remained a virgin before, during and after the birth of Christ.[10] But it was St. Ambrose and his great pupil and spiritual son St. Augustine who in clear and precise language pointed out that not only did Mary always remain a virgin, but the marriage was indeed a true and valid marriage.

That Mary and Joseph were not only united in a true marriage, but also lived according to a *"frater-soror"* arrangement is clearly maintained in the works of these great writers. It is even more significant that St. Augustine, later to become recognized as among the greatest doctors of the Church, pointed to the sanction which the Church extended to the practice of married couples who, advanced in grace and perfection, were following the example of Mary and Joseph by living according to this brother-sister arrangement.

St. Ambrose, in his commentary on the Gospel of St. Luke, pointed very definitely to both the virginity and the virginal marriage of the Blessed Mother. He inquired why, according to the wise plan of God, our Lord should have been born of a virgin betrothed to a man.

Divine mysteries are indeed hidden, and according to the saying of the prophets it is not easy for any man to know the plan of God. Nevertheless from the other deeds and precepts of our Lord and Saviour we are able to understand that this was also more in keeping with the divine plan, that she should be chosen to give birth to the Lord who was betrothed to a man.

---

[9] A classic definition of marriage existed at the time: "Viri et mulieris maritalis coniunctio inter legitimas personas individuam vitae consuetudinem retinens." This definition is classic, for it is taken almost verbatim from the Roman Law (*Inst.*, Lib. I. c. 9); also it is found in St. Augustine according to Gratian (c. 3, C. XXVII, q. 2); and in Gregory IX (c. 2, X *De Conversione Infidelium* III, 33) along with many Scholastics of the 13th century.

[10] Nothing explicit is said in the Scriptures about the virginity of the Blessed Mother *"in partu"* and *"post partum,"* but from the words *"virum non cognosco"* and others, the Fathers rightly concluded that there was a divine plan of perpetual virginity.

But why did she not become pregnant before her espousal? Perhaps lest it be said that she had conceived in adultery. And the Scripture clearly demonstrates that she would be both espoused and a virgin: a virgin, that it might be clear that she was free from intercourse with man; espoused, lest she be seared by the infamy of violated virginity, to which desecration the fact of the pregnant womb would seem to point ... A reason of no little weight is found in this, that the virginity of Mary should be kept from the knowledge of the prince of this world.[11] Even more clearly did St. Ambrose speak in two other passages.

Let it not disturb you that Holy Scripture calls Mary wife: for *it is not the deprivation of virginity, but the legally performed marriage contract that establishes the married state;* in fine, no one can dismiss a wife whom he has not taken to wife; therefore he who intended to dismiss her acknowledges thereby that he had taken her to wife.[12]

Nor let it disturb you where she says that Joseph took his wife and went into Egypt, for one espoused to a man has the name wife. For when the marriage is entered upon it gets the name of marriage: for it is not the defloration of virginity that constitutes the marriage, but it is the marriage contract. . . .[13]

Finally, as soon as the maid is joined by a legal act to the man, the marriage begins to exist, not when she is known by him in (sexual) cohabitation.[14]

----

[11] Ambrose, in his commentary on the Gospel of St. Luke, Book II, n. 1 and 3, translation by Anthanasius Dengler, O. S. B. as found in Mueller *The Fatherhood of St. Joseph* (St. Louis: B. Herder, 1952) p. 24. The following translations are taken from the same work.

[12] Ambrose, *ibid*. 5.

[13] Cum enim initiatur coniugium, tunc coniugii nomen adsciscitur: non enim defloratio virginitatis facit coniugium, sed pactio coniugalis." Cf. Ambrose, *De Institutione Virginum*, n. 42— MPL, XVI, 316; Gratian, cc. 5,9,C. XXVII, q. 2; St. Augustine, *De Bono Coniugali* I, c. 2. St. John Chrysostom said: "Matrimonium non facit coitus, sed voluntas." Cf. Migne, *Patrologiae Cursus Completus, Series Graeca* (161 vols., Parisiis, 1857-1866), LVI, 802 (hereafter cited MPG); c. 1, C. XXVII, q. 2.

[14] Cf. Ambrose, *De Institutione Virginum*, n. 42—MPL, XVI, 316.

From these few passages one notes that St. Ambrose definitely maintained the compatibility of the virginity of the Blessed Mother with her true marriage to St. Joseph.

St. Augustine perfected the teaching of his master St. Ambrose. In reading one of his sermons one notes that two reasons led him to a closer investigation of the marriage between Mary and Joseph. The first was the observation that already in his time there were quite a number of married people so far advanced in grace or perfection that with mutual consent for the sake of Christ they practiced continence and thus followed the example of Mary and Joseph. These people were actually living together as brother and sister, as did Mary and Joseph. The question arose whether such a way of life was still embodying the essential characteristics of a marriage, and thus could still claim the name of marriage in the proper sense.

It is not true that for the reason that Joseph had not carnally known the mother of the Lord he was not father, as if it were passion that made a woman one's wife, and not rather conjugal love. Pay attention to this well, dear brethern. Some time in the future the Apostle of Christ was going to declare in the Church: 'It remains that those who have wives be as if they had none.' (1 Cor., 7:29). We know many among the brethern who, advanced in grace, in the name of Christ and with mutual consent abstain indeed from carnal indulgence, but do not at all withhold from each other their conjugal love. The more the former is restrained, the more the latter increases in them. Are those who lead such a life perhaps not wedded because they do not demand from each other the carnal debt? Yet she is subject to her husband as is becoming (Col., 2:18), and this the more so, the more chaste she is; and he, on the other hand, loves his wife truly and, as it is written, in honor and holiness (1 Thess., 4:4) as coheir of grace (1 Pet., 3:7), just as Christ has loved the Church. (Eph., 5:25). *Therefore let no one put asunder those who can lead that life,* nor for that reason refuse the name husband and wife to those who are bound together, though not in the flesh, yet in their hearts.[15]

---

[15] Cf. Augustine, *Sermon* 51—MPL, XXII.

Here St. Augustine not only clearly stated that many married people did live this kind of life (a life of continence which, in effect, was cohabitation on a brother-sister basis), but also expressed his wish that "all could live that way." Especially did he point out in this sermon that Mary and Joseph were united in a true and virginal marriage.

Another occasion to discuss this question was furnished Augustine by the Pelagian and Manichean heresies with their errors concerning concupiscence, marriage and virginity. Augustine set out to explain the Christian position, and naturally this led to a discussion of the virginal marriage of Mary and Joseph.

If married people freely and with mutual consent have chosen to refrain from indulging carnal desires, the marriage bond between them is not loosened thereby: far from it. On the contrary, it will be all the stronger, the firmer that agreement is, an agreement to be kept with even greater love and concord, *not in the union of bodies,* but in the harmony of two hearts beating in unison. Hence there was no falsehood in what the angel said to Joseph: 'Do not be afraid to take to thee Mary thy wife, for what is begotten in her is of the Holy Spirit.' She is called wife ever since she had pledged her troth to him, although *he had not known her carnally, nor was ever to do so;* nor had the name 'Wife' lost its meaning or become a falsehood because there had never been, and never would be, any carnal intercourse. For this virgin was to her husband a source of joy all the more holy and wonderful, because she became a mother without man's intervention, differing from him as regards the offspring, but altogther like him in mutual fidelity . . .[16]

In this great doctor's teaching one finds a clear picture of the

---

[16] St. Augustine, *De Nuptiis et Concupiscentia,* Lib. I, c.2: "Quibus vero placuit ex consensu ab usu carnalis concupiscentiae in perpetuum continere, absit ut inter illos vinculum coniugale rumpatur... Neque enim fallaciter ab angelo dictum est ad Joseph: 'Noli timere accipere Mariam coniugem tuam.' Coniux vocatur ex prima fide desponsationis, quam concubitu nec cognoverat nec fuerat cogniturus."—*MPL,* XLIV, 420; Cf. also *Contra Julianum,* Lib. V, n. 47 — *MPL,* XLIV, 810; also *De Consensu Evangelistarum,* Lib. II, n. 2—*MPL,* XXXIV, 1071.

Church's attitude toward husband and wife living together as brother and sister. All of the ecclesiastical writers up to the time of Gratian in the 12th century recognized and acknowledged the facts that Mary and Joseph lived together and that Mary (and therefore Joseph also) remained a virgin. They witnessed, perhaps unwittingly at times, that these two divinely chosen people lived together as brother and sister. And yet, ostensibly because of a lack of acquaintance with Jewish and Roman law on matrimony, their writings concerning the essence of marriage, and in particular the marriage of Mary and Joseph, remained obscure and indefinite.[17]

Finally, Rupert of Deutz, a Benedictine abbot (d. 1135), following the lead of Ambrose and Augustine, acclaimed St. Joseph as a true husband of the Blessed Virgin Mary, and at the same time witnessed the *"frater-soror"* arrangement between them.

> Carnal corruption alone was absent. . . . but because the union of Mary and Joseph, like their whole life, was heavenly, and the Holy Ghost, engendering in them—for their conversation was in heaven—their conjugal love toward each other, and Himself reigning supreme in their hearts, had entrusted this wife to this husband. . .[18]

Also Hugh of St. Victor (d. 1141) stated explicitly that it was possible for Mary to contract a valid marriage in spite of her resolve or vow of perpetual virginity.

> She was, then, spouse and wife; she was also truly virgin and had not abandoned her resolve to remain a virgin. We declare, therefore, that she was an espoused virgin; we declare that she was a wife, though a virgin; we declare that later on also as mother and virgin she ever kept inviolate her vow of virginity, and that the unfading glory of chastity forever reigned side by side with the purity of the wife and the honor of motherhood. . . In whatever way it was done (how Mary found a vow of chastity compatible with the married state), we must never

---

[17] For a well documented treatment of the formation of Christian Marriage and of the much involved question of the essential factor of marriage (consensual or *copula* theory), see George H. Joyce, S. J., *Christian Marriage* (2. ed., London: Sheed and Ward, 1948), pp. 37-103.

[18] Cf. Rupert Deutz, *In Matth.*, Lib. I, 568—MPL, CLXVIII, 1319.

call in doubt that the Blessed Virgin Mary for definite and well-founded reasons, after having vowed perpetual virginity, entered the holy state of matrimony without changing her resolution to remain a virgin, so that she truthfully could claim the name of wife, and yet keep the vow of virginal integrity to the end.[19]

From all the ecclesiastical writings here considered, it can be reasonably concluded that the Church definitely sanctioned and in certain cases encouraged the living together of husband and wife in the relationship of brother and sister to each other. In fact, most of the early Fathers (with the exceptions of St. Ambrose, St. Augustine, and a few others), since they had a confused or mistaken notion of what constitutes the essence of marriage, seemed to sanction this "*frater-soror*" arrangement even in the case of what they regarded a non-true or non-real marriage—at least in the case of Mary and Joseph. For they did uphold the perpetual virginity of the Blessed Mother, and they did sanction her living under the same roof with Joseph, but some called into question the fact that theirs was a true and hence valid marriage. Regarding the "other couples" of whom St. Augustine spoke as imitating the life of Joseph and Mary, one finds that, while many Church writers did question the validity of the marriage, they did not condemn or rebuke the people who, by the grace of God, were able so to live.

The Church has always proclaimed Mary, Joseph and the Child Jesus as a model family, and lovingly refers to them as "The Holy Family". All of the Church's canonical history and legislation, including the Code of Canon Law, has made room for this way of life. Canon 1128 notes that a *iusta causa* may excuse married people from observing the community of conjugal life.[20]   It is generally accepted that *mutual consent* constitutes *a iusta causa*, provided that there is no

---

[19] Cf. Hugh of St. Victor, *De Beata Maria Virgine*, Cap. I—MPL, CLXXVI, 867.

[20] Cf. Can. 1128: "Coniuges servare debent vitae coniugalis communicationem. nisi iusta causa eos excuset."

danger of incontinence or threat of scandal.[21] Prümmer (1866-1931) pointed out that not only is such a "brother-sister" arragement permitted, but it also may be meritorious. For this conclusion he appealed to the words of Christ Himself, and mentioned that this applies both to the "*ratum*" and also to the "*ratum-consummatum*" marriage.[22] This has been the constant tradition of the Church through all the ages.

Article 2.   Continence Among the Clergy and Laity

In the first three centuries of the Church's history young virgins and widows as well as laymen and clerics consecrated themselves to God by vows of virginity and chastity. By necessity, these men and women spent their lives together as brothers and sisters. The clerics and laymen needed women to care for the household duties, and the women needed protection. Thus it became customary for virgins or widows with the vow of virginity to contract a "spiritual marriage" with unmarried men. They lived together, not in any carnal relationship, but for mutual spiritual encouragement and aid. These women were often called "*sisters*" (*sorores*) or "*agapetae*", in indication of the fact that they lived with men in this brother-sister relationship.

---

[21] Cf. Bouscaren, *Canon Law*, can. 1128, p. 570; Cappello, *De Matrimonio*, nn. 822-825 bis; Denzinger-Rahner, *Enchiridion Symbolorum*, n. 978 Coronata, *De Sacramentis*, III p. 914, nn. 655-657. The commentators mention that the Code is here speaking of separation in a sense which includes more than merely a "*separatio a toro*", for of this "*separatio a toro*" they say: "Cum res sit privata, fieri potest ex mutuo consensu studio perfectionis et orationis..." But if, as they say, the Code speaks here of a "*separatio a toro, a mensa et a cohabitatione*" then *a fortiori* it grants the same for a "*separatio a toro*" alone.

[22] "Huiusmodo divortium (i. e. quoad torum seu quoad cohabitationem) aliquando non tantum licitum, verum etiam valde meritorium esse docet ipse Christus dicens: 'Omnis, qui reliquerit domum... aut uxorem propter nomen meum, centuplum accipiet et vitam aeternam possidebit.'" In the footnote he added: "Haec verba (Matt., 19:29) Christi intelligenda sunt aut de matrimonio rato, aut, si agitur de matrimonio consummato, de separatione ex mutuo consensu facta." Cf. Prümmer, *Manuale Theologiae Moralis*, III, p. 492, n. 678.

Although this mode of life was in the beginning accepted without disapproval and was even considered edifying, it later developed into a life of many abuses and scandals of a very serious nature. As a consequence, several early councils of the Church enacted very definite laws regarding the abuse of a long-accepted and well-thought-of practice of permitting two unmarried people to live together as brother and sister. The laws were explicit in regard to clerics so living, and apparently were applied also to the lay men and lay women engaged in this same mode of life.

Thus the council of Ancyra (314) in canon 19 forbade virgins with vows of chastity to live as sisters with men. A council at Carthage (c. 349) in canons 3 and 4 forbade clerics and virgins, widows and widowers, to live together, *"sub praetextu caritatis et dilectionis'* as brothers and sisters.[23] St. John Chrysostom, Patriarch of Constantinople (d 407) wrote against the evils into which these people had fallen. In one of his pastoral letters he stated: *"Quod regulares feminae viris cohabitare non debeant."*[24]

The I General Council of Nicaea (325) absolutely forbade a bishop, a priest, a deacon or any other cleric to have living with him a woman (*suneisaktos*) other than his mother, sister, aunt or any such person on whom suspicion could not fall.[25]

But in all this one finds that it is not the way of life itself, or the practice of living together as brother and sister, that is condemned, but rather the abuse of a way of life that definitely had been approved for two hundred or more years.[26] The II Council of Arles (443 or 452) excluded all *"feminae extraneae"* from the cleric's home, but permitted him to keep under the same roof his grand-

---

[23] Cf. Mansi, *Sacrorum Conciliorum Nova et Amplissima Collectio,* (53 vols. in 60, Parisiis, 1901-1927), III, 154 (hereafter cited as Mansi.)

[24] Cf. MPG, XLVII, 495-532.

[25] *Apegoreuse katholou e megale sunodos mete episkopo mete presbutero mete diakono mete olos tini ton en to kaero ezeinai suneiskton eachein plen ei me ara metera e adelphen e theian e a mona prosopa pasan upopsian diapepseuge.* This same canon was repeated in the I General Council of the Latern (1123). Cf. Denzinger-Rahner *Enchiridion Symbolorum,* n. 360.

[26] Cf. Schroeder, *Disciplinary Decrees of the General Councils* (St. Louis: B. Herder, 1937), p. 26.

mother, mother, daughter, niece, or, if earlier he had entered marriage, his wife, provided that she took a vow of chastity. In the latter case, the married priest could legally live with his wife as a brother with his sister in spite of the other legislation for unmarried couples during that period. The Council of Arles understood the last part of canon 3 of the I Council of Nicaea to include such persons "on whom suspicion would not fall" as being a wife who had taken a vow of chastity.[27]

Pope Leo I wrote a letter to Rusticus, Bishop of Narbonne, in 443. In it he made it very clear that married men who wished to become priests were to keep their wives, but were to remain perfectly continent. What was for them a carnal union in marriage became a spiritual marriage. They were not to dismiss their wives, but were to "have them as if they did not have them." From this it was clearly understood that they were to have them as sisters.[28]

It is also quite clear that Gratian understood the letter of Pope Leo IX (1049-1054) to mean that the priests should not drive out their legitimate wives, but should keep them as sisters. The Letter of Pope Leo IX reads in part as follows:

> Omnino confitemur, non licere episcopo, presbitero, diacono, propriam uxorem causa religionis abiicere a cura sua, sed ut

----

[27] Cf. Mansi, VII, 879; This legislation should be viewed in conjunction with what is stated *Supra* pp. 10-11.

"Collectio ascripta concilio secundo Arelatensi, semi-officialis liber canonum, est opus alicuius jurisperiti, qui unitur dispositionibus concilii Nicaeni, Arelatensis a. 314, Arausicani I a. 441, Vasionensis a. 442, non sine quibusdam mutationibus. Tempus compliationis est circa a. 450, post allegatum concilium Vasionense a. 442, ante concilium Agathense a. 506. Locus probabiliter est civitas Arelatensis, tum propter momentum quod col-lector tribuit conciliis huius civitatis, tum propter fontes quibus utitur, qui provenire debent ex aliqua ecclesia maioris momenti qualis erat ecclesia Arelatensis. Van Hove, *Commentarium Lovaniense in Codicis Iuris Canonici,* Vol. I, *Tomus I, Prolegomena,* (ed. altera Mechliniae Romae: Dessain, 1945), p. 153, n. 149, (hereafter cited as *Prolegomena*).

[28] *Epistola* XCII, ad. II, c. 3, Cf c. 10, D, XXXI; Jaffé, *Regesta Pontificum Romanorum ab condita Ecclesia ad Annum post Christum natum* MCXCVIII (2, ed., Cura Wattenbach, Kaltenbrunner, Ewald, Loewenfeld, 2 vols., Lipsiae, 1885-1888), JK, n. 544 (hereafter cited as Jaffé).

ei victum et vestitum largiatur, sed non ut cum illa ex more
carnaliter iaceat. . . . scilicet ut mercede praedicationis susten-
taretur ab eis, nec tamen deinceps foret inter eos ulterius carnale coniugium.[29]

The first explicit reference to the brother-sister arrangement is
found in a letter of questionable origin.[30]

A question was asked as to what course of action should be
taken by those who, because of a frigid nature (impotence) could not
have intercourse. The Pope answered: *"If the husband cannot use the
woman as a wife, let him keep her as a sister."*

Requisisti de his, qui ob causam frigidae naturae dicunt se
non posse invicem operam carni dantes commiscere. Iste vero

---

[29] C. 11, D. XXXI; c. 14, D. XXXII; Berardi, *Gratiani Canones Genuini
ab Aprocryphis Discreti, Corrupti ad Emendatiorum Codicum Fidem Exacti,
Difficiliores Commoda Interpretatione Illustrati,* (4 vols. in 3 tomes, Venetiis:
P. Valvasensis, 1777), III, 310 (hereafter cited as *Gratiani canones*); c. 12.
D. XXXI; c. 1, D. XXXII.

[30] Gratian quoted this letter in c. 2, C. XXXIII, q. 1, under the words
"ex epistola eiusdem", which means that he regarded it as coming from the
same source as c. 1, C. XXXIII, q. 1. This c. 1 is listed as a letter of
Gregory 1 to John, Bishop of Ravenna, which would date it between 590
and 604. Friedberg (1837-1910) in discounting this said of it: "Caput
Incertum;" Berardi (1719-1768) in his *Gratiani Canones*, Pars II, Tomus II,
p. 23, wrote: "Duo adhuc supersunt Gratiani fragmenta, quae ex epistola
Gregorii ad Johannem Ravennatem laudantur--videlicet cc. 1-2, C. XXXIII,
q. 1. Neuter tamen aut in Epistolis ad Joannem aut in ceteris Gregorii monumentis legitur." Ivo of Chartres (1040-1117) held that Gregory II (715-731)
wrote it to John of Ravenna. Burchard of Worms (ca. 965-1025) did not
indicate its address, but he was the first who recorded the entire text of
the letter in the 11th century. Jaffé in n. +1934 (CCLXXI) stated: "Ran-
dulpho, principi Salernitano, respondet . . ." and in n. +1938: "*Venerio
Caralitano episcopo* (al. Johanni, Ravennati episcopo), respondet de his, qui
matrimonio iuncti sunt, et nubere non possunt, quod ille aliam vel illa alium
possit accipere. (*Est ex Epistola Rabani ab Heribaldum episcopum, c. 29;
vide Reginonis de syn. causis,* L. II c. 243)." This last reference in Jaffé
(n. +1938) refers to c. 2, C. XXXIII, q. 1, the section here in question.
Also see Mansi, X 446.

si non potest ea uti pro uxore, ha'beat eam quasi sororem.[31]

Though much doubt remains regarding the particular time at which this letter may have been written, its value is tremendously increased in that the outstanding canonists included it in their collections (although attributing it to different Popes) even before the Father of Science of Canon Law, Gratian, included it in his outstanding *Decretum*. The idea of the brother-sister arrangement certainly obtained at the time, and the mention of it was incorporated in the official collection of Gregory IX as a definite entity.

Another direct reference to cohabitation on a brother-sister basis seems to be found in a letter of Pope Gregory II (715-731). St. Boniface had asked a series of questions, one of which was: "What should a man do whose wife is unable to render the *debitum?*" Pope Gregory, in the letter of November 22, 726, responded: "As regards your question what a husband is to do, if his wife has been attacked by illness, so that she is incapable of conjugal intercourse, the rightful thing would be for him so to continue and to practice self-restraint."[32]

The II General Council of Nicaea (787) in canon 20 explicitly ruled out the practice known as a "double monastery." From the tone

---

[31] C. 2, C. XXXIII, q. 1; Jaffé, n. + 1934 (CCLXXI); n. + 1938; Mansi, X, 446; Burchardus, *Decretum Parisiis*, 1550), IX, 40; S. Ivo, *Decretum* (Migne: Parisiis, 1855), VIII, 182.

[32] "Nam quod posuisti, quod si mulier infirmitate correpta non valuerit viri debitum reddere, quid eius facit iugalis: bonum esset si sic permaneret, ut abstinentiae vacaret..." c. 18, C. XXXII, q. 7; JE, n. 2174: There was considerable discussion whether this was a *ratum-non-consummatum* marriage, since the Pope allowed the husbands to remarry. Cf. Ferraris, *Bibliotheca Canonica, Juridica, Moralis, Theologica, necnon Ascetica Polemica, Rubricistica, Historica,* (9 vols., Romae, 1885-1899), III, 248-249. There was also considerable discussion regarding the authenticity of this letter. The text says Gregorius Junior wrote it. The *Correctores Romani* noted that Greogry III wrote it. But today it is no longer disputed that the letter was written by Pope Gregory II. Cf. Cappello, *De Matrimonio,* n. 388 (3); Joyce, *Christian Marriage,* p. 332; De Becker, *De Sponsalibus et Matrimonis Praelectiones Canonicae* (2. ed., Louvain, 1903), p. 164. Berardi in his *Gratiani Canones,* Pars II, Tomus II, p. 164 wrote: "Jure optimo Gregorii II tribuendam esse demonstrat subiecta temporis nota incidens in annum 726, quo Gregorio II Summum Pontificatum tenebat."--JE, n. 2174.

and content of the canon, it seems that the monks and nuns were living in very close proximity, if not under the same roof. It explicitly stated that monks and nuns should not dwell together in the same monastery, for in such cohabitation adultery found its occasion.[33] If they had been living together as brother and sister, it is evident that abuses and scandal must have been the reason given for the discontinuance of the practice. The way of life as such was not condemned, but it was regarded as holding within it the danger or the occasion of sin.

Toward the middle of the 12th century a very important step was taken in the development of the science of Canon Law. Great universities came into operation at that time, and scholastic philosophy and theology were being formed. The study of Roman Law had received a new impetus with the discovery of the *Digesta* of Justinian at Pisa in the year 1070. With this discovery, schools of Roman Law with the medieval glossators of Roman Law began to flourish.

Bologna was the center of Roman Law study, and it was there that Gratian (d. before 1159) composed his monumental work, the *Concordia Discordantium Canonum,* otherwise known as the *Decretum Gratiani* or simply *Decretum.* By this work Gratian gave the world an organized system of juridic notions and forms. It was a comprehensively written juridical doctrine, both analytical and synthetical, of canon law.

Canonists and historians of Canon Law in later centuries accorded this work of Gratian a preeminent place, and regarded its author as the "Father of the Science of Canon Law." The *Decretum* soon became the universal handbook of the ancient canons. It was the best private compilation of existing ecclesiatical law which, along with the later and official collections of Papal decretals, formed the *Corpus Iuris Canonici* until 1917.[34] Although the *Decretum* was in-

---

[33] Me diaitasthosan en eni monasterio monachoi kai monasteriai moicheia gar mesolabei te sundiaitesei. Cf. Mansi, XIII, 205-363.

[34] Gregory IX (1227-1241) recognized the necessity of declaring collections of the Papal decretals authentic, which he did in 1234, by the Constitution *Rex Pacificus.*—Cf. Cicognani, *Canon Law* (2. ed., Revised English version by J. O'Hara and F. Brennan, Westminster: Newman, 1949; (Reprint of 2. ed., Philiadelphia; The Dolphin Press, 1935) p. 298.

cluded in the *Corpus Iuris Canonici*,[85] it was never officially approved by the Church as an authentic Code of law, and therefore the documents contained in Gratian's *Decretum* retained simply the same force or lack of force which in law attached to them before Gratian used them. However, since the *Decretum* was used in the Schools and in the Roman Curia, and was approved by custom, many of its decrees and canons did in effect have the force of universal law.[86]

The *Decretum* was divided into three parts, the first and third of which were composed of *Distinctions* and subdivided into canons. The second part of the *Decretum* was devided into thirty-six "Causae," which are subdivided into *questions* and *canons*. The canons were taken from papal decretals, conciliar statutes and patristic writings, and were incorporated by Gratian in explanation and support of his own *dicta*, in which he proposed and solved difficulties. Some time after Gratian both the canons and also the *dicta* of Gratian were explained and commented upon by way of *Glossae*. The principal gloss for the *Decretum* was composed by Joannes Teutonicus (d. 1245) and later revised by Bartholomew of Brescia (d. ca. 1258), and is called *Glossa Ordinaria*. It is in the canons and *Glossa Ordinaria* that one finds for the first time a clear and exact canonical teaching on the separation "*a toro*," which in effect reflected the cohabitation on a brother-sister basis as a distinct canonical entity.

In treating this particular phase of history the writer will confine his discussion to two related topics—Continence and Impotence. Under these headings one could rightfully expect that Gratian might in certain cases have permitted or even demanded that two people live together as brother and sister.

Gratian recorded considerable legislation in regard to the chastity and abstinence of priests, deacons and sub-deacons.[37] In the very first part of Distinction XXVIII Gratian pointed out that those who

---

[25] The *Corpus Iuris Canonici* was composed of: the *Decretum Gratiani*, the Decretals of Gregory IX, the *Liber Sextus* of Boniface VIII, the *Clementinae*, the *Extravagantes* of Pope John XXII, and the *Extravagantes Communes*. Cf. Bouscaren-Ellis, *Canon Law* pp. 1-13.

[26] Cf. Van Hove, *Prolegomena*, pp. 339-346.

[27] Distinctions XXVIII, XXXI, XXXII.

did not wish to remain continent could not be promoted to subdeaconship or to the higher ranks (deaconship and priesthood). He used a
letter of Pope St. Gregory the great to show that clerics were not to
be admitted to subdeaconship unless they took a vow of chastity.[38]
And in another *"dictum"* he pointed out that a lay person or one who
had minor Orders could have a wife and children, but could afterwards, with his wife's consent regarding continence, receive subdeaconship, deaconship, and even the priesthood, but had at the
same time to administer to the needs of his wife and children.[39]

Gratian, in these and the following canons pointed out that a
married man, if he promised to remain continent, could become a
priest and still take care of the needs of his wife and children. This
normally entailed living in the same house. However a priest or a
deacon could not marry after he had been ordained and then still
continue to serve at the altar.

Canon 6, D. XXXI, stated that those who abstained from the
"offitia uxoris" were to be permitted to participate in the sacrifice. In
support of this Gratian produced a letter of Pope Innocent I as his
authority. In this latter it was stated: *"Eos ad sacrificia admitti fas
sit, qui vel cum uxore non exerceant offitium carnale."*[40] In the third
part of this same *Distinctio* Gratian explicitly taught that a priest was
not to reject the love and care he had for his wife.[41] And in canon
10 he used the authority of Pope Leo I to say that bishops and priests
were under the same law of continence. What for them had been
a carnal union in marriage was to become a spiritual marriage. They
were not to dismiss their wives, but were to "have them as if they did

---

[38] *Dictum in Principio,* D. XXVIII, "Ecce ostensum est quod nolentes
continentiam, nec ad subdiaconatum, nec ad superiores gradus conscendere
possunt. Unde ad subdiaconatum accedentes, non sine voto castitatis iubentur
admitti, auctoritate, . . . (Lib. I, epistola 42 in fine) . . .". Cf. also JE n.
1112 and c. 1, D. XXXI.

[39] *Dictum post* c. 13, D. XXVIII (c. 14, § 2, D. XXVII).

[40] Cf. c. 6, D. XXXI, and c. 2, D. LXXXII, in which the same passage
of Innocent I is quoted a little differently, i. e. "neque eos ad sacrificia fas
sit admitti, qui excercent vel cum uxore carnale consortium."—JK, n. 293.

[41] Pars III, *Dictum post* c. 9, D. XXXI; ". . . quam (uxorem) nullus debet
contempnere, hoc est, ab animo et cura sua abicere, quin ei necessaria
provideat. . ."

not have them." And by this it was clearly understood that they were to have them as sisters.[42]

As if to take away any and all doubt about the ministers of the altar (if they were married before they accepted major Orders) living with their wives in the manner of brothers with their sisters, Gratian still further clarified his statement in the next canon and in *the dictum post* canon 11, as well as in the rubric. According to the rubric to canon 11, a bishop or a priest was not to exclude his own wife from his due care. "*Episcopus vel presbiter uxorem propriam a sua cura non abiciat.*" And then in the canon itself, which is a letter of Pope Leo IX, there follows the statement:

> *Omnino confitemur, non licere episcopo, presbitero, diacono, propriam uxorem causa religionis abicere a cura sua, sed ut ei victum et vestitum largiatur, sed non ut cum illa ex more carnaliter iaceat . . . scilicet ut mercede predicationis sustentaretur ab eis, nec tamen deinceps foret inter eos ulterius carnale conjugium.*"[43]

Then in the *dictum post* he says: "*Ut igitur ex his auctoribus apparet, sacerdotes, uxoribus, quas in laicali habitu vel in minoribus ordinibus constituti sibi legitime copularunt, necessaria subministrare, debita vero reddere non valent.*"[44]

In several other places Gratian pointed out that it was the mind of the Church, according to the writings of Jerome, Augustine, Ambrose, Chrysostom, etc., that husband and wife, during the time of solemn feasts and penitential seasons, should abstain from carnal intercourse. The Glossator pointed out that this directive was one of counsel and not of command.[45] And whenever they were to receive

---

[42] *Epistola XCII*, ad II, c. 3, Rusticus, Bishop of Narbonne, 443: "Lex continentiae eadem est altaris ministris, que episcopis aut presbiteris. . . Unde, ut de carnali fiat spirituale coniugium, oportet eos nec dimittere uxores, sed qui habent sic habere videantur *quasi non habeant,* quo et salva sit caritas conubiorum, et cessent opera nuptiarum."—C. 10, D. XXXI; JK, n. 544.

[43] C. 11, D. XXXI, Berardi in *Gratiani Canones,* III, p. 310; c. 14, D. XXXII.

[44] C. 11, D. XXXI. Cf. also c. 12, D. XXXI, and c. 1, D. XXXII.

[45] "Nullus debet uxorem suam cognoscere; quod est consilium."—c. 1, C. XXXIII, q. 4.

Holy Communion they were in like manner expected to abstain from carnal relations. " . . . *quod eo tempore quo carnes agni mand-ucaturi sumus, vacare a carnalibus operibus debeamus.*"[46]   Again in the very next canon, for which Augustine's sermon for the second Sunday of Advent is listed as the source, there was stated in the rubric: "*A coniugali concubitu in sanctorum solemnitatibus est abs-tinendum.*"   Then Augustine pointed out that, as he had frequently admonished them, they shoulld abstain not only from concubines, but also from their wives on the feast of Christmas and other feasts.[47]

In using an Advent sermon of St. Ambrose, Gratian recorded the following:

> *Fratres, non solum debetis ab omni immunditia abstinere sed etiam ab uxoribus propriis studiosissime contineatis.   Nullus om-nino uxori suae ieiuniorum diebus coniugatur.*[48]

Then Gratian cited another sermon as one of St. Ambrose,[49] in which the "abstinence" could appear to be more than a mere council, for he indicated that those who married for the purpose of having children enjoyed but a restricted period of time for the realization of the purpose in view of the fast and feast days, etc.[50]

---

[46] C. 1, C. XXXIII, q. 4.

[47] C. 2, C. XXXIII, q. 4.

[48] Cf. c. 3, C. XXXIII, q. 4; The glossator noted (s. v. *Fratres*) that this was a counsel, and not a command. Also (s. v. *Nullus*) the *Correctores Romani* added the words "*Diebus ieiuniorum*" in the rubric, and "nullus" in the canon, because they had access to this and other manuscripts of Ambrose's sermons in the Vatican Library. The other sermons used the words, "*Nullus uxori suae iungatur ante octavam Paschae,*" and "*ieiuniorum diebus.*"

[49] C. 4, C. XXXIII, q. 4. The *Correctores Romani,* however, in the *Corpus Iuris Canonici* stated that it was taken from Hilary the Deacon around the year 380.

[50] "Si causa procreandorum filiorum ducitur uxor, non multum tempus concessum videtur ad ipsum usum, quia et dies festi, et dies processionis, et ipsa ratio conceptus et partus iuxta legem cessare usum carnis debere his temporibus demonstrant."—C. 4, c. XXXIII, q. 4. The *Glossa, ibidem,* s. v. concessum, stated: "Et ita videtur, quod aliquod tempus prohibitum sit, in quo non debeat uxorem suam cognoscere causa sobolis (subolis) procreandae, et ita non est consilium. Sed fac vim in eo quod dicit, videtur. Non enim dixit, non est. Vel intelligas in casu, in quo loquitur cap., quando scilicet cognoscit eam causa sobolis: quia forte in eo casu non debet ad eam accedere; secus, si causa incontinentiae."

In a letter from Gregory the Great to Augustine, Archbishop of Canterbury (c. 604) it was stated that a husband should not sleep with his wife or have carnal relations, before the child was weaned or before the mother had been purified. The *Glossa* pointed out that this was to be observed both for the reason of health and for the purpose of religious devotion. But if there was danger of incontinence, then relations were granted as fully permissible.[51]

In two other places Gratian noted that there were many sources which authoritatively declared that a husband could not rightfully abstain from his wife or take a vow of continence without the consent of his wife. From this it is a reasonable deduction that there were times when rightfully they could live together as brother and sister.[52]

On the first night of the blessing of their marriage a husband and wife, so Gratian indicated, were out of a sense of reverence to remain in their virginity. But the *Glossa* pointed out that it was not a sin if they did otherwise.[53]

Thus it appears clearly that the Church commanded those who were in major Orders, if they were to perform the duties of that office, to live with their wives as brothers live with their sisters. Likewise husband and wife, on certain occasions and for various reasons, were brought under the necessity of living as brother and sister.

The Church, with the promulgation of a collection known as the Decretals of Gregory IX (1227-1241) in 1234, found itself with a valuable collection of authentic legal material. All the laws contained in this collection took on the force of universal law upon the

---

[51] C. 4, D. V.: "Antequam puer ablactetur, vel mater purificetur, ad eius concubitum vir non accedat." See also the *Glossa*, s. v. *ad eius*. It is to be noted that the mother was considered unclean for 33 days after birth if the child was a boy, and 66 days if the child was a girl, according to Jewish law. Cf. c. 5, C. XXXIII, q. 4.

[52] C. 24, C. XXVII, q. 2; *Dictum ante* c. 1, the rubric, and c. 1, C. C. XXXIII, q. 5.

[53] C. 5, C. XXX, q. 5: ". . . qui cum acceperint benedictionem eadem nocte pro reverentia ipsius benedictionis in virginitate permaneant."—*Glossa ibidem* s. v. *Reverentia*.

publication of the collection in the law schools of the Church, even though they were formerly of a particular nature.[54]

Again there is no particular section devoted to "*cohabitatio fraterna*" or the living together of husband and wife, or of a man and a woman, as brother and sister. But, as before, there are clearly expressed references to this mode of cohabitation as a juridic entity.

The first reference concerns the clergy, and is taken from a letter of Pope Alexander III (1159-1181) to the Bishop of Hereford. A married man was not to be admitted to the exercise of ecclesiastical Orders or to the administration of a benefice unless he promised chastity and was not a bigamist. In fact, he had to take a vow of chastity, and his wife needed to have been a virgin when he married her. The glossator mentioned that they had to cease sharing the same bed chamber, and if the parties were young, with the danger of in-continence threatening, the wife had to enter religion.[55]   ,

The same idea was expressed a little more forcefully when, in the Decretals of Gregory, it was forbidden that anyone be promoted to sacred Orders unless the wife promised continence, and unless the husband promised absolute abstinence from the wife. The glossator again made it clear that if the married couple were young, the wife had to enter religion. But this was not so if they were elderly. With reference to the married clergy, before a married man who had received sacred Orders could continue to live with his wife as a brother with his sister, he needed to be advanced in age. Apparently this arrangement was never permitted for younger couples.[56]

Thus it is seen that the Fathers, Popes, councils and outstanding canonists either explicitly or implicitly recognized and recorded the

---

[54] Cf. Cicognani, *Canon Law*, p. 303.

[55] C. 2, X, *de clericis coniugatis*, III, 3; ". . . nisi forte castitatem voveret perpetuam, et qui unicam et virginem habuisset uxorem." *Glossa* ad c. 2. X, III, 3, s. v. *castitatem*; JL, n. 13946.

[56] Rub. ad c. 5, X *de conversione coniugatorum*, III, 32: "Coniugatus non est ordinandus ad sacros ordines, nisi uxor continentiam promittat." And in the canon (5, X, III, 32): "Nullus coniugatorum est ad sacros ordines promovendus: nisi ab uxore continentiam profitente, fuerit absolutus." *Glossa* ad c. 5, X, III, s. v. *Ab uxore continentiam profitente* and the *casus*.

fact that the Church permitted, and at times even encouraged, men and women validly or invalidly married, or not married at all, to live together as brother and sister. The Church's sanction always hinged on the condition that no scandal or moral danger be present.

CHAPTER II

JURISPRUDENTIAL DEVELOPMENT

Article 1. First Explicit References

In treating of the notion of impotence, Gratian first asked whether, because of the impossibility of rendering the debt to her husband, a woman could separate from him. He set down two opposite points of view. In the first, no separation was permitted, and it seems that at least by implication this prohibition applied not only to a complete separation (*divortium plenum*) but also and especially with reference to the *separatio a cohabitatione,* so that, even though the debt could not be rendered, the parties were nevertheless to remain together. Gratian appealed to the Scriptures to show that a husband cannot dismiss his wife, nor a wife depart from her husband, except for the cause of fornication. Since impotence was not fornication, they were not to separate from each other.[1]

The second opinion was expressed in the first canon. In this Gratian stated that it is permissible for the wife to marry another if she can prove "*quod non possit coire cum ea.*" It is evident that the

---

[1] "Quod autem propter impossibilitatem reddendi debitum mulier a viro suo separari non possit, auctoritate evangelica et Apostolica probatur. Sic enim Christus ait in evangelio: 'Nulli licet dimittere uxorem suam nisi causa fornicationis,' vel qua alter eorum (sicut Augustinus exponit) fornicatus fuerit, vel ad quam alter alterum pertrahere voluerit. Item Apostolus (Rom. 7:1) 'Mulier, quanto tempore vivit vir eius, alligata est legi ipsius,' non legi reddendi sibi debitum, sed non transferendi se ad alium. Item (I Cor. 7, 10) 'His, qui matrimonio iuncti sunt, praecipio non ego, sed Dominus, uxorem a viro (suo) non discedere, nisi causa fornicationis.' Evangelica itaque et apostolica auctoritate prohibetur mulier a viro discedere, nisi ob causam illam cunctis notissimam, qua inter veniente si discesserit, oportet eam manere innuptam, aut reconciliari viro suo. Unde datur intelligi, quod impossibilitas reddendi debitum non facit discidium coniugii."— *Dictum ante* c. 1, C. XXXIII, q. 1.

matter was one of permissiveness and not of command. There seems
to be no law stating that she must separate (*a cohabitatione*) from
the one "*quocum non possit coire.*" The moral law could well demand that she separate "*a toro*" and not sleep with her husband, but
apparently, and especially in view of the next listed canon, they could
live as brother and sister.[2]

It is proper to note that two different situations were considered above. The first, in which Gratian said that they should
not separate, referred to what today would be called a "*ratum-
consummatum*" marriage. The impotence seemed to arise only after
the marriage had been consummated.[3] The second, in which Gratian
permitted the wife to leave the husband and to marry another, referred to what today would be called a *ratum non-consummatum*
marriage. To Gratian it was a simple *matrimonium initiatum*, or a
union not yet perfected through carnal intercourse. Accordingly if
the impotence arose before the *matrimonium initiatum* was consumat-
ed, the matrimonial bond ceased. But even then the "*separatio*" was
permissive, but not mandatory.[4]

The difference, therefore, between Gratian's and the modern
teaching regarding impotence in relation to marriage seems to rest on
the time element and on Gratian's notion of the essence of marriage.
Today, impotence incurred antecedently to the marriage is a diriment
impediment and nullifies the marriage. If it be incurred after the
marriage but before the marriage is consummated, then the marriage
is merely *ratum* and could be dissolved. Gratian did not seem to recognize antecedent impotence as a diriment impediment; rather, he
held that, if impotence was incurred before carnal intercourse ensued

---

[2] "...si se coniunxerint, et dixerit postea mulier de viro, quod non
possit coire cum ea, si potest probare, quod verum sit, per iustum iudicium,
accipiat alium."—C. 1, C. XXXIII, q. 1.

[3] "His ita respondetur: Coniugium confirmatur offitio, ut supra (D.
XXVII, q. 2) probatum est; postquam vero offitio confirmatum fuerit, nisi
causa fornicationis non licet viro uxorem dimittere, vel uxori a viro discedere."
Dictum ante, c. 1, C. XXXIII, q. 1.

[4] *Dictum ante* c. 1, C. XXXIII, q. 1; *Glossa ad* C. XXVII, s. v. *non
dubium* q. 1; C. XXVII, q. 2.

upon the contracting of the marriage, then the bond became dissolved · —the two individuals were not parties to a real marriage.[5]

Consequently, if the writer has correctly asserted that on a brother-sister basis cohabitation was permitted in 'both situations, it can also be said that such cohabitation was permitted in both valid and invalid marriages. In the one case a true marriage bond existed, and in the other *"apparet illos non fuisse coniuges."*

The first expressed reference to the brother-sister arrangement found in Gratian is given by him as the first of three solutions for a case of impotence.

> *Requisisti de his, qui ob causam frigidae naturae dicunt se invicem non posse operam carni dantes commisceri. Iste vero si non potest ea uti pro uxore, habeat eam quasi sororem. Quod si retinaculum voluerint coniugale rescindere maneant utrique innupti. Nam si huic non potuit naturaliter concordare, quomodo alteri conveniet? Igitur si vir aliam vult uxorem accipere, manifesta patet ratio, quia, suggerente diabolo odii fomitem, exosam eam habuit, et idcirco eam dimittere mendacii falsitate molitur. Quod si mulier causatur, et dicit: Volo mater esse, et filios procreare, uterque eorum septima manu propinquorum tactis sacrosanctis reliquiis iureiurando dicat, ut numquam per commixtionem carnis coniuncti una caro effecti fuissent, tunc videtur mulierem secundas posse contrahere nuptias. Humanum dico propter infirmitatem carnis eorum. Vir autem qui frigidae naturae est, maneat sine coniuge. Quod si et ille aliam copulam acceperit, tunc hi, qui iuraverant, periurii, crimine rei teneantur, et penitentia peracta priora cogantur recipere conubia.* (c. 2, C. XXXIII, q. 1.)

Permission for cohabitation on a brother-sister basis was explicitly

---

[5] "Verum ante, quam confirmetur, impossibilitas officii solvit vinculum coniugii."—*Dictum ante* c. 1, C. XXXIII, q. 1; "Ecce, impossibilitas coeundi . . . si vero ante carnalem copulam deprehensa fuerit, liberum facit mulieri alium virum accipere. Inde apparet, illos non fuisse coniuges." *Dictum post* c. 29, C. XXVII, q. 2.

given as the first of three solutions to the case of impotence as pre-sented by Gratian.[6]

Gratian lists this canon (2) as being part of a letter written to John of Ravenna by Pope Gregory the Great.[7]   But whatever the source may be, Gratian accepted the content of the letter, and as the first solution to the problem of a man with a "frigid nature" he ex-plicitly advised that the man keep his "wife" as a sister. *Iste vero si non potest ea uti pro uxore, habeat eam quasi sororem.* But he im-mediately pointed out that this was not a command, for he wrote: *Quod si retinaculum voluerint coniugale rescindere, maneant utrique innupti.*[8]

This is undoubtedly the most explicit reference to cohabitation on the brother-sister basis found thus far, which had some definite canonical authority behind it, i. e., Burchard, Ivo, and above all Gra-tian, the Father of the Science of Canon Law. As will be seen, cohabi-tation on a brother-sister basis was given as a solution for cases of im-potence in the official law of the Church, the Decretals of Gregory IX.   In the latter case, however, there was certitude regarding the antecedent existence of the impotence, and therefore certitude as to the nullity of the marriage, in which the solution of a cohabitation on a brother-sister basis was given.

The importance of this present reference to Gratian, however, is not to be minimized, as it is a definite indication of the mind of

----

[6] Harrington, *Impotency, The Notion and Impediment, A Historical Syn-opsis* (Typewritten licentiate disseration, School of Canon Law, the Catholic University of America: Washington, D. C., unpublished), pp. 41-50.

[7] Jaffé and others stated that this particular section (canon 2) is spuri-ous, JE, n. ✝ 1934; Friedberg said of it: "Caput Incertum;" Berardi, (*Gratiani Canones,* Pars II, Tomus II, p. 23); "Duo adhuc supersunt *Gratiani* fragmenta, quae ex epistola Gregorii ad Johannem Ravennatem laudantur— videlicet cc. 1 & 2, C. XXXIII, q. 1. Neuter tamen aut in Epistolis ad Joannem aut in ceteris Gregorii monumentis legitur." Cf., *Supra,* p. 13, ft. note 30.

[8] The glossator pointed out also that it was a counsel and not a command that they remain together. *Glossa ad c. 2, C. XXXIII, q. 1, s. v. pro uxore.* The glossator also pointed out that the husband was commanded not to marry another, and the woman was counseled to remain unmarried.—*ibidem,* s. v. *Innupti:* "Praeceptum est quantum ad virum, quantum ad illam consilium.

the Church toward the brother-sister arrangement as a solution for marriage difficulties in the 12th century . In giving the present solution, Gratian was expressing the practice followed in Rome, according to which those who were impotent were enjoined to live together as brother and sister.[9]

There are several other references in Gratian regarding impotence that should be mentioned. Inasmuch as they are not as explicit or as clear as the preceding, only mention will be made of them.

The first concerned a text already seen.[10] In this case the woman was impotent, and the man was advised to continue in his state of abstaining from the "wife." Authors are divided as to whether the word *"infirmitate"* referred to antecedent or subsequent impotence, but the more weighty opinion seems to be that it referred to antecedent impotence. In this invalid marriage cohabitation on a brother-sister basis seemed to be preferred to separation and re-marriage.[11]

Another case of impotence (*ratione sortiariae atque maleficae artis*) was considered to be caused by a just judgement of God or by the power of the devil. In this situation, Archbishop Hincmar of Rheims (860) called for the use of spiritual remedies.[12] But if there was no cure for the parties they could be separated. "*Quod si forte*

---

[9] Freisen, (1853-1932), quoting the *Exceptiones Petri*, stated the case of Emperor Henry IV (1069) who wished to dismiss his wife because of the impossibility of having carnal relations. The Archbishop of Mainz and other bishops thought Henry should be released from his marriage. But the case went to Rome and Pope Alexander II (1061-1073) forbade Henry to separate. Cf. Freisen, *Geschichte des Canonischen Eherechts,* (Paderborn, 1893), p. 337.

[10] Nam quod posuisti, quod si mulier infirmitate correpta non valuerit viro debitum reddere, quid eius faciat iugalis: bonum esset, si sic permaneret, ut abstinentiae vacaret."—c. 18, C. XXXII, q. 7; The better opinion is that Gregory II did write this letter. Cf. JE, n. 2174.

[11] Wernz-Vidal, *Ius Canonicum* (7 vols. in 8, Vol. V, *Ius Matrimoniale* 3 ed. a. P. Aguirre recognita, Romae: Universitas Gregoriana, 1946), Vol. V, n. 222, p. 266, footnote 21; Cappello, *De Matrimonio,* p. 387, n. 388; Joyce, *Christian Marriage,* p. 333; Gratian himself was not so certain about this, nor were the glossators. Cf. Esmein, *Le Mariagê en Droit Canonique* (2. ed., 2 vols, Paris: Recueil-Sirey, 1929-1935), II, 88 ff. (hereafter cited *Le Mariage*).

[12] C. 4, C. XXXIII, q: 1. The *Glossa ad* c. 4, C. XXXIII, q. 1, s. v. *nequibunt,* pointed out that the spiritual remedies of prayers, fasts, confession, alms, etc., should be applied for three years.

sanari non potuerint, separari valebunt." The glossator made a distinction when he said that they could be separated unless the "*maleficium*" was brought on through the woman's own fault. In that case
cohabitation apart from carnal relations seemed to be the only solution.[13] The glossator made the reference to this mode of cohabitation
even more clear when, in effect, he stated that if the man knew
beforehand that the wife was incapable of carnal relations, he could
not seek a separation. And if the wife knew beforehand that she
herself was impotent, she could not separate from the husband if
he wished to live with her, for she knew herself to be impotent.[14]
Now, if the woman was impotent, so that she couldn't have carnal
relations, and yet the man desired to cohabit or live with her, the
only possible solution was a cohabitation on a brother-sister basis.

Quite naturally the clearest references to cohabitation on a
brother-sister basis occurring in the Decretals of Gregory IX are under
the heading of Impotence or *Frigiditas*. In his Decretals Gregory
added the notion of "*knowledge of impotence*," and his Decretals
became the official law of the Church.

*Contrahens scienter cum impotenti ad copulam, ab ea non sep-
aratur.*[15] This is the rubric to the first of two canons which explicitly
permit cohabitation to the exclusion of carnal intercourse in an
invalid marriage. In the first canon, the Pope (Alexander III or Lucius
III) answered the question whether women who are "*clausae et im-*

---

[13] Glossa ad c. 4 C XXXIII, q. 1, s. v. *separari* "*nisi ipsa uxor dicatur*
procurasse maleficium, cum sua culpa . . .*"

[14] The Glossa referred to the decretal letter *Laudabilem* of Pope Celestine III (1191-1198). There it was the man who was impotent. "Sed quid si
mulier sciebat virum esse frigidum ab initio? Satis videtur quod tunc non
possit petere separationem . . . ; de viro autem potius videtur quod ille non
possit recedere a muliere, *si ipsa vult cohabitare ei, cum ipse sciverit se
frigidum.*" Cf. Bernardus Papiensis, *Summa Decretalium*, Lib. IV, Tit. 6. n.
10 (ed. E. A. Th· Laspeyres, Ratisbonae, 1860) p. 180, as quoted by P. A.
d' Avack, *Cause di Nullità e di Divorzio nel Diritto Matrimoniale Canonico*,
Vol. I (Firenze: Casa editr. C. Cya. 1952), p. 445, footnote: "Nec illud
omittendum puto, quod si mulier sciens virum impotentem nihilominus ac-
ceperit eum, occasione impossibilitatis coeundi non poterit ab eo divortium
postulars."

[15] Cf. Esmein, *Le Mariage*, I. 266 ff.

potentes commisceri maribus" can contract marriage, and whether, if they have contracted the marriage, it must be rescinded. The Pope answered that, although it seems incredible that any man would contract such a marriage, and although there is no express canon on the point, the Roman Church is accustomed in similar cases to judge that *these men should keep as sisters these women whom they cannot have as wives.*[16]

The glossator mentioned that this custom was to be regarded, not as involving a command, but simply as implying a council.[17]

The next canon refers particularly to the case in which the impotence of the husband may or may not be evident. If it was clearly shown, the parties could be separated immediately. But if it was not certain, the parties were to remain together for three years, after which they could separate, and then the one could remarry once it was proved *septima manu* that the marriage had not and could not have been consummated in consequence of the impotence.[18] But if

---

[16] "Consultationi tuae qua nos consuluisti, utrum foeminae clausae, impotentes commisceri maribus matrimonium possint contrahere, et, si contraxerint, an debeat rescindi, taliter respondemus, quod licet incredibile videatur, quod aliquis cum talibus contrahat matrimonium: Romana tamen Ecclesia consuevit in consimilibus iudicare, ut *quas tamquam uxores habere non possunt habeant ut sorores."*—c. 4, X, *de frigidis et maleficiatis, et impotentia coeundi,* IV, 15; Raymond of Pennafort listed this as a letter of Pope Lucius III, (1181-1185). But Friedberg demonstrated that Alexander III (1159-1181) wrote it. Cf. also Wernz-Vidal, *Ius Matrimoniale,* p. 267, footnote 27.

[17] *Glossa ad* c. 4, X, IV, 15, s. v. *iudicare.*

[18] "Si de impotentia coeundi constet, statim matrimonium separatur; alias cohabitabunt coniuges per triennium. Et si cum septima manu propinquorum iurant, quod dederunt operam carnali copulae, et non potuerunt coniungi; statim separantur. Ita communiter summatur."—Rubrica ad, c. 5, X, IV, 15; JL. n. 17649; JL, n. 10735.

both the "husband" and "wife" agree to remain together, the man is to have her, if not as a wife, at least as a sister.[19]

The decretal as found in Gregory IX, is certainly clear enough in itself, but Raymond of Penafort (1175-1275), Innocent IV (1243-1254, Hostiensis (d. 1271), Durandus (1237-1296), Panormitanus (1386-1453), Sanchez (1550-1610) and others, in treating of and commenting on this particular section, clarified and applied these canons to difficulties that did arise.

St. Raymond invoked a distinction between natural (*frigiditas vel arctatio*) and accidental (*castratio*) impotence or *maleficium*. He stated also that natural impotence is either temporal or perpetual, and that it impedes marriage: ". . . . quod quamdiu inest ei, non potest contrahere (c. 1, C. XXXIII, q. 1)." If it is natural and perpetual, *impedit matrimonium contrahendum, et dirimit* (c. 1, C. XXXIII, q. 1). Immediately thereafter he used the letter of "Gregory" to John of Ravenna (*Requisisti de his*) and of Celestine III to show "*quod si ambo consentiant simul esse, vir eam, etsi non ut uxorem, saltem habeat ut sororem.*"[20]

If accidental impotence or *maleficium* came after the marriage, there was no hindrance for the marriage. If it came before the marriage, then Raymond distinguished between temporal and perpetual. The first did not hinder the marriage, but perpetual impotence he regarded as a diriment impediment.[21] In order to determine

---

[19] "Quod si ambo consentiant simul esse, vir eam, etsi non ut uxorem, saltem habeat ut sororem."—c. 5, X, IV, 15; The glossator spoke for an arrangement in the same manner if the wife was the impotent one. *Glossa ad* c. 5, X, IV, 15, s. v. *separatur;* the glossator also mentioned that at least the consent of the woman was needed for them to cohabit as brother and sister, for if the man knew of his impotence before the marriage, he could not change his mind after the marriage. *Glossa, ad* c. 5, X, IV, 15. s. v. *Quod si ambo.*

[20] Raymond of Pennafort *Summa* (ed. nova, Veronae, 1744), Lib. IV, Tit. 16, n. 1, p. 513. It is evident here that Raymond regarded such a marriage as invalid, and consequently tolerated cohabitation on a brother-sister basis for invalid as well as for valid marriages. See also Panormitanus *Commentaria in Quinque Libros Decretalium* (5 vols. in 7, Venetiis, 1588), c. 4, Lib. IV, tit. 15: "Cum omnino impotenti ad copulam non potest consistere verum matrimonium; non desinit causa institutionis matrimonii."

[21] Raymond, *Summa*, Lib. IV, Tit., 16, n. 2, p. 515; c. 4, C. XXXIII, q. 1.

whether this element was of a temporal or a perpetual character, any *maleficium* was from the beginning (*a principio*) to be presumed temporal, inasmuch as all men were to be assumed capable of marriage relations. But if after three years in marriage this presumption remained unsubstantiated, then maleficium was to be presumed perpetual. He pointed out that certain doctors held a contrary opinion. They maintained that no *maleficium* severed the bond of a marriage already contracted. This opinion they based on the practice of the Roman Church which demanded that husband and wife in such circumstances live together as brother and sister.[22]

Regarding the case of antecedent knowledge of the impotence, Raymond offered a solution for three questions. In the first, if a man who knew he was frigid and incapable of marriage nevertheless contracted a union, he could not leave his partner in the union if she wished to live with him.[23]

The same applied to the case of a woman who under like circumstances contracted a union with a man. She could not leave him if he wished to live with her.

And in the case of a frigid man contracting with an impotent woman with each of them having knowledge of the impediment affecting them, Raymond believed that, unless both consented to the separation, they had to remain together and live as brother and sister.[24]

---

[22] Raymond, *Summa*, Lib. IV, tit., 16, n. 2, p. 515; Cf. *Consultationi* of (Lucius III) Alexander III, c. 4, X, *de frigidis et malificiatis, et impotentia, coeundi* IV, 15.

[23] "Ad primum videtur mihi dicendum, quod non potest vir recedere a tali uxore, si ipsa velit ei cohabitare."—Raymond, *Summa*, Lib. IV, tit. 16, n. 3, p. 517.

[24] "Quid, si frigidus contrahit cum arcta, et uterque sciat suum impedimentum? Credo, nisi ambo consentiant separationi, quod debent simul stare, sicut frater et soror, ut in praeall. *Consultationi* (ita ut neutri liceat altero invito resilire) ... Haec quae dicta sunt, restringendo ad ipsum casum, dicendum est, quod propter tale impedimentum, non posset quis petere separationem; aliter enim posset; puta si alter eorum viveret incontinenter; aut alter inhoneste, et male tractaret eam, et maritus nollet se corrigere et multo fortius, si alter, qui potens esset contraheret matrimonium cum alia persona."—Raymundus, *Summa*, Lib. IV, tit., 16, n. 3, p. 517.

Hostiensis (+1271) stated in his *Summa Aurea* that, if both knew of the impotence of either one or the other, and they both wished to contract marriage, or after they had contracted it to remain together, they indeed could. But he warned that the union could be regarded as a marriage, not in its actual nature, but only in consequence of the positive ecclesiastical law that favored the presumption for it, because if a man or a woman could not carnally know the other as wife or husband, then indeed they had to live as brother and sister. He also stated that, if there was proof of the possession of this knowledge, then the man had to retain the woman as a sister, because the Roman Church customarily demanded that. He also pointed out that it was quite understandable that the Church should regard this decree as a command, though others regarded it in the light of simply a counsel.[25]

Sanchez (1550-1610) still taught that for persons who were thus united but who lacked the capacity for marriage itself there remained the obligation of doing what they could, at least by leading their life in common as brother and sister. And if both were ignorant of the impotence at the time of the marriage, it seemed to him, that they were bound to live as brother and sister, so that neither could leave the common life as long as the other remained unwilling.[26]

---

[25] "Nam si ambo sciant impotentiam, et volunt simul contrahere vel post contractum simul remanere, hoc quidem poterunt; non tamen credas quod sit matrimonium sed est decretum, quia qui talem habere non potest ut uxorem, saltem habet ut sororem, aequa lance; mulier habebit maritum ut fratrem... Si sententia [scientia] probetur, cogitur [cogetur] eam retinere tamquam sororem, ut dixi, quia ecclesia Romana ita consuevit iudicare. Sic potes intelligere decretum praecipientem, quem alii dicunt consilium praebentem."—Hostiensis, *Summa Aurea* (Lugduni, 1568), Lib. IV, tit., 16, n. 6, p. 315.

[26] "Quod cum is contractus non possit vim matrimonii habere, videtur obligare ad id, ad quod potest, nimirum ad vitam sociorum et fratrum peragendam... Sed quid, si ambo coniuges tempore initi matrimonium ignorant impotentiam? Tunc enim videtur eos teneri tanquam fratres convivere, ac ad alimenta; ita ut neutri liceat altero invito resilire." Sanchez, *Disputationum de Sancto Matrimonii Sacramento Tomi Tres* (10 books in 3 vols., Antverpiae, 1626). Vol. II, Lib. VII. disp. 97, n. 11. (hereafter cited *De Matrimonii Sacramento*).

Article 2. The Revolt and True Reformation

The fourteeth and fifteenth centuries reflected a period of decline. This decline was accentuated by the long sojurn of the Popes at Avignon (1309-1377), by the Western Schism (1378-1417), and by the heresy of the Wyclifites as continued by the Hussites. The Church was in a very unhappy condition. Civil law in the form of anticanonical legislation began to arise. The lives of the clergy were often unworthy, if not also vicious. The practice of concubinage was rife. The law of residence was disregarded. The episcopate was regarded as the prerogative of nobles. All these and other spiritual diseases made reform a crying necessity.

As the Church's discipline declined and religious practices fell into desuetude, so also did civil society suffer from an epidemic of immorality, along with its evil train of ignorance, cruelty and disease. Superstition, usury, crime and general injustices were prevalent.

Attempts at reform were made, but even so a large part of the peoples of northern and central Europe was torn from the bosom of the Church in the beginning of the sixteenth century. Martin Luther (1483-1546), abetted by a corrupt political and civil power, presented false doctrines and lax moral principles to an already spiritually weakened world. By uttering invectives at the Papacy and the Church and by denying freedom of will he provided an occasion for a terrible division in the Church. Added to this new doctrine of Luther which was propagated in hatred and violence, the pagan element of humanism arose to demand absolute independence in philosophy, literature and law. This along with the lamentable economic conditions, the unbridled love of luxury, the widespread religious ignorance and hierarchical lethargy and corruption, helped spread the Protestant rebellion.

Germany, much of Switzerland under Zwingli, France under Calvin (Huguenots), England under Henry VIII and the treacherous Elizabeth, Scotland under John Knox, Holland, Denmark, Hungary and Transylvania, were all infected with Protestantism. All these nations were called by the name of Protestant. The Church, bewailing this sad state, saw the necessity of restoring ecclesiastical authority and discipline. After many difficulties, the Council of

Trent opened in 1545 and paved the way for true reformation and for the classic period of Canon Law. In this period after the Council of Trent (XVI to XVIII centuries), schools of canon law flourished and cultivated a highly organized system of law which blossomed into the modern Code of Canon Law.

Even so, there was developed but a minimum of pertinent legislation regarding the brother-sister arrangement. Only by the more recent authors was this topic consistently considered as one of the four remedies for invalid marriages. But even here it was little more than mentioned. By searching out the principles and laws concerning such topics as Adultery, Impotence, Divorce, Separation, Chastity, Abstinence, Second Marriages, Impediments, Presumed Death, Prior Bond, Cohabitation, Convalidation, and others, one can find some indirect and also some direct references to the brother-sister arrangement as a solution for an invalid marriage. In attempting to point out the legal existence and the justification and conditions for this mode of cohabitation during the period between the Council of Trent and the present day, the writer will discuss the topics of *Impotence* and *Presumed Death* in some detail in regard to the brother-sister arrangement.

Many corrections, helpful recommendations and strict regulations were enacted by the Council of Trent regarding marriage. The Twenty-fourth Session of the Council under the direction of Pope Pius IV (1560-1565) effected the necessary plan for restoring to the marriage state the order and the sanctity which had been lost in the preceding centuries.

The Council reiterated the evangelical and apostolic teaching that the sacrament of matrimony cannot be dissolved by reason of adultery on the part of one of the parties. In accord with the constant teaching of the Church, it was clearly stated that neither the guilty nor the innocent party can contract another marriage during the life-

time of the other without being anathematized.[27]In the very next
canon however, the Council repeated the law of the Church which
for various reasons permitted the partial separation of husband and
wife. This canon expressly stated:

> If anyone says that the Church errs when she declares
> that for many reasons a separation may take place between
> husband and wife *quoad thorum seu quoad cohabitationem,* for
> a determinate or indeterminate period, let him be anathema.[28]

The word *seu* was understood in a disjunctive sense, and consequently
also allowed a separation simply a *toro.* This amounted to the husband's and wife's living together as brother and sister for either a
determinate or an indeterminate duration of time, depending on the
cause of the separation, the will of the parties concerned, and the
particular decision of the ordinary.[29]

In the first chapter of this same session (XXIV) on the reform
of matrimony the Council exhorted the betrothed parties not to live
together in the same house until they had received the sacerdotal
blessing in the Church.[30] Obviously the Council here understood
"cohabit as brother and sister." In using the term "hortatur" the
Council seemed not to make its directive the equivalent of a command

---

[27] Sess. XXIV, *de matrimonio,* can. 7: "Si quis dixerit, ecclesiam errare,
cum docuit et docet juxta evangelicam et apostolicam doctrinam, propter
adulterium alterius coniugum matrimonii vinculum non posse dissolvi, et utrum-
que, vel etiam innocentem, qui causam non dedit, non posse altero coniuge
vivente aliud matrimonium contrahere, moecharique eum, qui dimissa adultera
aliam duxerit, et eam, quae dimisso adultero alii nupserit: anathema sit."
Quotations from the text of the Council of Trent are taken from H. J.
Schroeder, *Canons and Decrees of the Council of Trent* (St. Louis: Herder
Book Co., 1941) pp. 180-213, or, for the Latin text, pp. 451-481.

[28] Sess. XXIV, *de matrimonio,* can, 8: Si quis dixerit, Ecclesiam errare,
cum ob multas causas separationem inter coniuges *quoad thorum seu quoad
cohabitationem* ad certum incertumve tempus fieri posse decernit: anathema
sit.

[29] Cf.Prümmer, *Manuale Theologiae Moralis,* III, p. 492, n. 678, and p.
506, n. 695.

[30] "Praeterea eadem sancta synodus hortatur ut coniuges ante benedictionem sacerdotalem, in templo suscipiendam, in eadem domo non cohabitent. . ." In this same connection cf. c. 2, C. XXX, q. 5; cc. 3, 5, C. XXX,
q, 5; c. 19, C. XXXV, qq. 2, 3.

in any sense of the word. It was rather an exhortation, or an explicit encouragement that they remain separate *"quoad cohabitationem"* until they were married. The natural inference, then, seems to be that the Council showed its strong preference for non-cohabitation on the part of the betrothed persons even as between brother and sister, prior to the time of their marriage, but it did not necessarily disapprove or frown upon such an arrangement. Perhaps the Council intended the word *"hortatur"* in a stronger sense than the writer understands it, but at least it can be said that the Council did not absolutely forbid this arrangement.

The Council of Trent, however, dealt very severely with those who lived in adulterous concubinage and refused to heed the salutary admonitions of the Church.[31] No mention was made of the brother-sister arrangement. In fact, the Council gave expression to the principle: " ... he who has rashly despised the salutary precepts of the Church, is not worthy to enjoy without difficulty her beneficence."[32]

In one of the earlier sessions, however, the Council reminded the bishops of the manner in which the morals of the people were to be corrected.

In regard to those, however, who should happen to sin through human frailty, that command of the Apostle is to be observed, that they reprove, entreat, rebuke them in all kindness and patience, since benevolence toward those to be corrected often effects more than severity, exhortation more than threat, and charity more than force. But if on account of the gravity of the offense there is need of the rod, then is rigor to be tempered with gentleness, judgment with mercy, and severity with clemency, that discipline, so salutary and necessary for the people, may be preserved without harshness and they who are chastised may be corrected, or, if they are unwilling to repent, that others may by the wholesome example of their punishment be deterred from vices, since it is the duty of a shepherd, at once diligent and kind, to apply first of all mild anodynes to the disorders of his sheep, and after-

---

[31] Sess. XXIV, *de ref. matrim,* c. 8; sess. XXV, *de. ref.,* c. 14.

[32] " ... non enim est qui ecclesiae benignitatem facile experiatur cuius salubria praecepta temere contempsit."—Sess. XXIV, *de ref. matrim.,* c. 5.

wards, if the gravity of the disorder should demand it, to proceed to sharper and severer remedies; but if even these prove ineffective in removing the disorders, then he is to liberate the other sheep at least from the danger of contagion.[33]

Such was the guiding rule by which the Council governed its own disciplinary legislation. Such is the rule that has guided the Church in these past four hundred years in its dealing with misguided, fallen nature. It is this same seemingly paradoxical rule that governs modern moral and marriage problems, and grants permission in certain cases for the brother-sister arrangement.

Article 3. Impotence

Impotence has been the only cause for which the Church law as interpreted by canonists has since the twelfth century explicitly permitted the brother-sister relationship. The Council of Trent made no direct reference to impotence or to the impediment of impotence. Reiffenstuel (1642-1703), however, in his commentary on the Decretals, treated of it at length. He held the same teaching as the 12th and 13th century authors, and integrated his doctrine with considerable detail.

The fourth question he framed thus: "How can and must impotence be proved so that one may seek the annulment of marriage already contracted; and what is required before the marriage can be annulled or dissolved?" The answers were clear. Whenever either of the married couple was certain that the other was perpetually or permanently impotent, the potent party could not on his own authority, and without the previous legitimate approval in the external forum, dismiss the impotent party and marry another. But as all authors agreed, they were bound in the internal forum to abstain from all further attempts of copulation and from touches of a carnally stimulating character. He emphasized the need of certitude regarding the perpetual impotence and pointed out that with certainty in this there was certainty also that the marriage was to be regarded as

---

[33] Sess. XIII, *de ref.*, c. 1. Cf. also cc. 1-9, D. XLV; c. 6, D. XLV; cc. 16, 17, C. XXIV, q. 3.

null. Consequently the parties had to abstain from a number of actions that were licit in a true or at least a probably valid marriage. Accordingly in the external forum they were called on to live together until they proved the impotence in the external forum, but at the same time had to abstain from marital actions. This in actual fact was a cohabitation on the brother-sister basis.[34]

In order that they might separate in the external forum, Reiffenstuel further added that it was not enough that they both make known the perpetual impotence. According to the prescriptions of the canons, the perpetual impotence had to be established with proof through a *verum iudicium* before the judge could separate them or declare the marriage to be null.[35]

The same traditional decision was given by Reiffenstuel that had been given by Pirhing by Panormitanus, by Ioannes Andreae and in the decretal letter *Consultationi* of Pope Alexander III in regard to the law concerning those who knowingly contracted marriage with someone perpetually impotent. It is clear, said Reiffenstuel, that the impediment is diriment; nevertheless, one who had knowingly contracted an invalid union was bound to live perpetually with the impotent one, and to live chastely with her as with a sister, and minister to her necessities.[36] In the same place he quoted the famous decretal letter *Consultationi* in which the Pope had ordered: "...*ut quas tanquam uxores habere non possunt, habeant ut sorores.*"[37] But he added that if there was danger of incontinence on the part of the potent

[34] ...non potest pars potens propria auctoritate et absque praevia legitima probatione in foro externo facienda, impotentem repellere, et ad alias nuptias transire. Omnes tenentur nihilominus in foro interno ambo abstinere ab omni ulteriori attentatione copulae, et tactibus lascivis, . . . Reiffenstuel, *Ius Canonicum Universum* (5 vols. in 6, Romae: 1831-1834), Lib. IV, tit XV, n. 33 (hereafter cited *Ius Canonicum*).

[35] "... non potest eos Iudex separare, nec matrimonium illorum annullare, nisi prius legitima a S. S. Canonibus praescripta adhibeatur probatio... requiritur, ut id per verum iudicium probetur."—Reiffenstuel, *Ius Canonicum*, Lib. IV. tit. XV, n. 34.

[36] " . . . perpetuo habitare cum impotente, et cum illa tanquam sorore caste vivere, eique necessaria subministrare."—Reiffenstuel, *Ius Canonicum*, Lib. IV, tit. XV, n. 61.

[37] Reiffenstuel, *loc. cit.*, c. 4, X, *de frigidis et maleficatis, et impotentia coeundi*, IV, 15.

one, he might be given a dispensation for marrying another, but
"*manente nihilominus obligatione priorem alendi.*"

If, on the other hand, any married couples had in good faith, and
without knowledge of the antecedent and perpetual impotence of the
one or the other entered marriage and then learned of the impotence,
they could ask for a separation, but they were not bound to separate.
If they wished, as long as the danger of incontinence did not inter-
vene, they could indeed live together, not as consorts in marriage
(*coniuges*) but simply as brother and sister.[38]   In support of this, and
to show what was and what was not permitted to persons in such a
condition, Reiffenstuel then quoted from the decretal *Laudabilem* as
found in the Decretals of Gregory IX.

"*Quod si ambo consentiant simul esse, vir eam etsi non ut
uxorem, saltem habeat ut sororem, ut proin nec tactus, nec
aspectus, nec oscula lasciva, multo minus copula, eis sint licita,
hoc ipso quod nullum inter eos sit Matrimonium, quo solo tactus
praefati sint liciti.*"[39]

Special attention was paid to the condition *si abest periculum
incontinentiae.*   This same condition still is emphasized by modern
authors when they deal with the brother-sister arrangement as one
of the four solutions with reference to marriages which are null.
Reiffenstuel taught it as a common and certain teaching that, if the
danger of incontinence was present in such a putative marriage, the
parties were bound to procure a separation. According to the Scriptures, "*qui amat periculum peribit in illo,*" and hence anyone was
bound within the scope of his ability to remove the proximate

---

[38] . . . separationem petere possint, . . . tamen ad hoc non tenentur, sed,
si volunt, et periculum incontinentiae abest, simul cohabitare possunt non quidem ut coniuges, sed ut frater et soror."—Reiffenstuel *Ius Canonicum*, Lib. IV,
tit. XV, n. 62; Sanchez, *De Matrimonii Sacramento*, Lib. VII, disp. 97, n. 11.
Earlier mention of the danger of incontinence had been made by Raymond
of Pennafort (Supra, p. 31), and especially by Pope Sixtus V (1585-90). Reiffenstuel, being a moral theologian as well as a cannonist, emphasized the
absence of the danger of incontinence as being one of the fundamental conditions for the granting of the brother-sister arrangement in cases wherein
one or both of the parties were affected with impotence.

[39] Reiffenstuel, *Ius Canonicum*, Lib. IV. tit. XV, n. 62; c. 5, X, IV, 15;
Raymond of Pennafort, *Summa* Lib, IV, tit. 16, n. 1.

danger. He definitely insisted that the parties could not share the same bed.[40]

This last demand, namely that they could not share the same bed, had been made in the Epistle *Cum frequenter* of Pope Sixtus V (1585-90). This document, concise and specific, is worthy of careful consideration.

In the document itself the pope mentioned that he had duly considered the canonical sanctions and the natural law itself regarding those who by nature were frigid and impotent, and those who were who were not able to contract marriage, such as eunuchs, and especially those who could not have a woman as a wife and would not have her as a sister. The pope had learned that they married, not that they might live chastely, but that in their union they might nurture their base and libidinous intention under the pretext and appearance of marriage, in which the execution of their evil design became the occasion of sin and of scandal, and tended to the damnation of their souls. Of such practices he said: "*Sunt ab Ecclesia Dei prorsus exterminandae.*" With these considerations in mind he declared that no benefit could come from the unions of such impotent people, but rather only temptations and libidinous cravings. Accordingly he commanded that all impotent men and those who lacked both testicles be prohibited from contracting marriage with any woman, whether the woman possessed or lacked knowledge of the defect. Such men were to be declared incapable of contracting marriage, and all local ordinaries were forbidden in any way to permit such unions in the future. Those who had contracted such unions were to be separated, and all such unions were to be declared null and void.

The bishop was also to see to it that a separation was effected by those who had already contracted a union of this sort, if it appeared that they contracted it, not in order to live chastely, but with a view to indulging libidinous and carnal actions. The separation was also to be effected if they were convicted of sharing one and the same bed.

The Pope then decreed that any judgment or definition contrary

---

[40]". . . in eodem lecto cubare non possunt."—Reiffenstuel, *Ius Canonicum*, Lib. IV, tit. XV, n. 63.

to his statement stood null and void. This ruling was to apply to any cause or judicial instance. And it applied also to any and all judges and commissioners, no matter by what authority or dignity they held office. Accordingly he nullified any and every faculty that any of them may have had of judging or interpreting a case in a different way. He likewise indicated that if anyone attempted a decision different from this, either knowingly or unknowingly, that decision would prove null and void. This regulation applied to all contrary decisions, even if made in the past.

The rule here enacted was binding in character, notwithstanding all statutes, municipal laws or customs of any state, province, or kingdom whatsoever, to the contrary. Everything undertaken in opposition to this letter was to be considered as an abuse and a corruption even if it could be said for the practice that it had been observed from time immemorial.[41]

---

[41]Sixtus V. Motu proprio ad Episcopum Navariensem, Nuntium Sedis Apostolicae in regnis Hispaniarum, *Cum frequenter*, 27 iun. 1587: · . .

§ 1. "Nos igitur attendentes, quod secundum canonicas sanctiones, et naturae rationem, qui frigidae naturae sunt, et impotentes, iidem minime apti ad contrahenda matrimonia reputantur, quodque praedicti eunuchi, aut spadones, quas tamquam uxores habere non possunt, easdem habere ut sorores nolunt, quia experientia docet, tam ipsos dum se potentes ad coeundum iact-itant, quam mulieres, quae eis nubunt, non ut caste vivant, sed ut carnaliter invicem coniungantur prava, et libidinosa intentione, sub praetextu, et in figura matrimonii turpes huiusmodi commixtiones affectare, quae cum peccati, et scandali occasionem prabeant, et in animarum damnationem tendant, sunt ab Ecclesia Dei prorsus exterminandae. Et insuper considerantes, quod ex spad-onum huiusmodi, et eunuchorum coniugiis nulla utilitas provenit, sed potius tentationum illecebrae, ac incentiva libidinis oriuntur, eidem Fraternitati tuae per praesentes committimus, et mandamus, ut coniugia per dictos, et alios quoscumque eunuchos, et spadones, utroque teste carentes cum quibusvis muli-eribus, defectum praedictum sive ignorantibus, sive etiam scientibus, contrahi prohibeas, eosque ad matrimonia quomodocumque contrahenda inhabiles auc-toritate Nostra declares, et tam locorum Ordinariis, ne huiusmodi coniunctiones de cetero fieri quoquomodo permittant, interdicas, quam eos etiam, qui sic de facto matrimonium contraxerint, separari cures, et matrimonia ipsa sic de facto contracta, nulla, irrita, et invalida esse decernas.

§ 2. Eos etiam qui sic iam contraxerunt, si appareat illos non ut caste simul vivant, contraxisse, sed actibus carnalibus, et libidinosis operam dare simulve in uno, et eodem lecto cum praedictis mulieribus dormire convincantur, omnino similiter separari cures.

Cappello contends that this document not merely reflects a matter of discipline, but represents an authentic and infallible declaration of the natural divine law regarding impotence, which binds everyone, even infidels. According to Cappello, Pope Sixtus "*nihil novi ea inducit vel statuit.*"[42]

In line with the ruling of Pope Sixtus, one sees the point of Reiffenstuel was well made. Reiffenstuel also pointed out that other authors dissuaded such impotent and affected people from such cohabitation, which was ordinarily a very dangerous arrangement, that scarcely ever was free from danger of sin as resulting at least from touches, embraces and other carnal actions.[43]

In the same place, Reiffenstuel spoke of subsequent impotence. In the event of a supervening impotence for one or both of the married partners, it was again a common and certain teaching that the parties were to live together. The couple indeed had to abstain from any attempt at *copula* but under proper conditions they could indulge in the inchoate or incomplete acts of the marital life. The same actions are deemed allowable by modern authors also, but the conditions required by them are various. Some insist that there must be no danger of pollution, whereas others demand simply that there be no danger of consenting to the pollution.[44]

------

§ 3. Nos enim ita in praemissis, et non aliter, per quoscumque Iudices et Commissarios, quacumque auctoritate, et dignitate fungentes, sublata eis, et eorum cuilibet, quavis aliter iudicandi, et interpretandi facultate, in quacumque causa, et instantia iudicari, et definiri debere, et si secus super his a quoquam quavis auctoritate, scienter vel ignoranter attentatum forsan est hactenus, vel attentari in posterum contigerit, irritum et inane decernimus.

§ 4. Non obstantibus cuiusvis Civitatis, Provinciae, aut Regni statutis, legibus municipalibus, aut consuetudinibus, quae abusus potius et corruptelae censendae sunt, etiamsi ab immemorabili tempore observatae dicuntur, ceterisque contrariis quibuscumque."—*Codicis Juris Canonici Fontes, cura* Emi Petri Card. Gasparri editi. 9 vols. Romae: Typis Polyglottis Vaticanis, 1923-1939; (Vols.. VII, VIII, IX, ed. cura et studio Emi Iustiniani Card. Serédi,) n. 161 (hereafter cited *Fontes*).

[42]*De Matrimonio*, n. 343, pp. 351-352.

[43]*Ius Canonicum*, Lib. IV, tit. XV, n. 63.

[44]*Ius Canonicum*, Lib. IV, tit. XV n. 65; Cappello, *De Matrimonio*, pp. 809, 810; n. 814; Coronata, *De Sacramentis*, III, pp. 418-420: n. 328; Sanchez *De Matrimonii Sacramento*, Lib. VII, Disp. 102; Lib. IX, Disp. 17, n. 20 ff.; Lib. IX, Disp. 45.

Accordingly, though in strict principle and theory such parties need not live as brother and sister, they may if they so wish. But factually if they cannot avoid pollution, or, as some hold, preclude all consent to pollution, they must abstain even from unconsummated marital actions, and live together as brother and sister.

Article 4. Presumed Death

The only explicit historical reference to the brother-sister arrangement in regard to cases involving the impediment of *ligamen* is made under the heading of "Presumed Death." While the explicit reference is not made until most recently,[45] implicit references to the brother-sister arrangement under the heading of "*presumed death*" have been made at least from the time of Reiffenstuel and Sanchez. Reiffenstuel pointed out that the *mala* or *bona fides* plays an essential part in the solution of such cases, as does also the doubt or moral certitude concerning the life of the first spouse.

Reiffenstuel asked what the law was for those who entered a second marriage when they were in doubt or were favored only with probability concerning the death of the first spouse. He answered directly that, if both parties of the second marriage were in doubt regarding the continued life of the first spouse, they contracted in bad faith, and both were forbidden by law to either request or grant the marital *debitum*. The reason given was that, since both had contracted in bad faith, neither could claim possession of the other, and hence neither had a right to the conjugal *debitum*.[46] It is to be noted in this case that mention was made of the obligation of separating, not *a cohabitatione*, but simply *a toro*. Hence it seems that they were to live together as brother and sister as long as the death of the former spouse remained in doubt.

---

[45] Vlaming-Bender, *Praelectiones Iuris Matrimonii* (4. ed., Bussum, Holland: Brand, 1950), p. 202.

[46] "Accedit, quod, quamdiu ambo coniuges manent in dubio practico, an coniux prior adhuc vivat, consequenter an Matrimonium eorum mala fide contractum valeat, nec ne, hoc ipso debitum petere aut reddere non valeant; cum stante dubio practico operari non liceat, ut tenent communiter Theologi."·· Reiffenstuel, *op. cit.*, Lib. IV, tit. XXI, n. 25; f. Sanchez, *op. cit.*, Lib. II, Disp. 42, n. 7.

Reiffenstuel then solved the case in which both parties had entered the second marriage in good faith, but at a later time one or both began to have doubts regarding the continued life of the first spouse, and consequently doubts also about the validity of their marriage. In this case the one suffering the doubt had to inquire into the truth, and during the time of inquiry remained without the right to request the marital *debitum*. But the *debitum* was to be rendered if the other party was in good faith when requesting its exercise. If both were in doubt, both had to abstain from requesting or granting the marital debt while diligent inquiry was being made. If after the making of a diligent search the doubt still remained, the parties could nevertheless live as husband and wife.[47]

Finally, when a marriage had been contracted in the best of faith on the side of both spouses, they might, one or both, gain morally certified knowledge that the former spouse was still alive. The party gaining this knowledge could not ask for or render the marital debt. He immediately had to abstain from any and all carnal relations and forestall all danger thereof through a return to the former spouse. Even if proof could not be brought in court that the other spouse was still living, but there nevertheless was moral certainty that the first spouse was alive, then the knowing party could not live with the second spouse in the role of consort even when compelled under pain of excommunication or other grave penalties to do so.[48]

If one apply here the same principles that were given expression by Reiffenstuel in regard to proof of impotence in the external forum, one sees that the brother-sister arrangement was certainly contemplated in the case. In the internal forum, the parties having knowledge (moral certitude) that the first spouse was still living knew that the second marriage was invalid, and in consequence could not use the prerogative of marriage in this second union. In the external forum, since they could not prove that the first spouse was still living, they could be commanded to remain together, in which case they were

---

[47]Reiffenstuel, *op. cit.*, Lib. IV, tit. XXI, nn. 25-30; Sanchez *op. cit.*, Lib. II, Disp. 41, nn. 20-22, and 42.

[48]Reiffenstuel, *op. cit.*, Lib. IV, tit. XXI, n. 25-30.

under the necessity of living as sister and brother. However, it should also be pointed out, as Reiffenstuel had done before and again did here, that if they could not live together continently, then they had to separate (*a cohabitatione*) even though they might have been threatened with excommunication for so doing.[49]

Authors have explicitly spoken of the brother-sister arrangement with reference to impotence cases at least from the eleventh century onward.[50] They also seem to have expressly permitted or demanded the brother-sister arrangement in "presumed death" or *ligamen* cases. Modern authors, however, seem to make this remedy applicable not only for cases involving the element of impotence or of presumed death, but also for marriages invalid by reason of some diriment impediments deriving from ecclesiastical legislation. It must be immediately added that such an application of doctrine is subject to the most rigid rules and conditions. Each individual case must be scrutinized and investigated before it can be determined that the permission to live together as brother and sister may be granted, and then, when the permission has been made available, certain restrictions and rigid conditions must be verified.

Reiffenstuel appears to be the first author who explicitly extended the application of the brother-sister arrangement from marriages null by reason of impotence to marriages null by reason of any diriment impediment.[51]

He asked what was to be done by the married parties, if in a marriage already contracted they learn that it was invalidly contracted

---

[49]"Debet potius sententiam excommunicationis humiliter sustinere, quam per carnale commercium peccatum operari mortale. Ratio est: quia commercium carnale cum alio quam coniuge intrinsece malum est: consequenter *numquam* licet . . . " Reiffenstuel, *op. cit.*, Lib. IV, tit. XXXI, n. 30.

[50]The first explicit reference occurred, no doubt, much earlier, but the exact date and source cannot be established with more than probability. Cf., *supra*, pp. 13-14.

[51]Though the writer has spared neither time nor effort in seeking to determine the first author who made this transition explicitly, perhaps upon further research it could be found that before Reiffenstuel someone correlated the principles already explored by the more ancient writers, and arrived at the explicit conclusion that the brother-sister arrangement could possibly be used, or could even have to be used, as a remedy for marriages which are null by reason of a diriment impediment other than impotence.

by reason of a diriment impediment. In answering, Reiffenstuel first of all pointed out that, if they were certain that the marriage was null they could neither request nor grant the marital *debitum*. This obligation bound them, even though the impediment could not be established with full judicial proof, and even though they were perhaps compelled by an ecclesiastical judge under threat of excommunication to maintain a community of life between them. He pointed out that this was the certain and unanimous teaching, and based his assertion on the principles found in the Decretals of Gregory IX.[52] It is quite evident that, even though the parties might incur excommunication, they could not live together as husband and wife. The following paragraph shows implicitly that they had to live as brother and sister, at least in the internal forum, for they knew themselves not to be married and hence could not use marriage, but they also were forbidden to separate (*a cohabitatione*) on their own authority.

In his second response, Reiffenstuel stated that, even though one or both of the already married parties learned later of the impediment, they could not separate (leave each other) on their own authority, but with respect to the external forum needed the authority of the ecclesiastical judge.[53] If the impediment was such that the spouses could not furnish full judicial proof of its existence, or if they did not dare prove it because of a possible defamation of their character, they could, and in the forum of conscience had to, separate *if they could not live together as BROTHER AND SISTER WITH-OUT INVITING THE DANGER OF INCONTINENCE.* In the internal forum they were not bound in their obedience to the bishop to live as husband and wife, even though they were commanded under censure to cherish a community life between them.[54]

---

[52]"Debet potius sententiam excommunicationis humiliter sustinere, quam per carnale commercium peccatum operari mortale."—C. 44, X, *de sententia excommunicationis,* V, 39. "Quoniam omne, quod non est ex fide peccatum est; et quidquid fit contra conscientiam aedificat ad gehennam."—C. 13, X, *de restitutione spoliatorum,* II. 13.   ; Reiffenstuel, *Ius Canonicum,* Lib. IV, tit. XX, n. 22.

[53]Reiffenstuel, *ibid.,* n. 14.

[54]"Quamvis unus vel ambo coniuges certam notitiam impedimenti habentes, Matrimonio iam contracto, ab invicem propria auctoritate discedere nequeant, sed pro foro externo indigeant auctoritate Iudicis . . . Nihilominus si imped-imentum ita est constitutum, ut illud plene probare non possint, vel ob dif-

It is evident that if one or both of the parties learned with certainty that their marriage was null by reason of diriment impediment,
and if it was physically or morally impossible to prove the existence
of the impediment in the external forum, then they were to live together as brother and sister, provided that there was no danger of
incontinence. This was so for the reason that they could not in the
external forum separate (*a cohabitatione*) by their own authority,
and they could not prove the impediment in the external forum so
as to receive the proper judicial authority to separate. At the same
time they knew themselves to be invalidly married and that any
marital relations would be sinful. Consequently the only possible
solution under the law was for them to live together as brother and
sister. But even then, so Reiffenstuel pointed out, if there was danger
of incontinence in the brother-sister arrangement, they had to separate
a cohabitatione, even though the bishop might place them under censure for so separating.

It seems clear that Reiffenstuel was referring to diriment impediments from which the Church cannot or usually does not dispense.
For in the very next paragraph he limited the foregoing conclusions
by saying that, if the impediment was one from which the pope or
bishop can and usually does dispense, then the parties could have the
marriage dissolved on grounds of nullity if they wished, but they
were not bound to do so. They could procure a dispensation also.
In fact, they were sometimes to procure a dispensation if the good
of the children born of this union, or if some other grave cause,
demanded it.[55]

---

famationem sui non audeant: possunt, immo tenentur, in foro conscientiae ab
invicem discedere, si absque periculo incontinentiae ut frater et soror simul
cohabitare nequeant. Neque tenentur in foro interno obedire Episcopo, con-
trarium etiam sub censura praecipienti." -- Reifenstuel, *loc. cit.*

[55] Limitatur tamen conclusio casu, quo tale coniugis versatur impedimentum, in quo Papa, vel Episcopus potest, et solet dispensare; tunc, enim quamvis matrimonium utpote nullum dissolvere valerent, si vellent, tamen non tenerentur, sed, possent procurare dispensationem. Imo hanc procurare nonnum-
quam tenerentur, ut si bonum prolium ex simili matrimonio progenitarum, aut
alia, gravis causa id exigeret." Reiffenstuel, *ibid.*, n. 15.

A great deal was said by Reiffenstuel in this particular matter. In fact, these passages seem to contain three of the four solutions offered by all the modern authors in regard to marriages null by reason of diriment impediments.[56] The terminology employed and the conditions postulated by Reiffenstuel should be carefully considered, for the conclusions which he drew from the suppositions depended on the wording and the conditions invoked by him.

The first condition was *certain knowledge* by both of the parties concerning the nullity of the marriage, so that neither of them could render or request the marital *debitum*. The second was the *nullity* of the already contracted marriage by reason of some diriment impediment. The third was the impossibility in the external forum of separating from each other by their own authority... *necessity of the judicial authority for separating in the external forum*. The fourth was the *impossibility* (*physical or moral*) *of proving the impediment* in the external forum. The fifth was that the parties *were to live as brother and sister*. Finally, if there was danger of incontinence in this latter arrangement, they were to separate even in the external forum in spite of any threatened excommunication or penalty.

It seems quite obvious that Reiffenstuel was dealing in the case with a diriment impediment not yielding to any dispensation, for he stated that the conclusions arrived at would be different or limited if there were question of an impediment that could be or usually

---

[56]The four offered solutions are: cohabitation on a brother-sister basis, convalidation, declaration of nullity, and "dissimulation." (good faith). The one which is here omitted by Reiffenstuel is "dissimulation." It was omitted by Reiffenstuel inasmuch as he began with the supposition that one or both of the parties had a certain knowledge of the nullity. Cf. Reiffenstuel, loc. cit.; Coronata, *De Sacramentis*, III, n. 668; Gasparri, *De Matrimonio*, n. 841, p. 841; Chelodi, *Jus Canonicum de Matrimonio*, (5 ed., Vincenza: Societa Anonima Tepografica Editrice, 1947), n. 163, p. 207; Chretien, *De Matrimonio*, (2 ed., Metis, "*Le Lorrain*" apud J. Hocquard, 1937), p. 444 Wernz, *Ius Decretalium* (6 vols., Romae, 1898-1914; Vol. IV, 1904), IV, 943; Vlaming-Bender, *Praelectiones Juris Matrimonii*, pp. 519-523; *et passim*.

is dispensed by the bishop or pope. In this latter case, he said, the parties could have the marriage dissolved if they wished.[57] But they were not bound to dissolve it, since they could obtain a dispensation and enter the union validly. In the first case, if the diriment impedi-ment did not yield to any dispensation, they were bound to dissolve the union, for they could not obtain any dispensation. But even in the second case (in which they could have the marriage dissolved if they wished, or obtain a dispensation) they could by reason of other circumstances be bound to obtain a dispensation rather than a declar-ation of nullity, e. g., with a view to the good of the children, or some other grave cause.

These same conclusions were drawn also by the more recent authors. It seems freely admissible to maintain that their ideas and conclusions were more easily arrived at in consequence of the correlat-ing of principles accomplished at the hands of Reiffenstuel. Be that as it may, the more recent authors have clarified the problems of the use of the different solutions relating to invalid marriages by expressing and discussing more of the conditions, qualifications, and suppositions that enter such cases.

All the consulted authors who treat the four solutions agree, first of all, that there are four possible solutions, and they also agree that of these solutions the last one to be applied is the brother-sister arrangement. The normal reason assigned for the placing of this mode of cohabitation last in the order of choice is the danger of incontinence. But they do not say, nor is it felt that they intend to say, that this manner of solution is *in actuality* to be of less frequent use than any of the other three solutions. The authors also agree generally on the conditions and laws to be considered in the deciding of a particular case.[58]

---

[57]Although it is not mentioned here, he no doubt assumed that the nulllity could be proved in the external forum, for otherwise there would not have been any differnce between the cases.

[58] E. g. Gasparri, Cappello, Coronata, Noldin, De Smet, Chelodi, Chrétien, Wernz-Vidal, Vlaming-Bender, Becker, Ter Haar, Doheny, etc.

PART II

CANONICAL COMMENTARY

INTRODUCTION

With the recognition and establishment of diriment matrimonial
impediments of the positive and natural divine law and of ecclesiastical
law respectively, there is need of additional legislation, both general
and specific, regarding the solution of the particular cases affected
by these impediments. Recognizing the fallible and fallen nature
of man, the Church has endeavored to use every means at its disposal
for the salvation of souls. To this end the theologians and canonists
of the Church have labored incessantly, not only to forestall invalid
marriages or marriages detrimental to the souls of men, but, under
the loving providence of God, to find a happy solution or settlement
for those who, by fault or by error, have become involved in an
invalid and spiritually disastrous union. Priests in parochial work
are ever aware of and frequently heavily burdened with the problems
of their spotted and unspotted sheep. As a result, a detailed study of
the law regarding possible solutions (convalidation, declaration of
nullity with complete separation, or dissimulation) for invalid marriages has been made.

It is the purpose of this work to investigate the legislation and
requirements given for one of these solutions, which as yet has not
been investigated, developed or used to any great extent. It is that
permissible cohabitation in invalid marriages, otherwise known as the
"brother-sister arrangement," permitted by the proper authority as
a solution of *last resort* for invalid marriages that cannot be validated [1]
or otherwise adjudicated.

Little or no explicit legislation has been enacted regarding the
brother-sister arrangement, and few specific requirements have been
suggested or demanded by law. The writer wishes to offer a few
suggestions that may prove helpful in making the *"frater-soror"* ar-

---

[1] Cf. Doheny, *Canonical Procedure in Matrimonial Cases* (2 vols., Vol.II,
Informal Procedure, Milwaukee: Bruce, 1944), II, 604.

rangement not only a plausible solution for such invalid unions but a practicable one as well. At the same time he recognizes the dangers accompanying any attempt to set down any norms or standards of a definitive nature by which such delicate cases are to be handled. Perhaps the criticism of the present suggestions will produce an even more practical and safe method of approaching the problem ... a method that not only will prove beneficial to the individual couple, but also will safeguard the integrity and dignity of the sacrament of matrimony.

In the attempt to accomplish the purpose of this work there is, first of all, to be explained the nature of the brother-sister arrangement. Since there are five fundamental conditions or requirements that must be met and fulfilled in any case for which a possible brother-sister arrangement is sought, these same five factors are treated separately and in some detail. Since cases may differ, one or the other of these five conditions may need to be emphasized more than the rest, but all five are absolutely postulated for the proper and safe use of the brother-sister arrangement as a solution for invalid marriages. Secondly, a separate consideration is given to the diriment impediments from which there may arise the possibility for the application of the brother-sister arrangement on a permanent basis. Of less importance but of equal practicality in a work of this kind are the immediate details and lesser conditions involved in the granting of the needed permission. Finally, other considerations of interest, such as the question of Christian burial for those who had lived under the arrangement, or the temporary use of "fraternal" cohabitation in marriage cases still pending before the tribunal, will receive due treatment.

The writer spared no time or effort in attempting to enumerate all exigencies, conditions, suppositions and requirements which are frequently met in the application of the brother-sister solution. But, even after this considerable thought and research, the writer is forced to admit that the solution of any individual case depends fundamentally upon the inspected nature of the combined circumstances which attend the case and upon the subsequent prudent judgement of a competent confessor, pastor or ordinary. It would be foolhardy to attempt the impossible task of laying down a simple, hard-and-fast rule by which all cases must be solved. It is hoped that the present expression of norms, principles, suppositions and conditions will help to contribute to the formulation of a prudent and salutary judgement in the very complex matter of "fraternal cohabitation."

CHAPTER III

NATURE OF THE BROTHER-SISTER ARRANGEMENT

Article I. A Solution of Last Resort

It must be clearly understood at the outset that the brother-sister arrangement spoken of in this Part II necessarily and completely excludes any reference to the brother-sister arrangement freely agreed upon by those who have contracted a valid marriage. Such an arrangement, when freely entered for supernatural motives by those who in a valid marriage could lawfully exercise all marital rights reflects a praiseworthy endeavor and mode of life, and is plainly regarded as such by the Church.[2] The "fraternal" cohabitation or brother-sister arrangement here considered is the arrangement which the authors present as a solution for the union which has the appearance of a true marriage.[3]

"Fraternal" cohabitation, as permitted by the Church in invalid marriages, is not an arrangement established by the Church for the free use of persons who cannot contract a valid marriage in view of a diriment impediment that cannot be dislodged by means of a dispensation, or by way of its ultimate cessation.[4] It is not a *substitute* for marriage, nor is its use an optional matter.[5] For example, two young people desiring to marry each other learn that one or both parties have contracted a diriment impediment which cannot be removed. The mere desire of marriage or their professed love for each

---

[2]Cf. I Cor. vii, 5; Can. 1128. All authors agree that mutual consent furnishes the necessary "*iusta causa*," provided there is no danger of incontinence. Cappelllo, *De Matrimonio*, p. 819, n. 825 bis; Louis J. Nau, *Marriage Laws of the Code of Canon Law* (New York: Pustet, 1933), p. 193, n. 150.

[3]Cappello, *De Matrimonio*, p. 841, n. 841; Coronata, *De Sacramentis*, III, p. 929, n. 668.

[4]Special treatment of the diriment impediments that may occasion the use of the brother-sister arrangement is found in Chapter V of this work.

[5]Cf. John Krol, "Permission to Parties Invallidly married to Live as Brother and Sister," *The Jurist*, XI (1951), 22.

other is not sufficient cause to warrant substituting for their intended but impossible marriage a union in which the brother-sister arrangement would obtain instead. The unyielding diriment impediment, whether of the divine or the ecclesiastical law, bars all possibility of a valid marriage, and accordingly the moral law which calls on people to shun the proximate occasion of sin will not allow these parties to enter an unnecessary union in which the brother-sister arrangement could be countenanced.

The brother-sister arrangement is not an optional matter. It is very aptly called a solution of *last resort*[6] for an already effected invalid union. If any other solution for the existing situation is possible, such as the validation of the marriage, or a complete separation, or even dissimulation, then the brother-sister arrangement cannot be permitted. It is only in the event that all other solutions are found wanting that there is any possibility of using the brother-sister arrangement.[7] Although the authors are not in perfect agreement regarding other requirements or conditions in the use of the brother-sister arrangement, they are perfectly agreed that it is a *last resort* solution. If two solutions for the problem were equally possible, "fraternal" cohabitation and one other, "fraternal" cohabitation could not be permitted. All authors are agreed that the other solution would necessarily be the one to be employed.[8] The order, as recorded by the authors, of the four given solutions for invalid marriages which have the appearance of a valid marriage places the brother-sister arrangement in the last place.[9] It is only by reason of specific circumstances which rule out the adoption of the first of the three solutions that the brother-sister arrangement is permitted.[10]

---

[6]Cf. Krol, *loc. cit.*

[7]This matter is treated in greater detail in Chapter IV, Article I.

[8]Cappello, Gasparri, Chelodi, Chrétien, Payen, Coronata, Vlaming-Bender De Smet, etc·

[9]*Infra,* Chapter IV, article 1.

[10]Cf. De Smet, *Praxis Matrimonialis ad Usum Parochi et Confesarii* (2. ed., Burgis: Beyaert, 1939), pp. 141-142, n. 90 (hereafter cited *Praxis*); Gasparri, *De Matrimonio,* II, p. 249, n. 1181; Vlaming-Bender, *Praelectiones Iuris Matrimonii,* pp. 519-523; Chelodi, *De Matrimonio,* p. 207, n. 163; Chrétien, *De Matrimonio,* p. 444, n. 268.

The brother-sister arrangement is a canonical solution granted by the Church as a last resort for worthy persons involved in an invalid marriage. The words *"Matrimonium invalidum"* are to be interpreted in their fullest sense, so as to comprehend likewise a putative marriage (can. 1015), which in other respects produces the same effects as a valid marriage.[11] It is normally postulated, for the application of the brother-sister arrangement, that the parties actually attempted to contract marriage, and that their attempted contract bear the real appearance or figure of a marriage.[12]

---

[11] In the strict etymology of the words a distinction may be made between the terms *null* and *void* (*nullum et irritum*). The term null is more properly applied to a marriage that is invalid on account of the non-observance of the necessary juridical form. The term void, on the other hand, is more fittingly applied to marriage which is invalid on account of a diriment impediment (cf. canon 1036 §2) or on account of vitiated consent (cf. canon 1081, §1). Generally, however, no distinction of this kind is made in common usage and the law itself does not strictly hold to this distinction. The Code uses the terms *null, void, invalid* (*nullum, irritum, invalidum*) to designate a marriage that lacks validity. Cf. canons 1070, §1; 1072; De Smet, *De Sponsalibus et Matrimonio*, (4 ed., Brugis, 1927), n. 158; Payen, *De Matrimonio in Missionibus ac Potissimum in Sinis Tractatus Practicus et Casus*, (2. ed., 3 vols., Zi-ka-wei: In Typographia T'ou-se-we, 1935-1936), I, n. 139, (hereafter cited as *De Matrimonio*). It is in this same unrestricted sense that the terms are used in the present work.

[12] In a strict manner of speaking, the *figure* or *appearance* of marriage (*species vel figura matrimonii*) consists of the expression of marital consent according to the necessary external substantial form, the while the marriage itself is invalid. Accordingly, if the form required for the validity of a particular marriage is not externally observed, the union lacks the semblance or appearance of marriage in a strict canonical sense· Catholics bound by canon 1099 do not set up a union having the *"species vel figura matrimonii"* in the strict sense when they attempt marriage before a minister or justice of the peace. Cf. Gasparri, *Tractatus Canonicus de Matrimonio* (ed. nova ad mentem Codicis Iuris Canonici, 2 vols., Romae: Typis Polyglottis Vaticanis, 1932), I, n. 473, (hereafter cited *De Matrimonio*); De Smet, *De Sponsalibus et Matrimonio*, n. 158; Payen, *De Matrimonio*, I, n. 139.

In the present work, however, the phrase *appearance or figure of marriage* is not to be understood in a strict manner. Herein the phrase refers to any attempted marriage or to any union which is commonly regarded as a marriage, irrespective of the previous use of the proper juridical form of marriage.

This attempt could have been made before a civil magistrate or before a minister of a religious body.   Even an attempted common law marriage would suffice if the civil law in the locality in which the attempt was made sanctioned such marriages by attributing to them all the effects of a matrimonial contract, and provided that common law unions are regarded as means whereby licit marriage relations may be established between a man and a woman.   Also despite the many precautions taken by the Church, it may sometimes happen that the apparent "marriage" is attempted "*in facie ecclesiae.*"[18]

It is said that an attempted invalid marriage is normally postulated for the use of the brother-sister arrangement, for it could indeed happen that a man and woman, without benefit of any marriage ceremony whatsoever, begin to cohabit with each other and present themselves to the public as husband and wife. In this case there is question, not of an invalid marriage even in the widest sense of the term, but simply of a union in which the man and woman appear to be husband and wife, but in reality have not contracted even an invalid matrimonial union.

In either case, that of an invalid marriage, or that of a union with the appearance of marriage, the brother-sister arrangement finds possible application. The important point is that an invalid marriage or at least a union with the appearance of marriage is a definitely postulated antecedent to any consideration or application of the brother-sister arrangement. Legal records witness the previously attempted civil or religious marriage, whereas common knowledge or opinion testifies to the antecedent union which has indeed the appearance of marriage, but which in fact has remained without the benefit of any marriage ceremony.

The concept of a "previously effected invalid union" is not constituted simply through the commission of a single sinful act, such as adultery, fornication, incest or sacrilege. Nor is the concept of "an invalid union" evidenced even by a plurality of separate sinful actions,

---

[18] This is known to happen in cases of presumed death, of impotency, of mixed marriages in which the non-Catholic party erroneously or in bad faith declares himself to be unmarried when in reality he is bound by the impediment of *ligamen,* etc.

though these actions were of frequent occurrence with the same person and in the same place of residence. In order to fulfill the concept of an invalid union and hence to qualify for the brother-sister arrangement, the union must be one previously entered and one which has the appearance of a marriage. Such a union must reflect an element of continuity and an appearance of perpetuity. It must normally be supposed that the man and the woman have set up housekeeping and to all appearances have acted as husband and wife for some time previous to their application for the use of the brother-sister arrangement.[14]

The length of time for which the couple has been involved in the invalid marriage is an element of but relative import. Since the granting of permission for the brother-sister arrangement is more immediately dependent upon other circumstances, such as the presence of children, the state of ill health, the factor of economic security, etc., the time element may vary in individual cases. It is, nevertheless, of great importance that the "invalid marriage" reflect the status of an earlier entered union. Though the requesting of permission for the brother-sister arrangement is necessarily conditioned on a previously entered invalid union, people must nevertheless know that they are forewarned against entering invalid or impossible marriages with the precise purpose of receiving, at their own convenience, permission to live together as brother and sister. To permit them in this matter to acquire a false notion would involve the sin of giving scandal . . . serious scandal in the strict sense of the term.[15] Any likelihood of resulting serious scandal of this type would overrule any granting of permission for the brother-sister arrangement. Not only would the parties be placing their own eternal salvation in great jeopardy, but the Church itself would falter in its task and duty of fully responding to all the claims which Christ established for the

---

[14] The distinction between the invalid marriage, which presupposes some kind of ceremony, and the invalid union, which abstracts from the ceremony of marriage, will not be expressly adverted to in the course of this work. Both situations are to be understood under the one phrase ("invalid marriage") unless a closer distinction is expressly invoked.

[15] The element of scandal is treated in greater detail under Article 2 of Chapter IV.

benefit of Christian marriage. This could readily lead to a widespread disregard of both the divine and ecclesiastical law, and subsequently, by contributing greatly to the moral and physical breakdown of a Christian civilization, lead many to utter spiritual ruin. When considering the brother-sister arrangement, one must ever be mindful of the age-old principle that the common good supercedes the private good.[16]

"Fraternal" cohabitation must be regarded as a last resort solution. It is reluctantly tolerated rather than eagerly granted. It is tolerated indeed, but only if it is clearly evident that no other solution is possible,[17] that all the postulated conditions are fulfilled, and that the laws of God and His Church are preserved intact.[18]

Article 2.   Precautionary Elements

The material import of the brother-sister arrangement is clear from the very words by which there is designated this canonical solution for invalid marriages. The situation is one in which both the man and the woman, knowing that they are not and cannot be validly married, are permitted to continue living in the same house or dwelling place.[19] They may eat at the same table, sign their names as Mr. and Mrs., continue to minister to the spiritual and physical

---

[16] "Quibus addendum est, quod bonum commune maius est bono privato, quia bonum totius praestat bono partis." Cf. Noldin-Schmitt, *Summa Theologiae Moralis, iuxta Codicem Iuris Canonici* (26. ed., 3 vols., Oeniponte-Lipsiae: Typis et Siemptibus Feliciani Rauch, 1940-1941), II, p. 80, n. 74 (hereafter cited as *Summa*).

[17] "Porro cohabitatio uti frater et soror · . . in extraordinariis tantum adiunctis, quum alia remedia desint omnino permitti poterit." Cf. Cappello, *De Matrimonio*, p. 841, n. 841.

[18] Cf. Can. 855.

[19] An exception regarding the possession of knowledge by both parties is pointed out by Vlaming-Bender. If in a putative marriage the party who does not know of the nullity of the marriage is already in old age (*provectioris aetatis*) and lives as a brother with a sister, it seems that this party need not be told, but rather should be left to continue his adopted mode of life. Cf. Vlaming-Bender, *Praelectiones Iuris Matrimonii*, p. 523.

needs of their children,[20] and to all external appearances continue to live as husband and wife. But, since there is not and cannot be a valid marriage bond between them, they must refrain from any and all conjugal relations. In the matter of sexual thoughts, desires or actions, the relationship of the parties to each other must be that of a brother to his sister and that of a sister to her brother. Chrétien expresses the situation clearly when he says: "It consists in this, that a man and woman, when invalidly married, live in the same house and thus are publicly regarded as *coniuges,* but, inasmuch as they know their marriage to be null, live *de facto* as brother and sister." He makes it more explicit when he says: "This means that they do not perform the acts of conjugal life."[21]

In the light of the threefold distinction with reference to the idea of divorce or separation,[22] the brother-sister arrangement involves separation *a toro* on the part of the man and the woman, while they maintain a community of life regarding the *mensa et cohabitatio.*

If there is to be complete correspondence to the requirements of the brother-sister arrangement, there must be not only a complete abstinence from conjugal intercourse, but, as Reiffenstuel stated in agreement with all the authors, there must be complete abstinence from any and every direct approach to the act of intercourse as also from all touches of a carnally stimulating nature.[23] When, in connection with a permitted brother-sister arrangement, Reiffenstuel treated of marriages invalid by reason of antecedent impotence, whether entered in good or in bad faith, he quoted from the decretal

---

[20] The virtue of parental piety binds all parents to the proper support and care of their children, even though the children are born of an adulterous, sacrilegious, incestuous or otherwise invalid union. When a thing has been done wrongly, the consequences are not the same as if the thing had not been done at all.

[21] Cf. Chretien, *De Matrimonio,* p. 444; Payen, *De Matrimonio,* III, p. 479, nn. 2518-21.

[22] *Separatio a toro, a mensa, et a cohabitatione.,* *Supra,* Introduction to the Historical Synopsis.

[23] "Omnes tenentur nihilominus in foro interno ambo abstinere ab omni ulteriori attentatione copulae, et tactibus lascivis . . . " Reiffenstuel, *Ius Canonicum,* Lib. IV, tit. XV, n. 33.

Laudabilem, as found in the Decretals of Gregory IX, to further clarify what is and what is not permitted to persons in such a condition.

> " 'Quod si ambo consentiant simul esse, vir eam, etsi non
> ut uxorem, saltem habeat ut sororem,' ut proin nec aspectus,
> nec oscula lasciva, multo minus copula, eis sint licita, hoc ipso
> quod nullum inter eos sit Matrimonium, quo solo tactus prae-
> fati sint licita."[24]

While the question of purely internal sins of thought or desire is best left to the moralists, it should be mentioned that formal sin is in the will, so that the external action does not, of itself, add any new morality. It is not solely for the avoidance of externalized sins that canonists demand complete abstinence from both perfect and imperfect acts of conjugal love,[25] but also for the avoidance of purely internal sins of thought or desire. Consequently, if the parties find it impossible to avoid grave sins of thought or desire, as well as the externalized sin, precisely because of their proximity to whatever furnishes the occasion for these acts, the brother-sister arrangement could not be permitted. If the sins of thought and desire are occasioned by causes other than the brother-sister arrangement, i. e., by some other person or thing completely dissociated from the brother-sister arrangement then there would be no cause on that score to refuse permission for the brother-sister arrangement.

For the maintenance of the virtue of purity on the part of those who cohabit on a brother-sister basis, a majority of the canonical authors insist on the absolute and fundamental requirement that the parties use separate beds. This is the literal meaning of the phrase *"separatio a toro."* The necessity of using separate beds seems almost

---

[24]Cf. Reiffenstuel, *Ius Canonicum,* Lib IV, tit. XV, n. 62; c. 5, X, *de frigidis et maleficiatis, et impotentia coeundi,* IV, 15; Raymond of Peñafort, *Summa,* Lib. IV, tit. 16, n. 1.

[25]A perfect or complete act of conjugal love, as defined by canonists, is copulation or intercourse. The imperfect or incomplete acts are those acts which are mutually performed by husband and wife in preparation for the complete act of conjugal intercourse. Such imperfect acts are the touches, embraces, kisses, etc., which are of carnally stimulating nature. Cf. Reiffen-stuel, *Ius Canonicum,* Lib. IV, tit. XV, n. 65; Cappello, *De Matrimonio,* pp. 809-810, n. 814; Coronata, *De Sacramentis,* III, pp. 418-420, n. 328; Sanchez, *De Matrimonii Sacramento,* Lib. VII, Disp. 102; Lib. IX, Disp. 17, n. 20 ff; Lib. IX, Disp. 45.

self-evident, but because of its importance and absolute necessity it has been mentioned by the authors, ever since the brother-sister arrangement has been discussed, as a fundamental requirement.[26]

An explanation of what is meant by "*communio tori*," which is lawful for and even demanded of those who are validly married,[27] provides by way of contrast a clearer notion of the exact meaning of "*separatio a toro*." Coronata explains that marriage regularly and fundamentally implies a community of life between the married parties, which involves the elements of a common bed, board and dwelling place or house. . . . *tori, mensae et cohabitationis.* He points out that married parties have correlative rights and obligations in this common life. In order to satisfy the requirements for the "*communio tori*," they need not indeed share the same bed. It suffices that they sleep in the same room and thus create the ready opportunity for the use of the same bed. Some writers do not insist that the parties are required to sleep in the same room, provided that the rooms are easily accessible to each of the parties.[28] It seems, then, that a *separatio a toro*, which is the exact opposite of the *communio tori*, necessarily implies the negation of the three things mentioned above, i. e., that the parties do not share the same bed, nor the same room, nor even separate rooms which are easily accessible to both the parties. As a bare minimum, therefore, it appears that a separation *a toro* calls for the use of separate rooms not easily accessible to each of the parties involved in the brother-sister arrangement. Perhaps some emphasis should be placed on the relative accessibility or inaccessibility of the two rooms. In the one case the married parties could be satisfying the obligations of the "*common life*" even though they sleep in different rooms, provided the rooms are easily accessible to both parties. In the other case, in order not to live the "common life," but rather to live the life of a brother and a sister, they would probably have to use not only different rooms for sleeping

---

[26]" . . . in eodem lecto cubare non possunt."--Reiffenstuel, *Ius Canonicum*, Lib. IV, tit. XV, n. 63; c.2, X, *de clericis coniugatis*, III, 3; *Glossa*, ad. c. 2, X, III, 3, s.v. *castitatem*; JL, n. 9010; Sixtus V, *Cum frequenter*, 27 iun. 1587 Fontes, n. 161; De Smet, Praxis, pp. 141-142, n. 90; Chrétien, *De Matrimonio*, p. 444, n. 268; Gasparri, *De Matrimonio*, II, p. 241, n. 1170; Ter Haar, *Casus Conscientiae*, (3, ed., 2 vols., Taurini; Marietti, 1944) I, n. 158

[27]Can. 1128.

purposes but also different rooms not easily accessible to both the parties.

While separate, easily accessible rooms can serve to satisfy the minimum requirement for the observance of the common life, this arrangement is certainly not the most desirable under normal conditions.[29] Conversely, it is true that separate, not readily accessible rooms can best serve the purpose of those who cohabit on a brother-sister basis, in order namely that there may be maintained a strict separation *a toro*, but it frequently happens that household and financial conditions render the use of separate, not readily accessible sleeping rooms an impossibility. Since the only explicit demand made by the authors in regard to sleeping accommodations is that the parties use separate beds, and since separate and not readily accessible rooms are frequently unattainable, it seems that the use of individual beds in the same room can suffice for the fulfillment of this canonical regulation. If, in a particular case, it is found that separate rooms are possible or perhaps even necessary, then separate rooms are to be used. In either situation, the parties must take special precautions while dressing or undressing to preserve modesty, and also to maintain modesty even in the dress itself. This is especially true when the parties are not of an advanced age (*provectioris aetatis*).

Since the man and the woman who have been granted permission to live together as brother and sister can allowably sleep in the same room (but in separate beds), there seems to be no innate prohibition against extended family outings or vacations. Cases in which children are involved would almost demand that the family go together on their outings and vacations. Especially is this true in occult cases and in those cases in which the children are unaware of the parents' marital situation. Of course, the same precautionary measures concerning the type of dress, the act of dressing or undressing, and the matter of sleeping accommodations are to be observed on such outings or vacations. Parties, dances, theater-going, etc., seem to offer no great difficulty for those who live under the brother-sister arrangement. There are no greater restrictions or precautionary measures necessary than those which are demanded for the normal unmarried

---

[29] Disease, ill-health, pregnancy, etc., may rule otherwise in a particular case.

man and woman, except in so far as the parties of the brother-sister arrangement are to conduct themselves externally as husband and wife for the benefit of those who are unaware of their true status. If, however, their marital situation is known and their presence together at such social affairs would evoke or occasion serious scandal, the parties are bound to shun such particular affairs or places to the same extent that they are morally bound to shun the scandal which would result. If their attendance would occasion or give rise to slight scandal, they are slightly or venially bound to avoid it. If grave scandal would result, they are gravely or seriously bound to avoid the party, dance or similar affairs.

The required abstinence from imperfect conjugal acts, as mentioned above, does not demand that the parties of the arrangement forego those common, social courtesies which are normally expected of a husband and wife. Such courtesies would include those polite kisses and embraces which people quite generally expect to see exchanged in public between husband and wife. They may sign their names as *Mr. and Mrs.*, and on occasion may have even the obligation to do so. In order to preserve the secrecy of their true status and thereby to preclude scandal, they may also refer to each other as *"my wife"* or *"my husband."* Such social courtesies or amenities could be occasioned, for instance, at one's departure for work in the morning, or at one's return from the place of occupation in the evening. Anniversary parties or celebrations may call for these social amenities. The presence of children who have grown accustomed to seeing their parents kiss each other at the beginning or the close of a day may well furnish a solid reason for the continuance of such a practice.

Noldin (1838-1922), when explaining the moral theology regarding *"simulatio et dissimulatio"* as related to the seven sacraments,[30] stated that *"dissimulation"* is allowable if, for a proportionately grave

---

[30]Improprie dicta simulatio (dissimulatio), si mere materialiter permittitur deceptio aliorum, ex causa proportionate gravi permitti potest; talis enim simulatio non versatur circa sacramentum, quia vera materia et forma, i.e. signum sacrum non adest, sed aliquid simile. Propter deceptionem aliorum per se illicita est, nisi adsit ratio permittendi eam.—Noldin-Schmitt, *Summa* III, p. 36, n. 39; Cappello, *De Matrimonio*, p. 841, n. 841; Chrétien, *De Matrimonio*, p. 444; nn. 267-268; Coronata, *De Sacramentis*, III, n. 668.

cause, one merely permits the deception of others. A priest, therefore, who recognizes the invalidity of a marriage can, under certain
circumstances, permit the man and the woman to remain in good
faith and continue living as husband and wife.[31] By the same moral
principle it is also permissible to allow, under certain conditions, the
deception of others in cases in which the brother-sister arrangement
is employed. Two persons, therefore, who know themselves to be
invalidly married and who have been given permission to live according to the brother-sister arrangement may permit the deception of
others who regard them as actual husband and wife. Cases are known
to have existed in which even the parish priest was long unaware of
the marital status of the parties involved.

While all sexual relations, both perfect and imperfect, are to be
absolutely avoided by the parties, it would not be wrong in itself
for them to perform the common courtesies normally expected of a
husband and wife, as previously explained. By these actions they are
not directly to intend the deception of others, but merely to permit
it. Though it may be duly indicated to leave the solution of any
details regarding "mental reservation," "simulation" and "dissimulation" to the moral theologians, it seems, nevertheless, that the status
of secrecy attending the brother-sister relationship can be maintained
without serious difficulties or problems from a moral point of view.
In fact, it may well be that the parties have a moral obligation to
preserve the secret of their actual status in order to prevent the
emergence of scandal or of infamy.

Article 3.   Not a Canonical Dispensation or Privilege

Dispensation, in general, may be defined as "an act whereby in
a particular case a lawful superior grants relaxation from an existing
law."[32] In the field of matrimony it may be defined as "a legitimate

---

[31] This particular application of the principle of *dissimulatio* to the sacrament of matrimony, which in the terminology of Canon Law is properly
referred to as "*dissimulatio,*" is unanimously presented by canonists as one
of the four solutions for invalid marriages. After listing the canonical requirements for the use of this solution, canonists warn that it is not to be frequently
used. Some say "*raro,*" and others, "*rarissime.*" The major reason for its
infrequent use is the fact that both parties must be in good faith regarding
the invalidity of the marriage.—Cf. Cappello, *De Matrimonio,* p. 841, n. 841.

[32] Can. 80.

act of a superior by which the obligation prohibiting marriage, with or without the nullity of the contract, is relaxed in a particular case."[33] De Smet (1868-1927), offered a definition which further clarified the content of the term *dispensation*,[34] for it is simply defined as "the relaxation of the obligation of a law in a particular case." The law remains in force for the community in general, but its obligation is withdrawn in a particular case, that is, in favor of an individual person, physical or moral, or of a whole community, but for one act only, or for a fixed definite time.

Dispensation differs from permission in that a dispensation frees one from the observance of a law, whereas a permission does not free one from the observance of a law. One who receives permission to do or omit something actually observes the laws regarding the desired action or omission as well as the law of obtaining the legally required consent of authority. The proper authority, of course, may lawfully grant permission for those things only which are within the law. For example, if a superior granted permission for something which involved or, by reason of particular circumstances, would result in the violation of the moral law, that permission would be illicit and null.

A dispensation is always granted by way of an act of the will of a competent superior, since only in this manner can the obligation be lifted. (This act of the will need not necessarily be expressed by means of outward signs.) Because of the necessity of this act, a dispensation (unlike a permission) cannot be presumed.

In the brother-sister arrangement, there is no question of marriage between the parties concerned and consequently no call for a dispensation from laws governing matrimony. The brother-sister arrangement, however, does involve the problem of *cohabitation* (living under the same roof) on the part of two persons, a man and a woman, between whom marriage is an impossibility. The Church has enacted

---

[33]Cf. Vermeersch-Creusen, *Epitome Iuris Canonici cum Commentariis ad Scholas et ad Usum Privatum* (6. ed., 3 vols., Mechliniae-Romae: Dessain, 1937-46), II, p. 211 n. 301, (hereafter cited as *Epitome Iuris Canonici*).
[34]*De Sponsalibus et Matrimonio*, n. 732.

no explicit, positive legislation regarding "fraternal" cohabitation as such, and consequently a dispensation from any ecclesiastical law in regard to such cohabitation is impossible.

The natural and positive divine laws of morality, however, do find application in such cases of cohabitation, especially in regard to the elements of the *danger* of *incontinence* and of *scandal*, which may be present as a direct result of "fraternal" cohabitation or the brother-sister arrangement. But just as the Church has not the power to dispense from diriment matrimonial impediments of the natural or positive divine law, and simply declares in what cases the divine law forbids or invalidates marriage (Can. 1038), so also in reference to the natural or positive divine laws governing the morality of the brother-sister arrangement as a canonical solution for invalid marriages, the Church cannot properly grant a dispensation, but has only the right authentically to declare, interpret and apply them. In a particular case the Church investigates and judges whether the law forbids or permits cohabitation on a brother-sister basis, and then, in accord with that judgment, either grants or refuses permission to the couple to cohabit in the fashion of a brother and a sister.

This official judgement and the consequent permission are provided in a practical manner by the Church's lawfully appointed ministers. A bishop and a pastor have the care of souls in view of their offices, and the confessor has jurisdiction over the penitent in confession by delegated authority. All three, therefore, have the proper, fundamental authority to make the necessary and practical judgment regarding the morality of cohabitation on a brother-sister basis in a particular case, and therefore have the authority to grant or refuse permission for such cohabitation.[35]

---

[35]The relative powers of the bishop, pastor and confessor to grant permission for the brother-sister arrangement are discussed in Chapter IV, Article 5, *infra*, pp. 124-136. At present the writer wishes simply to clarify the juridic nature of the brother-sister arrangement.

It should also be mentioned that the bishop, pastor and confessor, in the manner explained above, are judges. As such they also have the right to exercise discretionary power. The law allows no dispensation and no choice, for if the laws of God (especially in regard to scandal and the occasion of sin) are not fulfilled in a particular case, the permission cannot be granted. However, after a thorough investigation and prudent judgment regarding the full observance of these laws as well as any laws of the Church which may indirectly affect this permission, the grantor may choose when or how to grant the permission. He may also establish certain conditions other than the ones explicitly mentioned for the normal case.

A *privilegium is defined as a "lex privata alicui specialem favorem concedens,"* and is either *"contra ius"* or *"praeter ius."* For approximately the same reasons as the ones mentioned above, it is found that "fraternal" cohabitation or permissible cohabitation in invalid marriages is not a privilege or *"privilegium"* in the sense of the Code. Since there are no positive ecclesiastical laws directly governing the brother-sister arrangement, one cannot say that permission to cohabit under this arrangement is either *"contra ius ecclesiasticum"* or *"praeter ius ecclesiasticum".* Hence, the brother-sister arrangement, although it may prove favorable to the parties concerned, is not in strict parlance a juridic privilege or *"privilegium."*[36]

Canonically taken, therefore, the brother-sister arrangement is an *official permission* granted by reason of some necessity. It is neither a dispensation nor a privilege, and hence is not determined by nor included in the Code of Canon Law under Titles V and VI of the First Book.

In the absence of specific legislation, however, regarding the brother-sister arrangement, it is found that some of the laws and principles governing a juridic "dispensation" and "privilege" can easily be adapted for application to this canonical solution for invalid

---

[36]Cf. Cappello, *Summa Iuris Canonici,* (3 vols., Vol. I, 5. ed., 1951; Vol. II, 4. ed., 1945; Vol· III, 3. ed., 1948; Romae; Apud Aedes Universitatis Gregorianae) I, pp. 130-144, nn. 152-165.

marriages. Just as a dispensation requires a qualified grantor,[37] so also does permission for the brother-sister arrangement require a grantor with the proper qualifications and authority. Both the canonical "dispensation" and the "permission for 'fraternal' cohabitation" require a just and reasonable cause . . . which cause must reflect a due proportion to the gravity of the situation.[38]

Strictness is the rule in the brother-sister arrangement. Even as a dispensation which has the continued force of a recurrent application, so also the permission for cohabitation when granted in the brother-sister arrangement, will cease with the total cessation of the motive cause or reason for which it was granted.[39] The status of the persons who are permitted to live under the brother-sister arrangement does not undergo any change, for there is simply an official declaration regarding it, and so the granted permission differs from a dispensation which does not have a recurrent application.

While "fraternal" cohabitation is juridically distinct from a "*privilegium*" in the sense of the Code, the arrangement is definitely beneficial to those concerned, as is a "*privilegium* (can. 68)." If cohabitation on a brother-sister basis proves harmful to those concerned, it is not to be permitted. If all the conditions and requirements for such cohabitation are met, then through the granted permission a more or less permanent way of life can be established. Once granted, the permission does not necessarily cease with the cessation of the jurisdiction or the authority of the one who granted the permission.[40] The permission ceases, however, just as a "*privilegium*" ceases, i.e., if, in the course of time, circumstances change in such a way that in the judgment of the superior the continuance of the permission becomes something injurious or illicit.[41] Similar to the "*privilegium*," a temporary or conditional permission for the brother-sister arrange-

---

[37]Cans. 80-83; 1040; Gasparri, *De Matrimonio*, II, n. 1181, p. 249.

[38]"A lege ecclesiastica ne dispensetur sine iusta et rationabili causa, habita ratione gravitatis legis a qua dispensatur; alias dispensatio ab inferiore data illicita et invalida est."-Can. 84.

[39]Cans. 50; 85-86.

[40]Can. 73.

[41]Can. 77.

ment ceases with the expiration of the appointed time or the non-continuance of the postulated conditions.[42]   Just as the abuse of a "privilegium" can call for the deprivation of that privilege,[43] so also may the abuse of the brother-sister arrangement call for its retraction. The code of Canon Law directs the ordinary to notify the Holy See of the grave abuse of a privilege which it has conceded. It seems that the pastor and confessor should notify the ordinary concerning grave abuses of the brother-sister arrangement which was permitted by the ordinary.[44]

While it is true, then, that the permission for the brother-sister arrangement is juridically distinct from a dispensation and a privilege in the strict sense, the legislation of the Code regarding the latter two canonical institutes can be gainfully adjusted and adapted to the brother-sister arrangement . . . especially since the Code contains no direct legislation concerning this arrangement as a solution for invalid marriages.

---

[42]Temporary permission for the brother-sister arrangement may be and frequently is given for the period of time in which a marriage case is in the process of being adjudicated, or while the "Pauline Privilege" is being sought, etc.

[43]Can. 78.

[44]In this as in all cases, the seal of the confessional must be strictly maintained. If, in the case mentioned, knowledge of the abuse of the arrangement is had only by way of confession, and the party refuses to permit the confessor to notify or consult with the ordinary concerning the abuse, the confessor is himself to decide the case. It should be pointed out that according to Król, one of the promises to be made by the parties when they seek permission to live on a brother-sister basis states "that under no circumstance will I ever attempt to live as husband (as wife) with my present consort; that if I violate this promise, I will not attempt to receive the Sacraments until I have separated, or referred the matter to the Bishop." Cf. Król, *The Jurist* XI (1951),32; cf. *infra.* pp. 131-133.

Article 4.   An Arrangement Beset with Danger

Modern authors have made it impossible to overlook or mistake the serious and dangerous nature of the brother-sister arrangement as a solution for invalid marriages.[45]   Unanimously they regard this arrangement as a *"res plena periculis."*   The two most common and most important dangers involved in the brother-sister arrangement are mentioned by most of the canonists who present this arrangement as a solution for invalid marriages.[46]   The first is the *danger of incontinence* for the cohabiting parties, and the second is the *danger of scandal* for the faithful in general.

The immediate danger, of course, is the danger of offering infinite offense to God by serious sin.   Along with this comes the correlative danger to the spiritual welfare of the couple involved.   It is common knowledge that one of the most effective means of avoiding sin is the avoidance of those persons, places or things that may easily lead one into sin.   In the brother-sister arrangement, two people who perhaps for years have lived as husband and wife, and who either sinfully or in ignorance of the nullity of their marriage had engaged in sexual relations, are called upon while they continue to live under the same roof, and to eat at the same table, and in general to maintain a rather intimate relationship, to abstain from all sexual relations and from all actions which for them are of a sexually stimulating nature.   In short, though they need not separate *"a cohabitatione"* or *"a mensa,"* yet by all means they must separate *"a toro."*

In consequence of the fallen nature of man himself, in view of the natural strength of the sex appetite, and finally in the wake of a possible, longstanding habit of indulgence, it is obvious that the brother-sister arrangement may easily be a dangerous way of life regarding the spiritual well-being of the parties themselves.   The

---

[45]Cf. Chrétien, *De Matrimonio*, n. 268; De Smet, *Praxis*, p. 140, n. 89.

[46]It should be stated that most of the authors mention this solution only in a passing manner. Perhaps because of its very nature and also because of its relative unimportance and non-necessity in past days as a solution for invalid marriages, no author has been found to give an exhaustive treatment of this subject.

immediate reason, therefore, for the extensive caution demanded in the granting of permission for the brother-sister arrangement is rightfully attributable to the danger of incontinence.

It should be mentioned that the authors do not say nor do they intend to say that the maintenance of chastity is an impossible task. They do say that the brother-sister arrangement, by the very nature of things, may offer the danger of incontinence. Certainly they agree that it is both normally and continuously difficult for two people under this arrangement to remain chaste. At the same time, however, they indicate that this difficulty can be overcome by means of the grace of God and through a use of the necessary precautionary measures. The authors repeatedly mention that the use of separate sleeping accommodations, or at least of separate beds, is one of the fundamental requirements for the efficacious avoidance of the danger of incontinence, and therefore for the licit use of the brother-sister arrangement.

The second danger, and indeed a very real danger, although not as proximate or easily discernible as the danger of incontinence, is the danger of *scandal* in the strict sense of the term. If people generally learn that the Church permits such cohabitation even when a marriage is clearly invalid, the discipline of the Church regarding the dignity and honor of the sacrament of matrimony may be jeopardized. Persons who have difficulty in their married life, or who perhaps already have separated, could easily feel encouraged to attempt another marriage, or persons who propose to contract a union could seek to conceal the presence of some unyielding diriment impediment, with the hope that the Church would eventually grant them the permission of living together as brother and sister.

This particular danger of scandal, while it cannot be overlooked, seems to be a remote danger at present, since in fact there are very few who have any knowledge of a possible brother-sister arrangement. There is also some question in the writer's mind whether a knowledge of the possibility of the arrangement would engender such dire effects. A new idea is frequently frightening at first, but frequently too those fears are unfounded. The history of dispensations from matrimonial impediments is a point in fact. It does not appear that the granting of dispensations has lessened the dignity and sacredness of the sacrament of matrimony. It seems, rather, that dispensations and the increased legislation and publication regarding dispensations have served to alleviate a definite need which arose in the Church. The brother-sister arrangement is a much less drastic measure than the granting of dispensations.

Unless the Holy See issues an instruction forbidding use of the brother-sister arrangement, history will expose the presence or the absence of this particular danger. In the absence of any general ecclesiastical legislation, it is the writer's opinion that the arrangement will prove to be a happy solution for an ever increasing problem, and will serve to aid those unfortunate or weak individuals who find themselves involved in an invalid marriage for which there is no other solution. The writer does not advocate a wholesale publication of the possibility of this arrangement, but he sees no valid condemnation of the guarded and prudent application of the arrangement whenever the occasion presents itself. If, in a particular case, the circumstances demand a public explanation, it is felt that a reasonable explanation can be given without undue harm.

The scandal which offers a more proximate danger and cause for concern is that scandal which may be caused in a particular case and locality. There are two sources from which scandal may arise in the individual case; the first is the fact of cohabitation in an invalid marriage, and the second is the public reception of the sacraments by the parties of an invalid marriage.

This more proximate danger of scandal is one that must be carefully considered, but like the danger of incontinence, it too is not to be over emphasized. The authors emphasize this danger of scandal, but not to the extent of rendering the application of the brother-sister arrangement a practical impossibility. The likely occurrence of scandal and the probable risk of incontinence constitute the two immediate reasons for saying that the brother-sister arrangement is a *"res plena periculis."* But these possible dangers, since they can in many cases be overcome (although admittedly with considerable difficulty), do not warrant either the frame of mind or the procedure apparently followed in some dioceses, which views the brother-sister arrangement as an impossibility and hence as of no practical value.

Granted, the major authors speak in a most hesitant manner and with the utmost restrictive concession when they seek to gauge the frequency with which the brother-sister arrangement may find application. Chrétien states that there is occasion for the brother-sister arrangement only *"rarissime,"* but that it can be tolerted as a favorable solution upon previous consultation with the bishop.[47] Coronata says that the arrangement is *"rarissime"* to be counseled,[48] whereas Gasparri used the phrase *"fere numquam."*[49] DeBecker (1857-1936) stated: *"Neque absolute reiicienda esset solutio quae tenderet ad hoc, ut contrahentes vivant deinceps tamquam frater et soror . . ."*[50] Chelodi (1880-1922) pointed out that, when the other remedies are not available, then the brother-sister arrangement is permitted.[51] Payen(+1941) also was very explicit when he wrote: *Cohabitatio ut frater et soror excludit omnem vitae conjugalis usum, non vero communionem mensae et habitationis. Non est ei locus nisi, in casu rarissimo, certe remotum sit, praeter scandalum, incontinentiae periculum."*[52]

While the authors have been consistently explicit in pointing out the dangers of incontinence and scandal connected with the brother-sister arrangement, and while they have used such phrases as *"fere numquam,"* *"rarissime,"* etc., apparently to express the number of cases in which the brother-sister arrangement may licitly be used as a solution for an invalid marriage, they do not say, nor do they intend to say, that it is *most rare* for two people to find it possible under the brother-sister arrangement to remain in the state of grace. Chrètien for example, insists that there must be no danger of incontinence in the brother-sister arrangement, but he immediately adds that there is no danger of incontinence between the *"pseudo-conjuges"* if they are old, or impotent, or *de facto* know themselves to be true brother and sister, or father and daughter. He goes even further when he says that

---

[47]*De Matrimonio,* n. 268; De Smet, *Praxis,* p. 140, n. 89.
[48]*De Sacramentis,* III, p. 929, n. 668.
[49]*De Matrinonio,* II, p. 249, n. 1181.
[50]*De Sponsalibus et Matrimonio,* p. 359.
[51]*De Matrimonio,* n. 163.
[52]*De Matrimonio,* III, p. 479, nn. 2518-21.

of itself or inherently the brother-sister arrangement is not to be considered as entailing the danger of incontinence.[53]

For the better understanding of the modern authors' treatment
of the brother-sister arrangement, and also for the purpose of off-set-
ting any unreasonable fears held by some with reference to the practicable use of the arrangement, the writer feels that the precise relationship between the phrases *"res plena periculis"* and *"fere numquam"* or *"rarissime,"* as used by the authors, should be accurately determined.   For the achieving of this it should also be determined
whether the authors were speaking in a relative or an absolute sense
when they used such terms as *"fere numquam"* and *"rarissime"* to express the frequency of the actual application of the brother-sister arrangement.

If the authors were speaking in an absolute sense and actually intended to say that objective cases in which the brother-sister arrangement could find application are most rare or that such cases could
practically never be found, because the arrangement is a *"res plena
periculis,"* it seems obvious then, that the authors intended to include
under the phrase *"res plena periculis"* not only the dangers of scandal and incontinence, but also all of the conditions, suppositions and
requirements for the arrangement as enumerated by the same authors.[54]
This inclusive meaning seems intended by these same authors, who in-

---

[53]*De Matrimonio*, p. 444, nn. 267-268 Cf. also Gasparri, *De Matrimonio*,
II, p. 241, n. 1170; Coronata, *De Sacramentis*, III, n. 659.

[54]Vlaming-Bender give a fairly complete list of the considerations that call
for an appraisal. It must be determined whether the impediment which causes
the invalidity is known or unknown by the parties, or by only one of them;
whether the impediment is public or occult; whether the union was contracted
also civilly; whether a civil divorce is being or may be sought, or perhaps has
been obtained; whether the parties can live together peacefully; whether
they are with or without children; whether there would be scandal in the
applying of this solution; whether the impediment yields to dispensation;
whether it is both a canonical and a civil impediment, and whether the nullity
must be made known to the parties. Other authors advert to such circumstances as the danger of incontinence; the age of the parties; the health and
financial condition of the parties concerned. Cf. Vlaming-Bender, *Praelectiones Iuris Matrimonii*, pp. 519-520; Cappello, *De Matrimonio*, p. 841, n.
841. Wernz, *Jus Decretalium* (6 vols., Romae, 1898-1914) IV, n. 646;
Gasparri, *De Matrimonio*, II, n. 1180; Wernz-Vidal, *Ius Matrimoniale*, p.
851, n. 651.

dictate that the dangers of incontinence and scandal likewise can be removed or made sufficiently remote, and they even mention some precautionary measures to insure the removal of these two dangers.

With this understanding of the phrase *"res plena periculis,"* and on the supposition that the authors were speaking in an absolute or objective sense, they were no doubt quite accurate when they said that the arrangement could *"fere numquam"* be used. The accuracy of their statement is enhanced by the fact that at the time in which they wrote there were relatively few invalid marriages which could not be handled and settled according to one of the other three solutions for invalid marriages. Today, however, there are far more invalid marriages than there were 30 or 40 years ago, and the people (at least in the larger cities in America) are far less susceptible to the elements of scandal. Consequently, at least by reason of these two basic elements, the *"fere numquam"* of the authors cannot possibly, in an absolute sense, mean today what it meant in the first quarter of the present century.[55]

The more plausible explanation of the authors' use of the terms *"fere numquam"* or *"rarissime"* seems to be that they were speaking in more of a relative than in an absolute sense. Most of the authors treat the brother-sister arrangement as one of four possible solutions for invalid marriages. In listing these four solutions, they indicate the relative frequency with which the individual solutions may or may not be used. Consistently they list the brother-sister arrangement as the solution to be chosen last in relation to the other three solutions. They point out that convalidation, complete separation and perhaps even dissimulation are to be preferred, and consequently more frequently to be used, than *"fraternal"* cohabitation as a solution with reference to invalid marriages. In any particular case, it is only after the first three solutions have failed that the brother-sister arrangement can be used, and hence in this relative sense is *"rarissime"* applicable.

For example, Cappelo speaks of *"convalidatio"* as the *"remedium ordinarium."* Regarding the declaration of nullity and complete

---

[55] One of our larger dioceses reportedly receives requests for use of the brother-sister arrangement at an average of one a week, and the majority of these requests are granted.

separation, he says that *"raro"* is there occasion for its use.   *"Raris-sime"* is the term he uses in reference to dissimulation as a solution. Finally when speaking of the brother-sister arrangement, Cappelo says that it is a *"res plena periculis"* and *"fere numquam"* permissible but that in extrordinary circumstances, and when the other remedies are lacking, it can be permitted.[56]

Coronata lists the remedies in the same relative order, but uses a different terminology.   For him, too, the *"convalidatio"* serves as the *ordinary* solution.   He employs the term *"raro"* in reference to the declaration of nullity coupled with complete separation.   He says that sometimes dissimulation can be used, and uses the term *"rarissime"* in reference to the brother-sister arrangement.[57]

Perhaps of the four possible solutions with reference to invalid marriages the brother-sister arrangement will always remain the solution most rarely (*rarissime*) used.   Its relatively infrequent use, however, gives no indication of the absolute or numerical frequency with which the brother-sister arrangement may be used.   In days past it was most rare that all three preferred solutions (convalidation complete separation, dissimulation) would fail, and hence most rare that the brother-sister arrangement could even be considered.   The present age, however, because of its increasing divorce rate among other causes, is witnessing a change.   More and more often it is found impossible to solve a particular marriage case by one of the three preferred solutions.   As a result, the brother-sister solution is receiv-ing more and more consideration.

The only valid conclusions that can be drawn from this discussion are that the brother-sister arrangement is indeed beset with danger (especially that of scandal and of incontinence) and therefore an extensive investigation is called for and a profound caution must always be employed in its use.   Since the arrangement is a last resort solution with reference to invalid marriages, and since there are many dangers, conditions and suppositions involved, it will find relatively infrequent use.   It may, however, and often should find a more

---

[56]*De Matrimonio,* pp. 841-842, n. 841.
[57]*De Sacramentis,* III, p. 929, n. 668.

frequent and less fearful consideration on the part of those who currently need to deal with the increasing problem of invalid marriages for which there is no other solution. It is felt that there are many existing cases worthy of consideration.

In view of the dangerous nature of the arrangement it seems that the matter of the brother-sister arrangement should be a matter of positive diocesan legislation. The writer is of the opinion that the matter is sufficiently urgent and important to warrant consideration in the diocesan synod, or perhaps even in the provincial council.

CHAPTER IV

FUNDAMENTAL REQUIREMENTS FOR
ALL BROTHER-SISTER CASES

Article 1.   No Other Solution

Since the brother-sister arrangement is a *last resort* solution, it must be determined antecedently to any consideration of this arrangement whether there is any other possible solution for the invalid marriage in a particular case. Four solutions are listed by modern authors as possible remedies for invalid marriages. They are: convalidation, declaration of nullity and complete separation, dissimulation and, finally, cohabitation on a brother-sister basis.[1] For the practical use of any one of these remedies all the authors demand a thorough investigation in regard to several elements. Cappello has compiled an extensive list of these elements. He says that the solution must be chosen in accordance with the diverse circumstances that may occur. It must be determined whether the nullity is unknown by both or by at least one of the parties; whether the impediment is public or occult; whether the marriage was contracted as a civil union; whether the parties live together peaceably; whether there are children; whether the impediment yields to the possibility of a dispensation; whether the solution chosen can be applied without scandal to others, or without danger of inviting the occasion of sin for the parties

---

[1]Cf. Cappello, *De Matrimonio,* pp. 841-2, n. 841; Gasparri, *De Matrimonio,* II, p. 249, n. 1181; Wernz-Vidal, *Ius Matrimoniale,* p. 852, n. 651; Coronata, *De Sacramentis,* III, p. 929, n. 668; Chelodi, *De Matrimonio,* p. 207, n. 163; Wernz, *Ius Decretalium,* IV, 943; Vlaming-Bender, *Praelectiones Iuris Matrimonii,* n. 519; Chretien, *De Matrimonio,* p. 444, n. 268; De Smet, *Praxis,* p. 140, n. 89.

involved. He indicates that this is only a partial list of the elements that at times must be considered.[2]

While the ultimate solution of any individual case depends, therefore, upon the particular circumstances and combination of circumstances surrounding the case, it is generally agreed among the authors that *convalidation* is the ordinary and the most desirable solution for an invalid marriage.[3] If the cause of the invalidity can be removed, the normal procedure is to accomplish just that and to obtain the convalidation of the marriage.

Practicality, therefore, demands that the priest or pastor handling, any particular case determine, first of all, that a union or a marriage was previously attempted by the parties, and, secondly, that the attempted marriage is truly invalid, or the union at best doubtfully valid. Legal records, both civil and ecclesiastical, as well as the fact of cohabitation, the presence of children, or even the established reaction of a common opinion can point to the existence of a previously attempted marriage between the two parties seeking the brother-sister arrangement.[4] Canonical proof, as explained by the Code,[5] is not needed nor is it usually employed, since all that needs to be established

---

[2]*De Matrimonio*, p. 841, n. 841. Cf. also Wernz, *Ius Decretalium*, IV, 646, and Gasparri, *De Matrimonio*, II, n. 1180. Vlaming-Bender (*Praelectiones Iuris Matrimonii*, pp. 519-520.) furnish a list which is even more inclusive than that of Cappello.

[3]In a particular case in which the parties do not wish to remain together, or also when it is evident that the marriage would not last because of constant bickering or quarreling, the authors are agreed that a complete separation is preferred to a convalidation of the union. For any consideration of the brother-sister arrangement it is presumed that the parties to the invalid marriage recognize the moral obligation which calls for a simple cohabitation on their part, or at least that the parties desire to remain together.

[4] Care must be taken not to confuse the necessity of establishing the fact of an attempted marriage between these two parties seeking permission for the arrangement with the necessity of establishing the existence of a previous, sacramental and consummated marriage, which gives rise to the diriment impediment of prior bond and is presented as the reason or the cause for the invalidity of the subsequent attempted marriage here in question.

[5]Cans. 1747-1836.

is the existence of a union which is commonly regarded as a marriage, or in some cases merely regarded as an attempted marriage.[6] The fact of a civil or religious ceremony can usually be determined with comparative ease, but the existence of a specific ceremony is not essential to the ultimate solution of the case. It is, however, a circumstance that should be determined, as it is of some value regarding the final disposition of the case according to the brother-sister arrangement.[7]

In order to accomplish the second practical step, viz., to establish the invalidity of the attempted marriage, one must discover the reason or the cause of the invalidity as well as the precise nature of the reason or the cause.[8] Authors point out that a marriage can be null for reasons generally classified under three headings: 1) the lack of personal capacity or the presence of a diriment impediment; 2) the lack of a mutual consent, and 3) the lack of compliance with a prescribed juridical form.[9] This classification is clear from the Code itself, which under canon 1081, §1, states that the consent of the parties, when legitimately manifested by persons capable before the law, makes the marriage. Consequently, whenever any one of these three essential elements is missing, there is an invalid marriage. If the invalidity is caused by a defective consent [10] or by lack of compliance with the proper form prescribed for the sealing of the matrimonial contract,[11] there is usually no great problem. Such marriages can normally be convalidated according to the rules of the Code dealing with simple convalidation[12] or the *sanatio in ra-*

---

[6]*Supra*, Chap. III, pp. 57-59.

[7]Cf. Cappello, *De Matrimonio*, p. 841, n. 841; Vlaming-Bender, *Praelectiones Iuris Matrimonii*, p. 519: *infra*, pp. 140, 169.

[8]I.e., whether or not the cause of the invalidity can be obviated for the purpose of permitting a convalidation.

[9]Cf. Cappello, *De Matrimonio*, p. 843, n. 843.

[10]Cans. 1081-1093.

[11]Cans. 1094-1109.

[12]Can. 1136.

dice.[13] In special cases of this type "dissimulation" may be the proper solution to use, or perhaps there may be cause even for a juridic declaration of nullity and a complete separation. But there is never room for the brother-sister arrangement on a permanent basis if the invalid marriage can be convalidated.[14] On the other hand, if the marriage is invalid by reason of a diriment impediment, the impediment must either cease or be removed by way of dispensation if the convalidation of the marriage is to be rendered possible. It is precisely in this that the problem lies, for some impediments do not cease, and others either cannot or usually will not be removed by way of dispensation. It is this type of diriment impediment—one that does not cease or one that cannot or usually does not yield to dispensation—which gives rise to an invalid marriage in which the brother-sister arrangement finds possible application on a permanent basis.

Canonists usually classify diriment impediments as deriving from the natural or the divine law, or simply from the ecclesiastical law. This distinction between diriment impediments as deriving from the divine or the ecclesiastical law is of importance with reference to the factor of dispensation, for the Supreme Authority of the Church cannot dispense from impediments of the divine law, but simply has the right to declare authentically in which cases the divine law forbids or disaffirms the marriage.[15] On the other hand, this same Supreme Authority has the power to dispense from those diriment impediments which the Church itself has created. There are, however, some impediments of ecclesiastical origin from which the Holy See does not dispense, even though it has the power. The brother-sister arrangement finds possible application only in those marriages which are invalid by reason of an impediment of the divine law, or which are invalid by reason of an ecclesiastical impediment from which the Church usually does not grant a dispensation. Use of the brother-

---

[13]Cans. 1138-1141.

[14]The arrangement can be used on a temporary basis, i.e., during the time needed for the convalidation of the marriage, provided that a complete separation during that time is impossible, that there is no new scandal, and that no proximate occasion of sin results.

[15]Can. 1038.

sister arrangement also presupposes that these impediments have not in any way been obviated.[16] The five diriment impediments for which no dispensation is given which frequently cause or occasion invalid marriages in which the brother-sister arrangement finds possible application are: Prior Bond, Impotence, Holy Orders (Priesthood), Consanguinity and Specific Criminality (*Crimen*).[17]

It is only after all efforts to find a means by which the attempted marriage can be validated have failed that it is possible to consider any other of the four solutions advanced by canonists for invalid marriages.

The Church is certainly not in favor of declaring attempted marriages null, especially those which it has witnessed and apparently approved. Whenever possible, it is the Church's usual policy to con-validate or sanate attempted marriages. This, however, is not always possible or advisable, and the Church at times finds it necessary by judicial or administrative processes, to declare attempted marriages to be null. Cappello says that only rarely is there occasion for a juridic declaration of nullity. He lists several reasons for using this remedy when the marriage cannot be healed, viz., if the parties are determined to separate or get a divorce, or if there is danger of the perversion of one of the parties, or perhaps grave causes demand that a new marriage be entered.[18] As far as the subject at hand is concerned, however, there is no need for a detailed consideration of the law regarding a declaration of nullity. The important point is that a declaration of nullity along with a complete separation, or simply a complete separation in itself, is the second solution for in-valid marriages. If the attempted marriage cannot be convalidated, the general rule is that a complete separation must take place. It is only in the event that a complete separation is morally impossible

---

[16]V.g., the impediment of prior bond ceases upon the death of one of the parties, in which case the surviving party could convalidate the earlier marriage, so that the brother-sister arrangement would become inapplicable.

[17]The particular cases wherein no dispensation is granted for these five impediments, in consequence of which these cases can furnish the occasion for a possible application of the brother-sister arrangement, are delineated in the following chapter.

[18]*De Matrimonio*, pp. 841-2, n. 841.

that one or the other of the remaining two solutions finds possible application.

A complete separation is absolutely demanded in cases in which the parties know of the invalidity and find it impossible to avoid grave sin, even though no danger of grave scandal be present. If the invalid marriage is formally public[19] and scandal would result from continued cohabitation, a complete separation is demanded, even though there is present no danger of grave sin. Finally, a complete separation is demanded if there is no proportionately grave reason for continued cohabitation. This remains true even though there be absent all danger of scandal and every proximate occasion of sin.[20] Obviously the brother-sister arrangement finds a possible application only if a complete separation is morally impossible, and then only if the postulated necessary conditions and requirements are met.

Dissimulation is listed by the authors as a third possible remedy for invalid marriages. This is not dissimulation of the sacrament of matrimony in the strict sense, since dissimulation strictly taken involves a positive, non-sacramental sign or action which takes place at the time of the ceremony or apparent administration of the sacrament.[21] *Dissimulation* as a solution or remedy for an invalid marriage, on the other hand, implies that the marriage ceremony has already taken place and that the nullity of the marriage was discovered only afterwards. Dissimulation in this sense does not involve a positive sign or action; rather, it simply connotes that the *"coniuges"* are not to be informed of the nullity of their marriage, even though the priest or the confessor recognizes that it is invalid. If the necessary conditions are verified, the deception of both the *"coniuges"* and the public regarding the invalidity of the marriage is allowed to continue.

Dissimulation, as a solution or remedy for invalid marriages which cannot be convalidated, requires that both parties of the

-----

[19]*Infra*, p. 101.

[20]In such cases, however, the scandal or the loss of reputation resulting from a complete separation usually becomes sufficient cause for warranting the continued cohabitation.

[21]Cf. Noldin-Schmitt, *Summa*, III, pp. 35-36, nn. 38-39; Cappello, *De Sacramentis*, I, pp. 58-60, nn. 66-67.

invalid marriage be in good faith as to the invalidity. It requires, not only that the parties be ignorant of the nullity of their marriage, but also that the invalidity be materially and formally occult. Cappello points out, therefore, that *dissimulation* cannot be allowed if one or both of the parties are conscious of the nullity, or if the invalidity of the marriage is notorious.[22] Even if both of the stated conditions are fulfilled, Cappello further insists that the parties are most rarely (*rarissime*) to be left in good faith. It is only in the event that grave injury, or formal sin, or scandal is foreseen to result from one's informing the parties of the nullity of their marriage that dissimulation can be permitted as a solution.

The final solution mentioned by authors for invalid marriages is the brother-sister arrangement. This arrangement can be considered only after it is found impossible to apply one of the previous three solutions, viz., convalidation, complete separation or dissimulation. Truly, the brother-sister arrangement on a permanent basis is a solution of last resort for invalid marriages. The arrangement can be considered as a possible solution only upon the failure of the previous three remedies, but even then it cannot be used unless there is simultaneous verification of the other four requirements proper to the arrangement itself, viz, that no grave scandal emerge, that no proximate occasion of sin arise, that a proportionate reason be present, and finally that the proper permission of a competent ecclesiastical authority be granted.

Article 2. No Grave Scandal (Actual or Virtual)

Perhaps the zenith of difficulty regarding the application of the brother-sister arrangement is reached in the problem of scandal. Convincing proof and positive assurance of the absence not only of scandal but also of the serious danger of scandal must be had before the permission for the brother-sister arrangement may be granted. Even though the concept of scandal may be clearly defined, it is frequently difficult to make a practical judgment regarding its presence or absence. In one set of circumstances a thing may be scandalous, but upon the change of merely one of the conditions the

---

[22] *De Matrimonio,* p. 841, n. 841.

same thing may be a source of edification. Scandal frequently depends heavily upon the time, place, temperament and character of the people involved as well as upon the nature of the act or objective fact. The multiplicity of contingencies and possibilities frequently tax the judgment of a prudent man.

In view of the inherent difficulties involved in a practical application of the principles of theology regarding scandal, it is indicated here to define scandal, and to point out the ways or modes in which scandal may enter into the brother-sister arrangement, and consequently determine the practical application of the arrangement.

Scandal, in its strict and proper sense, is defined by St. Thomas as a "*dictum vel factum minus rectum praebens alteri occasionem ruinae spiritualis.*"[23] This is distinct from scandal in a broad or improper sense, which signifies the wonderment (*admiratio*) or common talk (*rumor*) which an unusual action excites in people, but which does not incite anyone to sin. It is scandal in the strict sense with which we are here concerned, for it is the presence or the proximate danger of this type of scandal alone which rules out the application of the brother-sister arrangement as a solution for invalid marriages.

Mere cohabitation (living under the same roof) on the part of two invalidly married persons is not necessarily evil in itself, but it normally has the appearance of evil when the nullity of the marriage is public, especially when the parties cohabiting are young and are known to have had previously either materially or formally sinful marital relations. The presumption is that the couple is living in sin, and hence such a cohabitation may qualify as a *factum minus rectum.* If the invalidity of the marriage is public and the Church permits the parties involved to receive the sacraments publicly, the apparent ecclesiastical sanction of a presumably sinful relationship would also fulfill the concept of a *factum minus rectum.*

Scandal does not arise from a formal sin as such, since the formal sin can be purely internal. Scandal does arise in the common estimation of men, however, and the cohabitation permitted in the brother-

---

[23]*Summa,* IIa IIae, q. 43, a. 1; Merkelbach, *Summa Theologiae Moralis* (3 vols., Vol. 1, 3. ed. aucta et emendata, Paris: Descleé de Brouwer et Soc., 1938), I, p. 729, n. 958; Noldin-Schmitt, *Summa,* I, p. 106, n. 102.

sister arrangement for those whose invalid marriage is public may give
rise to scandal even though the parties are living a completely sinless
life.   If the invalidity of the marriage is public, and the nature of the
cohabitation on a brother-sister basis is not explained and shown to be
without sin (thereby destroying the presumption of a sinful union),
the brother-sister arrangement could indeed offer "*alteri occasionem
ruinae spiritualis.*"

Most of the authors do not make any allowance for an exception
to the general rule that the brother-sister arrangement is inadmissible
in cases in which the nullity of the marriage is formally (*formaliter*)
public.   Consequently there would be no occasion for an explanation
to the public regarding the sinless nature of the cohabitation in a public
case.   There are, however, some authors who indicate two exceptions
to the general rule.   Since they point to these two exceptions not as implying a complete accounting of the possible exceptions, one can readily
contemplate others which are similar in nature.

Coronata lists one exception when he says that, if the nullity or in-
invalidity of the marriage is publicly known, and is already so commonly divulged that it reflects a notoriety of fact, or will readily be divulged (virtual scandal), the remedy of cohabitation in the fashion of a
brother- and sister is excluded as a possible solution for the case because
of the scandal that would be caused, *unless* the parties were of advanced age, and it thus would not test the credulity of the public to
believe that they were living continently. [24]   In this Coronata posits
the necessity of advanced age (*provectioris aetatis*) and in reference
to the sinless nature of the arrangement implies for the public an explanation which does not test or tax the credulity of the people.   If
the nullity of the marriage is *formaliter* public and the parties who are
granted the permission to cohabit after the manner of a brother and
and sister are young, it seems that such cohabitation would be an
occasion for the spiritual ruin of others.   For even though an explanation were given in the case, the credulity of the people would
be tested or taxed, and the presumption of a sinful life would remain.

De Smet gave expression to the second exception in cases which
are formally public.   He taught that, if the nullity is already known,

---

[24] *De Sacramentis*, III, p. 930, n. 669.

the parties must separate *a tecto* or from cohabitation immediately But, if the separation cannot be undertaken here and now, v.g., because the man is gravely ill, and needs the nursing of the woman in such a manner that he cannot get along without her help, then the "*pseudo-conjuges*" must be prepared to declare before two witnesses that they will obtain a convalidation or a separation as soon as they are able. In the meantime they must carefully avoid the occasion of sin and follow the instructions of the pastor.[25] The exception, however, contemplates merely a temporary granting of the brother-sister arrangement, and consequently the declaration of the involved parties before two witnesses is sufficient publication of the nature of the case. If the illness were protracted and it were foreseen that grave scandal would otherwise result, a public explanation of the sinless cohabitation which would not tax the credulity of the people would be in order.

With possibly the two exceptions mentioned above plus a few similar ones, cohabitation on a brother-sister basis in formally public cases is not permitted by the Church (or at least the parties involved are not permitted to receive the sacraments in the presence of those to whom the nullity of the marriage is formally public). Consequently, there is little occasion in such public cases for scandal to arise from what may be termed the *apparent* approbation by the Church of a presumably sinful cohabitation. In these few exceptions, however, the temperament of the people might be such that the administration of the sacraments to the parties involved would easily be interpreted as ecclesiastical approbation of a presumably sinful union. This apparent approbation would thus offer "*alteri occasionem ruinae spiritualis*," unless a public explanation of the case is made and it is demonstrated that the Church in no wise relaxes its doctrine and legislation regarding the virtue of purity, the dignity of marriage and the worthiness required for the reception of the sacraments.

Scandal, in the strict sense of the word, does not require that the sin of another actually take place. It suffices that from the

---

[25]*Praxis*, p. 139, n. 88. Cf. also Gasparri, *De Matrimonio*, II, n. 1183; Chrétien, *De Matrimonio*, p. 444.

"*factum minus rectum*" the sin of another can easily follow or is, perhaps, foreseen to follow.[26]

It is clear, therefore, that the brother-sister arrangement can in two different modes be a source of scandal strictly understood. In the first, scandal may be given by the continued and apparently sinful cohabitation of the parties involved in an invalid marriage, when the nullity of this union is a matter of public knowledge. In the second, scandal may result from the unexplained and apparent sanction of the Church in permitting persons, when the invalidity of their marriage is a matter of public knowledge, to continue cohabiting while repeatedly and publicly receiving the sacraments.

These two modes of giving scandal are distinct from the single act of entering an invalid marriage, in that these two modes can be a source of continuous scandal. The single act of entering an invalid marriage, especially when this involves the impediment of prior bond, may indeed be a source of scandal, but the single act may soon be forgotten. After the initial shock has been sustained and the parties obtain some degree of seclusion, for example by moving to another town or to a different section of a large city where their marital status is unknown, the act itself does not remain long in the memory of the majority of men. In a small town a divorce and a subsequent remarriage may still be a shocking affair, but they frequently pass unnoticed in our larger cities because of the wholesale divorce rate that plagues our nation. The individual scandalous act of entering an invalid marriage, therefore, is not of concern at present except in so far as the scandal, if it has perdured, must be repaired.[27] The scandal here to be considered is that which results from the presumably sinful cohabitation and from the apparent sanction of this cohabitation by the Church in administering the sacraments to the parties involved.

The ultimate solution of the question regarding scandal (and therefore of the brother-sister arrangement) depends primarily on whether the nullity of the marriage is public or occult, and whether

---

[26]Cf. Noldin-Schmitt, *Summa,* I, p. 106, n. 102; Merkelbach, *Summa Theologiae Moralis, I,* n. 958.

[27]Can. 855, § 1.

the impediment preventing the convalidation of the marriage is public or occult.

The very mention of the words *public and occult* brings to mind an oft discussed problem. In the Code itself the term public is given a twofold meaning. In canon 1037, where there is question of matrimonial impediments, public is given a meaning different from that which is given in canon 2197, 1°, where there is question of delicts. Since any application of the brother-sister arrangement must be preceded by a thorough investigation regarding the *public* or *occult* nature of both the invalid union as such and the impediment which occasioned or caused the invalidity of the union,[28] a correct undersanding and application of the terms *public* and *occult* are of paramount importance.

Is the term *public* to be understood according to the definition of canon 1037, which states that an impediment is public if it can be proved in the external forum? And if it is to be so understood, does the phraseology of canon 1971, 2°, have any bearing on the interpretation of canon 1037?[29] Or is the term *public,* in its application to the brother-sister arrangement, to be understood in accord with its definition in canon 2197, 1°?[30] Canon 1037 states that an impediment which can be proved in the external forum is considered public. Accordingly, if the term *public* in its relation to the brother-sister arrangement is to be taken in the sense defined in canon 1037, the nullity of the marriage or the extant impediment need only be provable in the external forum in order to prohibit the use of the brother-

---

[28]Cf. Vlaming, *Praelectiones Iuris Matrimonii ad Normam Codicis Iuris Canonici* (3· ed., 2 Vols., Bussum in Hollandia, 1919-1921), n. 757; De Smet, *Praxis,* p. 139, n. 88; Coronata, *De Sacramentis,* III, p. 930, n. 669; Vlaming-Bender, *Praelectiones Iuris Matrimonii,* pp. 519-520; Chrétien *De Matrimonio,* p. 444, n. 267.

[29]Can. 1037. ·"Publicum censetur impedimentum quod probari in foro externo potest; secus est occultum. Can. 1971, 2°,·Promotor iustitiae in impedimentis natura sua publicis [habilis ad accusandum est.]

[30]Can. 2197, 1° Publicum, si iam divulgatum est aut talibus contigit seu versatur in adiunctis ut prudenter iudicari possit et debeat facile divulgatum iri. The words of this canon are taken almost verbatim from Wernz, *Ius Decretalium,* IV, n. 17·

sister arrangement in a particular case. Such proof could be furnished by the testimonies of two trustworthy and oathbound witnesses[31] who, by reason of a close connection or relationship with the parties, know of their invalid marriage (and perhaps sinful association), although otherwise it remains entirely hidden. Legal records or even private documents,[32] such as private letters exchanged between the parties, would contribute much to the making of the invalidity of the marriage or the existance of the impediment itself public in the sense of canon 1037. It is of interest to note that the Commission for the Authentic Interpretation of the Code declared on June 25, 1932, that to make an impediment of marriage public in the sense of canon 1037 it is sufficient that the fact from which the impediment arises be public.[33]

If this undersanding of the term *public* were applied to the application of the brother-sister arrangement, as it does apply in regard to dispensations from matrimonial impediments, the brother-sister arrangement would indeed be a speculative thing rather than the practical remedy which it is. With possibly the few exceptions mentioned above,[34] it would mean that cohabitation on a brother-sister basis could not even be considered if there were extant any legal records or two witnesses capable of proving the nullity of the marriage or the impediment involved. Even though such records are buried in the files of the city hall or even in a foreign country, and even though the fact of a previous marriage, of the reception of holy Orders, or of the existence of impotence would remain unknown to all but one or two persons, the brother-sister arrangement would nevertheless be impossible because the nullity or the impediment could be proved in the external forum. As Bishop Król pointed out, however, scandal does not arise from records buried in archives,[35] and hence a different understanding of the term *public* is called for.

Canonists who wrote before the Code distinguished impediments as public by their very nature and as occult by their very nature. The Code makes use of this distinction when it states that the *promotor*

---

[31] Cf. can. 1791, §2.

[32] Cf. can 1817.

[33] *AAS*, XXIV (1932), 284.

[34] *Supra*, pp.89-90.

[35] Cf. his article "Permission to Parties Invalidly Married to Live as Brother and Sister," *The Jurist*, XI (1951), 24.

iustitiae has the right to challenge the validity of a marriage in the case of an impediment public of its very nature.[36] Although the phrase does not occur in the Code regarding the impediments of marriage, it was common among the pre-Code canonists, and its insertion in canon 1971 has been responsible for a limited return on the part of some commentators to the old distinction of *public* and *occult* impediments.[87]

It seems that the Sacred Penitentiary made use of this distinction even after the Code in relation to matrimonial impediments, and according to Gasparri the Code Commission was asked whether the words *pro casibus occultis* of canon 1045, §3, included only those matrimonial impediments which were occult both by their nature and *de facto*, or also such impediments as were public in their nature but occult in fact. On December 28, 1927, the response was made: *"Negative ad primam partem, affirmative ad secundam partem."*[88]

According to the pre-Code canonists an impediment was public *de facto* if it was known by the public, and occult *de facto*, or actually, if it was unknown by the public. If there were no competent witnesses, and if only the parties, the confessor and one or two persons knew of the impediment, it could not be proved in the external forum and was therefore called *omnino occultum*. It was *simpliciter* occult if only five or six persons in a town knew of the impediment, and in a city it was the same if only seven or eight persons knew of the impediment. The pre-Code canonists based this distinction not only on the number of persons who knew of the impediment, but also upon the character of these persons. If they were talkative or frequently engaged in gossip, then the impediment could not be regarded as occult.[89]

---

[36]Cf. can. 1971, 2°.

[87]Cf. Gasparri, *De Matrimonio*, I, p. 127, n. 209; S. R. Rotae *Decisiones seu Sententiae, ab anno* 1909—(Romae: Typis Polyglottis Vaticanis, 1912‑‑), XX (1928), 402; Woywod, *A Practical Commentary on the Code of Canon Law,* (Revised and Enlarged Edition, 2 vols., Wagner, Inc. : New York, 1948), I, p. 672, n. 1008 (hereafter cited *Commentary.*)

[88]Cf. Gasparri, *De Matrimonio*, I, pp. 234‑235, nn. 398, 401; Woywod, *Commentary,* I, n. 1008.

[89]Gasparri offers a short summary of this distinction as made by the pre-Code and post-Code authors. Cf. *De Matrimonio,* I. pp. 126‑129; Petrovits, *The New Church Law on Matrimony* (J. J. McVey: Philadelphia, 1921), pp. 72‑74.

This description of the terms *public* and *occult* is better suited to the demand here in question than the definition given under canon 1037 of the Code, but the definition which is most aptly and accurately applied to the brother-sister arrangement is that which is found under canon 2197, 1°, of the Code. A crime is held to be public, if it has already been divulged, or if it was committed under or attended with such circumstances that its divulgence can and must prudently be considered as readily occurring.[40] Since the element of scandal arises not from records buried in archives, and since this same element is of paramount importance in any application of the brother-sister arrangement, it is obvious that the invalidity of the marriage or the extant impediment itself must be regarded as a matter of public knowledge only when it is public in the sense of canon 2197, 1°.

Again, since the invalid marriage or union for which the brother-sister arrangement is a possible solution can be and frequently is concubinage in the true canonical sense, it is evident that the term *public* must be understood as defined in canon 2197, 1°. The matrimonial impediment of public propriety is of greater juridic import and the dispensation therefrom requires a higher ecclesiastical jurisdiction than the authorative judgment and subsequent permission involved in the granting of the brother-sister arrangement. In order to give rise to the impediment of public propriety,[41] concubinage must be public in the factual sense of canon 2197 rather than in the juridical sense of canon 1037.[42] A *fortiori*, therefore, the concubinage or the invalid marriage for which the brother-sister arrangement is a possible solution must be regarded as public in the sense of canon 2197 rather than in that of canon 1037.

---

[40] "Publicum, si iam divulgatum est aut talibus contigit seu versatur in adiunctis ut prudenter iudicari possit et debeat facile divulgatum iri."

[41] Can. 1078.

[42] Payen, *De Matrimonio*, I, n. 1541; Gasparri, *De Matrimonio*, I, p. 450, n. 738; Chelodi, *Ius Matrimoniale iuxta Codicem Iuris Canonici* (4. ed., recognita et aucta a Vigilio Dalpiaz, Tridenti; Libreria Moderna Editrice A. Ardesi, 1937), n. 104; Vlaming, *Praelectiones Iuris Matrimonii*, I, n. 361; Noldin-Schmitt, *Summa*, III, p. 603 n. 597; Cappello, *De Sacramentis*, III, p. 516, n. 544.

Other passages in the Code serve to confirm the necessity of understanding the term *public* in the sense of canon 2197. As previously mentioned,[43] cohabitation on the part of those whose marriage is notoriously public is offensive to the public sense of decency and they are normally presumed to be living in sin...as public sinners. When there is question of *public sinners* in the Code, they are such when their evil life stands divulged according to canon 2197, and not simply when proof of their sinful life can be established in the external forum according to canon 1037. Thus, according to canon 1240, 6°, public and manifest sinners are to be deprived of ecclesiastical burial.[44] Those who are publicly unworthy, such as the excommunicated, the interdicted and manifestly infamous, are to be debarred from the reception of the Holy Eucharist.[45] Similarly canon 693, §1, states that non-Catholics, those who belong to condemned sects, those who are notoriously under censure, and also public sinners in general, cannot be admitted into associations of the faithful.[46]

In regard to the brother-sister arrangement it is not a question of proving in the external forum something which already exists (viz. the invalidity of the marriage); rather, it is a question of whether the invalidity of the marriage or the extant impediment is a matter of public knowledge, and therefore a source of scandal. It is obvious that the definition of "*public*" according to canon 1037 does not suffice, and that the term *public* must be understood as defined in canon 2197.

The Code further divides crimes into those which are formally or materially public.[47] A crime may be public materially the while it remains occult formally. That is to say, the fact or happening of a crime may be public, but the imputability of the fact as something criminal may be occult. It is in this way that a public crime

---

[43]*Supra*, pp. 88-89.

[44]"Alii peccatores publici et manifesti."

[45]"Arcendi sunt ab Eucharistia publice indigni, quales sunt excommunicati, interdicti manifestoque infames . . ." Can. 855, §1.

[46]"Acatholici et damnatae sectae adscripti aut censura notorie irretiti et in genere publici peccatores valide recipi nequeunt."

[47]Can. 2197, 4°.

differs from a notorious crime.[48] The imputability of a notorious crime cannot be occult. A crime is notorious by notoriety of fact if it is publicly known and if it was committed under such circumstances that it cannot be concealed by means of any artifice, or excused by means of any reason or remedy honored as admissible in law.[49]

An adaptation of this distinction can be aptly made with reference to the invalid marriage or union for which the brother-sister arrangement is a possible solution. The invalid marriage may be formally or materially public. It may be public materially, the while it remains formally occult. That is to say, the fact of the invalid marriage or union may be public, but the nature of the impediment preventing the convalidation of the marriage remains occult. It is in this way that an invalid marriage which is public differs from one which is notorious. An invalid marriage may be said to be notorious by notoriety of fact if it is publicly known to be invalid and if the reason for the invalidity—the impediment—is attended with such circumstances and is of such a nature that it cannot be concealed by means of any artifice or presented as one which yields to dispensation or juridic cessation. If an invalid marriage is notoriously public, there is usually no possibility of applying the brother-sister arrangement because of the scandal that would result (cf. infra, pp. 101-105). Whereas, if the invalid marriage is simply public (materially public and formally occult), an application of the brother-sister arrangement is frequently possible.

For example, the invalidity of a union which is invalid by reason of a previous marriage bond may be either materially or formally public. If the second marriage is commonly known to be invalid, or if because of circumstances of place and persons it can and must prudently be judged that it will easily be divulged that the marriage

---

[48]In the earlier law the use of the terms *public* and *notorious* was not as precise as it is today in the law of the Code. The *Corpus Iuris Canonici* sometimes used the terms public and notorious indiscriminately and interchangeably. Cf. cc. 7-8, X, *de cohabitatione clericorum et mulierum*, III, 2; Reiffenstuel, *Ius Canonicum*, Lib. V, tit. I, n. 234; D'Annibale, *Summula Theologiae Moralis* (4. ed., 3 vols., Romae, 1896-1897), I, n. 242; Augustine, *A Commentary on the New Code of Cannon Law* (8 vols., Vol. VIII, *Penal Law*, 3. ed., 1931, St. Louis: Herder), VIII, 16.

[49]Can. 2197, 3°.

is invalid, and yet it is not known and will not be known that a previous *ratum et consummatum* marriage bond is the cause of the invalidity, the nullity of the second marriage is materially public, but
formally occult.[50] As such, the invalidity is frequently but erroneously ascribed simply to a lack of the observance of the prescribed
proper form. The subsequent reception of the sacraments, in many
cases, allows the false conclusion that the marriage has been convalidated. If this is the case, then there is no scandal and the brother-
sister arrangement can afford a reasonable and happy solution.

On the other hand, if the two parties of a former marriage are
living in the same locality and are known to be husband and wife,
or if the previous marriage is publicly known to have been a ratified
consummated marriage and still in existence, then a second and invalid
marriage is not only materially public, but formally or notoriously
public as well. Since it is common knowledge among Catholics and
also among many non-Catholics that the impediment of prior bond
does not yield to dispensation and that it can cease only through the
death of one of the parties, the second and invalid marriage is formally or notoriously public and thus becomes a source of grave
scandal. Grave scandal rules out any consideration of the brother-
sister arrangement.

With good reason the Code has avoided a more precise definition
of the amount of publicity postulated for a public crime. Authors
both before and after the Code, have attempted a more specific explanation. In doing so they take into account not only the size or
population of the community but also the temperament or garrulous-

---

[50]The passage of time, the fact that many people involved in divorces
make every effort to conceal their divorce and remarriage, and also the reality
that many divorces granted in larger cities pass entirely unnoticed even though
no effort is made to conceal them, combine to make possible the numerous
prior bond cases which may indeed be materially public but remain formally
occult. Cf. Krol. in *The Jurist,* XI (1951), 24.

ness of the persons who have knowledge of the crime.[51] It is maintained by many canonists that at least six persons in a small town or community must know of the crime before it can be called public, and at least eight persons in a city. It is not clear to the writer just how the authors arrive at the numbers "six in a town" and "eight in a city." There seems to be no objective and clear standard from which to judge. The terms "town" and "city" are also of nebulous import, since a community is often designated a town or a city in accordance with varying norms, viz., by the size of its population, by the form of its government, by the fact of its incorporation, etc.

Santamaria even offered a schema in which he said that in a community of one hundred the knowledge of fifteen made the crime public; of twenty, in a community of one thousand; and of forty, in a community of five thousand. Since there is no arithmetical or geometrical progression in these figures, they are of little practical value. It is impossible to calculate from these figures the number of persons necessary to make a crime public in a city of fifty thousand or a hundred thousand population, etc. The matter is such a relative one in regard to crime as well as with reference to the brother-sister arrangement that no absolute mathematical or numerical norm can be established.[52]

While these attempts of the authors to clarify the matter are not without value, there is question in the determination of crimes, in the appraisal of infamy, and in the acceptance of the brother-sister arrangement, of a fact for which the estimation of upright men in a community should be the criterion.[53] A more precise definition of the term *public* according to indications in the Code and canonical authors

---

[51]Cf. Beste, *Introductio in Codicem* (Editio altera, St. John's Abbey Press: Collegeville, Minn., 1944), pp. 875-876; Woywod, *Commentary*, II, p. 449, n. 2028; Coronata, *De Sacramentis*, III, n. 413; Lega, *De Delictis et poenis* (2. ed., Romae, 1910), n. 244; Gasparri listed a number of earlier writers of the sixteenth and seventeenth centuries who treated this problem, Cf. *De Matrimonio*, I, pp. 127-129, n. 210. Cf. also Bouscaren-Ellis, *Canon Law*, p. 431.

[52]Cf. Santamaria, *Commentarios al Codigo Canonico*, (6 vols., Madrid; 1919-1922), VI, 54.

[53]Cf. D'Annibale, *Summula Theologiae Moralis*, I, n. 242; Wernz-Vidal, *Ius Canonicum*, Vol. VII (altera editio, Romae, 1951), p. 52, n. 35, note 12.

is best left to the prudent judgment of upright men in a particular case, and also to the prudent judgment of the man upon whom falls the obligation of deciding in a particular case whether the brother-sister arrangement is possible or not.

It must be remembered, as Beste and others point out,[54] that a thing may be public in one place the while it remains occult in another. The brother-sister arrangement, therefore, may find possible application in a place where the invalidity of the marriage is formally occult, even though it may be formally or notoriously public in another town, or also in another section of a large city. The brother-sister arrangement and the subsequent, public reception of the sacraments is scandalous and therefore forbidden only in the place where the invalid marriage is materially and formally public. If it is possible to move to a place where the invalidity of the marital status of the couple is not publicly known, or in some cases to receive the sacraments in a place where the invalidity of their status is an occult matter, it is possible that the brother-sister arrangement and the reception of the sacraments would not be a source of scandal and hence could permissibly be granted.

By way of summary, it becomes evident that a considerable number of possibilities must be kept in mind for a prudent and practical judgment regarding the element of scandal in its determination of the brother-sister arrangement.

1. Scandal must be understood in its strict and proper sense: "*dictum vel factum minus rectum praebens alteri occasionem ruinae spiritualis.*"

2. Scandal may arise in two ways: from the cohabitation itself or from the subsequent reception of the sacraments.

3. Scandal results not from the *dictum vel factum* itself, but from the public reaction of men regarding the status that has resulted. The element of scandal, therefore, rests primarily upon the public or the occult nature of the *dictum vel factum*.

4. The term *public* must be understood in the sense of canon 2197, 1°. An invalid marriage and the extant impediment causing the invalidity are public if they have already been divulged, or if

---

[54]Cf. Beste, *Introductio In Codicem*, p. 875.

they are attended with such circumstances that their divulgence can and must prudently be considered as readily occuring.

5.   An invalid marriage is *materially public* if only the fact of invalidity is public.

6.   An invalid marriage is *formally public* or *notorious* if the impediment or the reason for the invalidity of the marriage is public and is commonly known to be an impediment for which there is no dispensation or juridic cessation.

7.   By reason of the distinction between invalid marriages which are materially public and those which are formally public there is a threefold possibility regarding the emergence of scandal in a particular case.   An invalid marriage may be:

      a. materially public and formally public (notorious);
      b. materially public and formally occult:
      c. materially occult and formally occult.

Each of these possibilities is treated in reference to the scandal and other possible juridic effects which it engenders.

A.   *Materially and formally public invalid marriage.*

It is difficult to see how scandal can be avoided in an invalid marriage which is both materially and formally public, unless the parties involved move to an entirely new locality.   A few possible exceptions were mentioned above (*supra* pp. 89-90,) but the writer hesitates to allow, not only any exceptions to the general rule which forbids cohabitation on a brother-sister basis, but also the public reception of the sacraments in that place where the invalidity of the marriage is materially and formally public.

Continued cohabitation in a union when its invalidity is formally public subjects the parties to various juridical consequences.   They incur *infamia* and are usually *manifesto infames.*[55] As such they are regarded as *publice indigni* or *publici peccatores.*

Infamy (*infamia*) is divided into infamy of law (*infamia iuris*) and infamy of fact (*infamia facti*).   Infamy of law is that which is declared in the cases fixed by the common law.   Infamy of fact is contracted when, through the commission of an offense or as the result of bad conduct, one has lost his good repute with righteous and

---

[55]In pre-Code editions of the *Roman Ritual* (tit. IV, c. I, n. 8), persons living in concubinage were enumerated among those who were manifestly infamous in the sense of canon 855, §1.

serious Catholics. The judgment whether infamy of fact exists in a given case rests with the ordinary.[56]

The Code states that bigamists, that is, those persons who attempt marriage—even though it be only the so-called civil ceremony of marriage—while they are already subject to a matrimonial bond, are *ipso facto infames.* [57] And if, disregarding the warning of the ordinary, they continue to live in concubinage, they are to be excommunicated if that be warranted according to the gravity of their guilt, or punished with personal interdict. [58] As bigamists they *ipso facto* incur the *infamia iuris,* which ceases only in consequence of a dispensation granted by the Holy See.[59] If the bigamous, incestuous, adulterous or sacriligious union is entered or continued in bad faith, and the invalidity of the marriage is materially and formally public, they no doubt also incur (in accord with the judgment of the ordinary) an *infamia facti.* Infamy of fact ceases only when the ordinary after considering all the circumstances and especially the prolonged amendment of the guilty party, prudently judges that the person has regained his good repute among righteous and serious Catholics.[60] If the invalid marriage is materially and formally public, the case is indeed notorious, and the illicit cohabitation brands the parties as notoriously or manifestly infamous. As such they are, in the terminology of the Code, public sinners and *publice indigni* (canon 855).

In general, therefore, the parties to an invalid marriage which is materially and formally public are subject to that legislaton of the Code which relates to the infamous and to those who are publicly unworthy (*publice indigni*) as long namely as the cohabitation continues and irrespective indeed of the internal disposition of the parties. These juridical consequences cannot be offset by means of the secret application of the brother-sister arrangement and it is

---

[56]Can. 2293, §1-3.

[57]I.e., they incur infamy of law. The same is true for anyone guilty of incestuous, adulterous and sacrilegious concubinage.

[58]Cf. canons 2356, 2256 (765, 2°; 795; 1448); 2357, §2.

[59]Cf. can. 2295.

[60]Can. 2295. The prolonged amendment (*diuturna emendatio*) could possibly postulate the continuance of a laudable conduct for as long as three years, as in the case spoken of in canon 672.

most rare that the use of the brother-sister arrangement in a particular case can be made a matter of public knowledge.[61] Accordingly they cannot be admitted into Pious Associations of the faithful;[62] they cannot licitly or validly act as sponsors at baptism or at confirmation;[63] they cannot receive ecclesiastical or Christian burial unless they have given some sign of repentance before death.[64] Of greater importance is the legislation which debars the *publice indigni* or those who are manifestly infamous from the reception of the Blessed Eucharist until they have repented and also have amended their lives and repaired the scandal which was given.[65] The problem of scandal and notorious infamy of fact in a formally public invalid marriage is not overcome by the public reception of the sacraments, as it might be in cases which are materially public but formally occult. In a particular case it may be true that the parties have repented of their sins (if formal sin was committed)[66] and have amended their lives to the extent of making an efficacious promise to avoid the voluntary proxmiate occasion of sin (*infra*, pp. 109-115). But the third condition of canon 855, §1, (the adequate reparation of the scandal caused by continued cohabitation in a formally public case) can usually be verified only after a complete separation has taken place.[67] Consequently, the public reception of the sacraments is always inadmissible in formally public cases in which the continued cohabitation brands the parties with the mark of infamy and public unworthiness.

A private solution for a case of this kind was rendered by the

---

[61]*Supra*, pp. 89-90.

[62]Can. 693, §1·

[63]Cans. 765-766; 795-796.

[64]Cans. 1240, 6°, 1241; *supra*, p. 96; *infra*, pp.161-163.

[65]Can. 855, §1.

[66]It is possible that the parties were in *good faith* until the invalidity of their marriage became materially and formally public. E.g., there are known cases of presumed death in which the husband or the wife was erroneously declared dead and then unexpectedly and publicly returns.

[67]The third condition could also be verified if the parties were to move to a place where their marital status is unknown. In this event, however, the case would no longer be materially or formally public.

Sacred Congregation of the Council in 1922.[68] The facts of the case showed that a missionary admitted to the reception of Holy Communion, after hearing her confession, a woman who was living in open concubinage with a relative. The action of the missionary was unacceptable to the pastor, who immediately reported the incident to the local ordinary. The latter, in turn, reversed the decision of the missionary and forbade that Holy Communion be given the woman until she separated from the man with whom she was living. The case came to the Sacred Congregation through the recourse interposed by the missionary-confessor. The ultimate solution was that the authority of the local ordinary is paramount in the external forum in determining the question involved.

The administration of Holy Communion to persons living in an invalid marriage which is materially and formally public, or to other manifestly infamous persons, is abhorrent because the conscience of the public is affronted by the conflict between the public state of the recipient and the holiness demanded by the reverence due the Blessed Sacrament. With the few possible exceptions mentioned above (*supra*, pp. 89-90), continued cohabitation makes the theory of repentance publicly unacceptable. It is of the public acceptance of repentance that the minister of Holy Communion must judge, and it is on this likewise that the local ordinary must render his decision. Even in danger of death, Holy Viaticum cannot be administered to a dying man unless he either marries his concubine or, if that is impossible, repudiates her in the presence of witnesses or, at least, authorizes the confessor to make known the fact of his repentance and of his repudiation of her as a concubine.[69]

But what is to be said of the *private*[70] and of the *secret* reception[71] of the Blessed Eucharist. It is true that the sincere promise to repair

---

[68]S.C.C., 18 nov. 1922-Bouscaren, *The Canon Law Digest*, (3 vols., Milwaukee: Bruce, 1934-1943-1949-1953), I, 408-9 (hereafter cited *Digest*).

[69]Cf. Vermeersch-Creusen, *Epitome Iuris Canonici*, II, pp. 78-80, nn. 116-117; Coronata, *De Sacramentis*, I, n. 313.

[70]The term *private* is used to indicate the reception of the Eucharist in the place of cohabitation, but without the knowledge of the public.

[71]The term *secret* is used to indicate the reception of the Eucharist in a locality other than the place of cohabitation and in which the invalidity of their marriage is materially and formally occult.

the scandal suffices to permit the private or secret reception of the Blessed Eucharist by a truly repentant person. But if the parties continue to cohabit in the place in which their invalid marriage is materially and formally public, even though the cohabitation is on a brother-sister basis, the scandal continues, and the sincerity of their promise to repair the scandal arising from the cohabitation is in question. It seems, therefore, that the parties must move to a different locality, in which they are unknown. If it is morally impossible[72] for them to move immediately, their promise may be regarded as being sincere, and they should be admitted to the private or secret reception of the sacraments. If, on the other hand, it is morally possible for them to move to another locality and they neglect or refuse to do so, the scandal of their cohabitation continues, their promise is insincere, and they are unworthy to receive the Blessed Eucharist either privately or secretly. Briefly stated:

· 1) the public reception of the sacraments is not permissible for persons involved in an invalid marriage which is materially and formally public, the reasons being that the continued cohabitation brands them as infamous and publicly unworthy, and the public reception of the sacraments by them would add greater scandal.

2) The private or secret reception of the sacraments by persons whose invalid marriage is materially and formally public is not permissible if it is morally possible for them to remove the scandal caused through their continued cohabitation (e.g., by moving to a different place) and they neglect or refuse to do so. If it is morally impossible (because of grave illness or grave financial difficulties) for them to remove the scandal of continued cohabitation by moving to a different location, they may be admitted to the private or secret reception of the sacraments provided that they have seriously promised to move as soon as they are able.[73]

---

[72]E.g., because of serious illness or extreme financial difficulties.

[73]If the parties actually move to another locality in which their invalid marriage is not materially or formally public, there is no problem of continued scandal, but the parties may be called upon to perform some private penance to help satisfy for the scandal which they had caused. This would at least indicate the good will of the parties, in that they would repair the past scandal if it were possible. The ordinary, in accord with canon 2295, will have no special difficulty in making a judgment regarding the cessasion of the *infamia facti.*

B. *Materially public and formally occult invalid marriage. . .*

In this case it is comparatively easy to find possible the application of the brother-sister arrangement and the subsequent public
reception of the sacraments. In the first place, only the fact of
the invalidity is public, the while the cause or the precise nature
of the cause of the invalidity remains occult. In this situation
the public is either unconcerned with the nature of the invalidating cause or the impediment, or it erroneously ascribes the invalidity of the marriage simply to the lack of the prescribed
marriage form, or perhaps to the failure of acquiring a dispensation which erroneously is regarded as being easily obtainable. In any
event, it can be reasonably and prudently assumed that the public
reception of the sacraments will be regarded by the public as pointing
to the convalidation of the marriage. If this assumption can be
prudently made in the individual case (and usually it is a safe presumption), the brother-sister arrangement is allowable.

A case which most likely conforms to the type described above
(materially public and formally occult) was solved by the Holy Office
in the year 1900.[74] Bertha, a Catholic girl, lived in concubinage with
Titus, a non-Catholic, for five years. During this time two children
were begotten by them. One of them survived and was baptized a
Catholic. Two years after the birth of the second child, Bertha and
Titus attempted marriage before a civil magistrate. Sometime later
Bertha's pastor endeavored to have the marriage convalidated with
the proper dispensation from the impediment of mixed religion, but
Titus claimed that by an operation performed two years before the
civil marriage he had been made perpetually impotent by the removal
of both testicles. Since the marriage could not be convalidated, but
since a complete separation would have proved very difficult and
likewise very grave scandal was feared, they asked the Holy Office for

---

[74]S·C.S. Off., 8 mart. 1900·-Cf. *Coll.S.C.P.F.*, II, n. 2078; *ASS*, XXXII,
639-40.

a happy solution. The response of the Holy Office indicated that, since a convalidation was impossible, the *"coniuges"* should separate. But if a complete separation was morally impossible and the danger of incontinence was removed, they could cohabit on a brother-sister basis. It was also pointed out that the child could receive canonical legitimation by way of rescript.[75]

In order to arrive at a prudent decision, it is the opinion of the writer that it must be determined, first of all, that the invalid marriage is only materially public, and that it is in fact formally occult. This requires that the priest handling the case make a proper and discreet investigation of the case to the extent deemed necessary.[76] This investigation should normally extend to the pastors of nearby parishes in a city, and to neighboring towns if the case occurs in a small town. From this investigation the one handling the case should arrive at positive conviction that the case is, indeed, only materially public the while it remains formally occult. These requirements cannot be presumed, and mere probability will not suffice. There must be moral certitude regarding the public or the occult nature of the case. If after due investigation this moral certitude cannot be had, the case should be handled as one which is both materially and formally public.

After it is morally certain that the invalid marriage is only materially public, it can be prudently assumed that the public reception of the sacraments will be regarded by the public as pointing to the convalidation of the marriage. Thereafter, the invalid marriage must remain occult both materially and formally. The parties involved in

---

[75] Resp. "In casu exposito sanationem in radice concedi non posse; et ad mentem: Mens est, quod cum matrimonium revalidari nequeat, putati coniuges illico separari deberent. Si vero hoc moraliter impossibile sit, dummodo absit periculum incontinentiae, (saltem) adhibitis cautelis, sub eodem tecto cohabitent uti frater et soror. Quod vero ad canonicam prolis legitimationem, eam per rescriptum Principis rite expediendum concedi posse . . ."

[76] Cases involving the impediment of a prior bond usually require a more thorough investigation.

the union should be instructed and forewarned that a solution other than the brother-sister arrangement will be necessitated if the invalidity of their marriage does not remain occult.

If the invalid marriage is one that has caused considerable scandal previous to the application for the brother-sister arrangement, there seems to arise another problem for consideration. On the one hand, it is said that the public reception of the sacraments will put a stop to the scandal caused by the invalid union which is materially public and formally occult. On the other hand, canon 855 rules that the sacrament of the Blessed Eucharist cannot be received until the scandal caused by the cohabitation has been repaired. It appears to be a vicious circle . . . as if one were trying to repair something with a tool that cannot be used until that something is repaired.

It seems, however, that this difficulty, if it exists in a particular case, is a technical one and can be solved in a practical manner without inevitable offense to the law. The public reception of the sacrament of penance (which is not restricted by canon 855) can in itself repair a considerable amount of scandal which had been caused by the illicit cohabitation. The repeated reception of this sacrament of penance by one or both parties in such a manner that it becomes known to the entire parish may be sufficient to point to the (erroneous) conclusion that the marriage has been convalidated, and thereby may stop any future scandal. This repeated public reception of the sacrament of penance could simultaneously remove some or even all of the past scandal. By way of absolution they will be freed of any censures they have incurred, and by reason of their frequent public reception of the sacrament of penance they will no longer be regarded as *publici peccatores,* so that all *infamia facti* can lapse from this basis.[77] No longer regarded as public sinners, they are eiligible for membership in Pious Associations (canon 693) and can engage in edifying works and prayers, which will soon repair the harm of the past scandal to such an extent that the restrictions of canon 855 will no longer apply . . . i. e., they will be regarded as publicly worthy to receive the Most Blessed Sacrament.

Again, in those localities wherein a public apology is still de-

---

[77] The latter in accord with the judgment of the ordinary (can. 2295).

manded for the attempting of marriage before a minister or a civil magistrate, this apology could be made by the parties to help repair the scandal.[78]

The entire difficulty regarding the reception of the sacraments in the case proposed is, in the writer's opinion, a technical one. In many cases it may not exist at all, and if it does exist in other cases it seems readily surmountable through the adoption of means similar to the ones mentioned above.

C. *Materially and formally occult marriage* . . .

In this case the question of scandal is non-existent, or it is at least sufficiently remote that no problem is created. The brother-sister arrangement finds readier application, and the subsequent public reception of the sacraments in such cases presents no problem from the aspect of scandal.

Article 3.   No Proximate Voluntary Occasion of Sin

A thorough consideration in the light of moral theology concerning an occasion or danger of sin is best left to the moral theologians. A brief summary, however, is not without merit in this work, since any applicaion of the brother-sister arrangement from either a canonical or a moral point of view, gives explicit warning concerning the occasion or danger of sin.[79] The sin which is here of primary concern or import is that of incontinence—the violation of the mutual and perfect chastity to which the parties are bound—which finds its oc-

---

[78]The practice of demanding a public apology seems to be falling into disuse, since the apology has itself been found to be a source of increased scandal in some cases.

[79]Reiffenstuel, *Ius Canonicum*, Lib. IV, tit. 15, nn. 61-63; and Lib. IV, tit. 19, n. 14; Gasparri, *De Matrimonio*, I, n. 549, and II, nn. 1180-1183; Sanchez, *De Matrimonii Sacramento*, Lib. VII, Disp. 97, n. 5; St. Thomas, *Summa Theologica*, Suppl., q. 58, art. 1, in fine; S.C.C. *Maurianen*, 15 dec. 1877—ASS X. 504; S.C.S. Off., 8 mart. 1900—Coll. S.C.P.F., II, n. 2078; Cappello, *De Matrimonio*, p. 372, nn. 266-68; Ter Haar, *Casus Conscientiae* (3. ed., 2 vols., Taurini: Marietti, 1944), I, n. 158; Wernz, *Ius Decretalium*, IV, n. 646; Wernz-Vidal, *Ius Matrimoniale*, p. 851, n. 651; Coronata, *De Sacramentis*, III, n. 668; De Smet, *Praxis*, p. 141, n. 90; Chrètien, *De Martrimonio*, p. 444, nn. 267-8.

casion as a result of the cohabitation on a brother-sister basis. The absence of a voluntary and proximate occasion of sin is one of the five conditions absolutely postulated in any application of the brother-sister arrangement.

For the most part, the moral distinctions regarding an occasion or danger of sin are not expressly adverted to by the authors in their presentation of the brother-sister arrangement. Without exception however, these same authors absolutely demand the absence of the danger of incontinence in the arrangement.[80] If, therefore, the brother-sister arrangement is to be a practical solution for invalid marriages, a consideration of the distinctions and principles of moral theology regarding the occasion or danger of sin is indispensable. Krol, in his splendid treatment of the brother-sister arrangement,[81] devoted considerable space to this precise point. The same general considerations are offered here.

The licit reception of the sacrament of baptism by an adult requires contrition or at least attrition for all his mortal sins.[82] The Council of Trent clearly defined contrition "as a sorrow of mind and a detestation for sin committed with the purpose of not sinning in the future."[83] This purpose or intention of not sinning in the future is essential to contrition, and according to the theologians it must extend not only to the sin itself but also to the voluntary proximate occasion of sin. From a proposition condemned in 1679 by Pope Innocent XI, it is clear that anyone who can but does not want to avoid the proximate occasion of sin must be denied the sacraments.[84]

An occasion of sin is generally defined as some external circumstance—a person, place or object—which attracts to and affords

---

[80]Cf. the preceding footnote.

[81]Cf. "Permission to parties invalidly married to live as brother and sister," *The Jurist*, XI (1951), 12-19.

[82]Can. 752, §1; Conc. Trident, sess. VI, *de justificatione*, c. 6; S.C.S.Off., instr., 3 aug, 1860—Coll. S.C.P.F., I, nn. 1050, 1198.

[83]Sess. XIV, *de poen.*, caput 4, can. 5.

[84]"Potest aliquando absolvi, qui in proxima occasione peccandi versatur, quam potest et non vult omittere, quin immo directe et ex proposito quaerit aut ei se ingerit."-Denzinger-Rahner, *Enchiridion Symbolorum*, n. 1211.

a facility for sin.[85] According to some, the occasion is entirely external, and not to be identified with the internal propensity arising from fallen human nature with its inordinate passions, evil habits, etc.[86] Merkelbach (1871-1942)[87] and Aertnys (1829-1915)-Damen (1881-1953),[88] however, offer a definition which proves better suited for our consideration of the brother-sister arrangement, and which seems to conform more closely to the warning extended by the authors regarding the danger of incontinence in the arrangement. According to Merkelbach and Aertnys-Damen and others, an occasion of sin is an external circumstance which induces the danger of sinning—*periculum peccandi*. This definition indicates a combination of both the internal (relative) elements and external (absolute) elements.[89] Applying this definition to an invalidly married couple, who because of advanced age and illness have lived in continence for some time, one could presume that they are not living in the occasion of sin. This is not so for the normal, young and healthy couple.

An occasion of sin can be either *proximate* or *remote* A remote occasion of sin is one which presents only a slight probability or danger of sinning, or in which a person rarely commits sin. These remote occasions are universal in this life, and they neither can nor need be avoided.[90]

[85]Cf. Jone-Adelman, *Moral Theology* (3. ed., Westminster, Maryland: Newman Bookshop, 1947), p. 444, n. 607.

[86]Cf. Prümmer, *Manuale Theologiae Moralis* (3. ed., 3 vols., Friburgi Brisgoviae: Herder, 1936) III, n. 449; Jone-Adelman divide an occasion of sin into *absolute* and *relative* by reason of the external and intenal elements (*Moral Theology*, p. 444, n. 607).

[87]*Summa Theologiae Moralis*, III, n. 667.

[88]*Theologia Moralis* (14. ed., 2 vols., Taurini: Marietti, 1944), II, n. 476.

[89]Napholc insists that both the external and internal elements are essential components of an occasion of sin, and that there is no occasion unless both are present. Cf. "De Vera Proxima Occasionis Peccati Notione," *Periodica,* XXI (1932), 150.

[90]Cf. Noldin-Schmitt, *Summa,* I, p. 319, n. 325; Jone-Adelman, *Moral Theology,* n. 607; Ter Haar, *De Occasionariis et Recidivis* (ed. altera, Taurini: Marietti, 1939), p. 11 (hereafter cited as *De Occasionariis*). Any reasonable or useful cause justifies a remote occasion of sin, according to most of the authors.

There are two schools of thought regarding the definition of a proximate occasion of sin.[91] This controversy, however, between the two schools is of practical value only when there is question of a single or a disjunctive occasion of sin. Since the brother-sister arrangement involves the question of a continuous occasion of sin, an account of the controversy would be of mere academic value. Without wishing to become involved in that particular discussion, the writer uses the safer definition or explanation proposed by the school of St. Alphonsus. An occasion of sin, according to the school of St. Alphonsus, is proximate when something external to a person—whether it be another person, or place, or thing—places him in grave danger (serious probability) of sinning mortally, even though it is at least probable that, despite the occasion, sin will be avoided.[92]

Whether or not one has a serious obligation to avoid even the single proximate occasion is a question best left to the moralists. All theologians agree that one has a serious obligation to avoid the continuous voluntary occasion in which there is grave danger of committing mortal sin. As far as the brother-sister arrangement is concerned, and for practical purposes, it must be taken for granted that, as long as the couple invalidly married are in a voluntary occasion in which there is grave danger (serious probability) of committing mortal sin, a complete separation is the only solution.

A proximate occasion of sin is *voluntary* if it can easily be avoided; otherwise it is a *necessary occasion*. A *necessary occasion* of sin can be either physically or morally necessary. Physical necessity is exemplified in the case of a prisoner or a soldier who is not free to remove himself from the occasion. The same is true of a lawful wife, if she be exposed to the danger of sin by living with her husband. Moral necessity is exemplified, according to the general agreement of the authors, in the company keeping or the period of engagement

---

[91]Cf. Król, "art. cit.," *The Jurist*, XI (1951), 13, 16.

[92]The followers of St. Alphonsus reject the more liberal view which says that a proximate occasion of sin is one in which a person always or almost always (moral certitude) falls into sin. Their primary reason for this rejection seems to be that no allowance is made for the subjective or relative element. Cf. Ter Haar, *De Occasionariis*, pp. 6-11, 47-168; Noldin-Schmitt, *Summa* I, pp. 319-321, nn. 325-326.

between a young man and woman with a view to marriage in the near future. It is a proximate occasion which indeed can be avoided, but not without grave harm or grave inconvenience.

In spite of the difference of opinion regarding the nature of the proximate occasion of sin, theologians rather commonly agree that there are proximate occasions of sin which normally must be avoided, but which nevertheless can lawfully be frequented, provided that the avoidance of them is morally or physically impossible, and provided also that sufficient means are seriously employed for the rendering of the occasion remote. St. Alphonsus is to be numbered among these.[93]

In defining a proximate occasion of sin as something external to a person—whether it be another person, or place, or thing—which places him in grave danger (serious probability) of repeatedly sinning mortally, even though it is at least probable that, despite the occasion, sin will be avoided, one may safely set down the following general rules regarding the brother-sister arrangement:

1. The brother-sister arrangement is permitted:
   a. when there is no occasion of sin;
   b. when the occasion of sin is remote;
   c. when the occasion of sin is proximate but necessary, and provided that the parties take efficacious precautionary measures to render the proximate occasion remote.
2. The brother-sister arrangement is not permitted:
   a. when the proximate occasion is voluntary;[94]
   b. when the proximate occasion is morally necessary, but

---

[93]Davis, *Moral and Pastoral Theology* (4. ed., 4 vols., London: Sheed & Ward, 1943), III, 293, 294; Noldin-Schmitt, *Summa*, III, p. 413, n. 401.

[94]This is clear from the propositions condemned by Pope Innocent XI. Cf. Denzinger-Rahner, *Enchiridion Symbolorum*, nn. 1211-1213:

61. "Potest aliquando absolvi, qui in proxima occasione peccandi versatur quam potest et non vult omittere, quin immo directe et ex proposito quaerit aut ei se ingerit."

62. "Proxima occasio peccandi non est fugienda, quando causa aliqua utilis aut honesta non fugiendi occurrit."

63. Licitum est quaerere directe occasionem proximam peccandi pro bono spirituali vel temporali nostro vel proximi."

the proper precautionary measures to avoid sin are not taken or are not efficacious;[95]

c. when the proximate occasion, even though necessary. constitutes a proximate danger to eternal salvation.

Ter Haar (1857-1939) listed the fundamental precautionary measures which the parties must employ in order to render a proximate necessary occasion remote. He stated that they must not sleep in the same bed or even in the same room, and that they must abstain from all signs of special affection, and finally avoid being alone with each other as much as possible.[96] There are many other measures that can and should be employed by those who find the convalidation of their marriage, or also a complete separation, impossible. Some of these measures are: ejaculatory prayers at the moment of temptation; special prayers in the morning and at night, in which the firm purpose of amendment is renewed with great force of will, with humility and confidence; frequent reception of the sacrament of penance, from the same confessor if possible; frequent Holy Communion; frequent meditation and consideration of the eternal truths; etc. There are various intermediary stages between the remote and the proximate occasions of sin. The more proximate the occasion is, so much the more seriously should one employ the proper measures to render it remote.[97]

Ter Haar also, in an exemplary manner, furnished a list of the causes which may suffice to render a proximate occasion of sin

---

[95]Ter Haar, *Casus Conscientiae*, I, n. 62: "Poenitens, qui in occasione moraliter necessaria, adhibitis etiam remediis, eodem fere modo semper re-labitur, ita ut probabilis spes eius emendationis iam non supersit, hanc oc-casionem physice relinquere debet, etiam cum gravissimo suo incommodo aut damno." Cf. Davis, *Moral and Pastoral Theology*, III, 291; Noldin-Schmitt, *Summa*, III, 413.

[96]Si neque matrimonium, neque separatio physica fieri potest, *alia remedia* efficacia sunt praescribenda, quibus periculum peccandi e proximo reddatur remotum; de hisce vide *Opus.* n. 142. Imprimis nitendum est, ut in separatis lectis vel etiam cubiculis dormiant, ut a signis specialis amoris omnino se abstineant, imo etiam ut solum cum sola esse, quantum possint, evitent." Cf. Ter Haar, *Casus Conscientiae*, I, n. 158.

[97]Cf. Noldin-Schmitt, *Summa*, III, p. 413, n. 401; Davis, *Moral and Pastoral Theology*, III, 279; Jone-Adelman, *Moral Theology*, p. 445, n. 608.

morally necessary. He prefaced this list with the remark that by all means a physical (complete) separation must be demanded unless cohabitation and the proximate occasion are truly necessitated in a given case. This necessitation can be present, for example:

    a) if the parties have already entered a civil marriage in which the obtaining of a divorce is precluded;

    b) if there are children for whom a proper education must be provided;

    c) if, in consequence of a complete separation, the parties are subjected to serious injury or suffer harm to their reputation;

    d) if the woman is unable to support herself by means of work or through begging on the assumption that the latter can be done without shame or grave inconvenience.[98]

Article 4. Proportionate Reason

In view of the considerations and principles enumerated in articles two and three of the present chapter it is clear that a proportionate cause or reason must be had if the brother-sister arrangement is to be rendered permissible. In so far as the danger of scandal is more or less grave, and in so for as the occasion of sin is more or less proximate in an individual case, the reason or the cause for which the brother-sister arrangement can be permitted must be proportionately grave.[99]

---

[98] ". . . omnino insistendum est *separationi physicae,* nisi cohabitatio et occasio proxima sit vere necessaria. Haec necessitas adesse potest, v.g.: a) si complices iam inierunt matrimonium civile quod rumpi nequeat; b) si iam nati sunt infantes quorum educationi providere debeat; c) si cui ex separatione damnum valde grave vel gravis infamia oriatur,—haec tamen ratio non facile admittatur, utpote saepe ob passionem exaggerata; d) 'si femina' inquit St. Alphonsus, 'nequiret manuum labore se alere, aut in aliqua domo servire, aut mendicare sine dedecore aut aliquo gravi incommodo' (III, 437): in hoc autem casu femina saepe in aliquo instituto locari potest." Cf. Ter Haar, *Casus Conscientiae,* I, n. 158.

[99] Cf. Noldin-Schmitt, *Summa,* I, pp. 180-1, n. 179; Sabetti-Barrett, *Compendium Theologiae Moralis* (22, ed., Cincinnati: Frederick Pustet & Co., 1915), p. 87, n. 93.

Most of the authors regard the brother-sister arrangement as a *res plena periculis*.[100] Though they do not specifically consider the moral principles involved, they do demand at least a grave reason for the granting of permission for the use of the brother-sister arrangement in any instance. Actually, it is a proportionate cause which they demand but they do not envisage a case in which less than a grave cause would suffice. While it is possible to have a case in which there is no proximate occasion of sin, or another case in which the danger of immediate scandal is non-existent, such cases are not common. It is even more exceptional for a case to be had in which both the danger of scandal and the occasion of sin are completely absent.

The usual case is one in which a number of slight or more or less remote dangers combine to form a situation in which nothing less than a grave cause or reason suffices for the licit use of the brother-sister arrangement. Still other cases may involve a proximate necessary occasion of sin which, in order to be a necessary occasion, presupposes a grave cause or reason. In any event, the authors list several causes or reasons, each of which is commonly regarded as sufficient to permit a use of the brother-sister arrangement. In mentioning these causes they point out that other similar causes may be had. It is likewise true that frequently there are more than one proportionate cause in a single case. Chelodi (1880-1922) seems to have expressed the entire situation in general terms when he said that cohabitation on a brother-sister basis is a very dangerous thing, and that it is permitted only in extraordinary circumstances and when there is no other remedy.[101]

---

[100]Cappello, *De Matrimonio*, p. 841; Chelodi, *De Matrimonio*, p. 207, n. 163; Gasparri, *De Matrimonio*, II, n. 1181; De Smet, *Praxis*, p. 140, n. 80; Chrétien, *De Matrimonio*, p. 444, n. 268, etc.

[101]"Cohabitatio uti frater et soror est res perculis plena, in extraordinariis dumtaxat adiunctis, quum alia remedia praesto non sunt, permittenda."-*De Matrimonio*, p. 207, n· 163; cf. also Cappello, *De Matrimonio*, p. 841.

1. *Presence of Children*

The first example of a proportionate cause, and perhaps the strongest of all, is the presence of minor children for whom a home, education and training are necessary. It is a matter of common knowledge that parental love and home training are essentials in the formation of a well-balanced character. One minor child can suffice to constitute a grave cause or a cause which renders the brother-sister arrangement permissible. If there are more than one child the cause or the reason for finding the arrangement permissible is that much more grave.

A minor, according to the Code, is a child who has not completed his twenty-first year.[102] For purposes of the brother-sister arrangement, a minor is one who has not completed his twenty-first year and is living with and dependent upon his parents. Obviously, minor children do not constitute a grave cause if they are self-supporting and living away from home. It is equally evident that an infant (can. 88, §3) who in fact is not and will not be living with his parents does not create a sufficient cause for the use of the brother-sister arrangement. After the children reach adulthood they no longer constitute a grave cause for their parents to remain together (on a brother-sister basis). It should be noted, however, that if the parents have been living according to the brother sister arrangement for some time by reason of the minor children, it is not usually necessary for the parents to separate completely when the children reach adult-hood. It is most likely that the period of cohabitation has given rise to another grave cause, i. e., the invalid marriage is now regarded as a valid marriage by the public, and grave scandal or serious harm to their reputation would result from a complete separation.

2. *Scandal Arising from Complete Separation*

Chrètien explicitly points out that the arrangement is tolerated when there is danger of scandal if the parties separate completely.[103] For example, if two people have been living together for a long time and are commonly regarded as husband and wife, scandal would be

---

[102]Can. 88, §1.
[103]*De Matrimonio*, p. 444, n. 268.

given if they were to separate. Coronata indicates that, if the parties of an invalid marriage which is materially and formally occult find it necessary to separate completely for some pressing reason, they should do so under some other pretext, such as that of a journey, in order that all scandal and infamy may be duly forestalled.[104] If the invalid marriage is formally public in character, even though it is not as yet *de facto* known by the public, the brother-sister arrangement could not be granted on the basis that scandal would be caused in consequence of a complete separation. Although the invalidity is not as yet known, it is prudently foreseen that it soon will be, and the resulting scandal would be greater than the scandal caused in consequence of the immediate and complete separation. It is, in this case, a matter of tolerating the lesser of two evils.

The danger of scandal resulting from a complete separation is certainly a grave cause and forms a sufficient basis for permitting the brother-sister arrangement in a case which is materially and formally occult. The same is true for a case which, although materially public, will be made completely occult through the parties reception of the sacraments.

3. *Serious Injury to Reputation*

One's good reputation has always been regarded as a very precious possession. Ter Harr stated that the inescapable emergence of serious harm or injury to one's reputation is regarded by the authors as a sufficient reason for rendering a proximate occasion of sin a moral necessity.[105] If, therefore, all the other conditions are verified for the licit use of the brother-sister arrangement, the fact that one's reputation is subject to serious harm or injury furnishes a sufficient cause for the granting of permission to use the brother-sister arrangement.

Obviously, if anyone has already lost his good reputation (as

---

[104]*De Sacramentis*, III, n. 670. Vlaming-Bender (*Praelectiones Iuris Matrimonii*, p. 520) point out that if the nullity is public "*in sensu iuris*" only then, in order to avert all scandalous talk that would be brought on by this separation *a cohabitatione*, the parties can be permitted to live together as brother and sister, provided that their character and disposition warrant it. Cf. also Gasparri, *De Matrimonio*, II, n. 1180.

[105]*Casus Conscientiae*, I, n. 158.

in a materially and formally public case), or if it is impossible for him
to regain his good reputation (through the use of the brother-sister arrangement in a materially public but formal occult case), then the
safeguarding of his reputation cannot furnish a sufficient cause for
the use of the arrangement. Ter Haar also made the observation that
this danger of the loss of one's good name is frequently exaggerat-
ed.[106] Great care should be taken, therefore, to see that an objective
judgment is made. Especially is this true if the loss of reputation is
the only cause presented in support of one's attempt to receive permission for the brother-sister arrangement.

It also is evident that the element of good or bad faith on the
side of the parties when they entered the invalid union, or when possibly they still continue in it, plays a major role in regard to the factor of good reputation.[107] One's good reputation is not usually lost
if it is clear that the invalid marriage was entered in good faith. Therefore, materially public but formally occult cases in which good faith
was always a present factor may leave room for the application of the
brother-sister arrangement on the basis of the serious harm to one's
reputation through a complete separation.

4. *Conversion of One or Both Parties*

The Church has always been, and will continue to be, most so-
licitous regarding the spiritual welfare of persons not yet within the
fold. The Church's history gives ample testimony of its many endeav-
ors to bring the Word of the Gospel to all men, and of its unlimited

---

[106]*Loc. cit.*

[107]A person who has entered an invalid union in good faith certainly
merits more consideration, indulgence and sympathy from the Church in regard
to the entire question of the brother-sister arrangement, than does the person
who entered or continued in an invalid marriage in bad faith. This does not
mean to say that a truly repentant person is not to receive a full amount of
consideration and sympathy· A majority of the cases in which the brother-
sister arrangement finds a possible application are those in which the parties
have become matrimonial casualties through their own weakness or recklessness.
It is only subsequently that they return to their senses and seek readmittance
into the fold. These, however, by reason of their very weakness and self-in-
dulgence, will find it more difficult to measure up to the rigid requirements of
the brother-sister arrangement. Cf. Król, in *The Jurist*, XI (1951,) 9.

compassion and mercy in making it possible for the stray sheep to enter or return to communion with the one true Church.

The conversion and salvation of each individual soul is indeed a task of untold importance. Our Divine Savior pointed the way by dying not simply for the entire human race, but for each and every human soul. The conversion of a single soul, therefore, is truly a grave matter, and offers a sufficient cause in itself for rendering the application of the brother-sister arrangement permissible. Every priest in the active ministry wastes no time in discovering invalid marriages in which one or both of the parties are desirous of entering the Church. Frequently the invalid marriage can be convalidated, and frequently a complete separation is morally possible, either of these solutions may clear the way for entrance into the Church. But not infrequently it happens that neither of these solutions is possible. It is then that the brother-sister arrangement finds a possible application, based on the likely conversion of one or possibly both of the parties.

It is not absolutely necessary that the parties be exceptionally old or gravely ill. It suffices that the requirements regarding the avoidance of scandal and also of the occasion of sin are fulfilled, and that the parties sincerely desire to enter the Church.[108] It frequently happens that the invalidity of a marriage between two non-Catholics results from the impediment of a previous bond. It may be that the invalidity is materially public, and it may also be that the public has some vague knowledge of a previous civil or non- Catholic marriage ceremony on the part of one or both of the parties seeking the brother-sister arrangement. This vague or even clear knowledge of a previous bond between two non-Catholics does not in itself make the present invalid marriage formally public. It is quite probable that the public will look upon the baptism and subsequent reception of the sacraments as pointing to the convalidation of the present marriage. Most Catholics have some idea of the Pauline and so-called Petrine privileges, to which they might easily attribute the apparent convalidation of the subsequent marriage. This supposition is not plausible if it is publicly

---

[108]It is granted, however, that these requirements are more easily fulfilled if the parties are advanced in age or are afflicted with some grave illness.

known that the previous marriage bond was entered by way of a Catholic ceremony.

If, however, the invalid marriage is prudently regarded as being formally public, the only manner in which the brother-sister arrangement can be a plausible solution is for the parties to move to a locality in which their marital status is materially and formally occult.[109] In any event, it is generally admitted that the conversion of one or both of the parties offers a sufficient cause to warrant the use of the brother-sister arrangement, provided, of course, that the other requirements postulated for the arrangement are fulfilled.

5. *Grave Financial Inconvenience*

If the woman involved in the invalid marriage is unable to support herself by means of work, or of service in another's household, or by begging (if this can be done without shame or grave inconvenience) it seems that a sufficient cause is had for the application of the brother-sister arrangement.[110] In order licitly to plead this cause it is not necessary that the parties be destitute. It is sufficient that they would otherwise suffer grave inconvenience from a financial standpoint. If the woman is wealthy or fully capable of supporting herself, it would not be a grave inconvenience for them to separate. The ability to support oneself normally means to be able to acquire sufficient means to live according to one's state in life. In reference to the brother-sister arrangement, it means the ability to provide all the necessities of life in a shameless manner. Ter Haar pointed out that it is frequently possible for the woman to lend her services to some institution, and thereby to obtain her livelihood. It is evident, however, that this would be a grave inconvenience if the woman is in old age or also when she is sickly.

If financial difficulty is alleged as the sole reason in the request for the brother-sister arrangement, a prudent judgment can be made only when the grantor has a thorough knowledge of the locality, its opportunities, the financial status of the parties, their age, health, etc. Although the writer must agree with Ter Haar that this cause is

---

[109]*Supra*, pp. 101-109.
[110]Ter Haar, *Casus Conscientiae*, I, n. 158.

seldom verified to the extent that it is sufficient in itself to allow the brother-sister arrangement, it is, nevertheless, a cause which can be sufficient in itself.

6. *Grave Illness.*

This cause was presented by De Smet (1868-1927), as sufficing to permit the use of the brother-sister arrangement by two persons whose invalid marriage is materially and formally public. He said that if a complete separation cannot take place here and now, v. g., because the man is gravely ill and needs the nursing of the woman in such a manner that he cannot get along without her help, then the *pseudo-coniuges*" must be prepared to declare before two witnesses that they will separate as soon as possible. . .[111]

It seems that the arrangement was contemplated on a temporary basis in this case by De Smet, but no specific limitation of time was set, and accordingly one may reasonably conclude that he regarded the use of the brother-sister arrangement operative as long as the grave illness continued. If the illness is of a chronic or even of a permanent character, the parties are permitted to cohabit as brother and sister on that more or less permanent basis, and are also, according to De Smet, permitted to receive the sacraments in public.[112]   Indeed, if serious illness can provide a sufficient cause for permitting the brother-sister arrangement in a case which is formally public, it is all the more certain that serious illness can furnish a sufficient cause in a case which is occult.

In regard to the nature of the illness, it seems that any permanent or frequently recurrent serious illness proves sufficient. Any sickness, disease or crippling condition which confines a person to bed or to a wheel-chair is certainly serious or grave. A serious heart condition, although not completely confining its victim, may offer a sufficient cause in some cases. Certain mental disturbances or aber-

---

[111]*Praxis*, p. 139, n. 88.

[112]The writer sees need for very special precautions in this exception to the general rule regarding formally public cases. It is readily conceivable that the private or secret reception of the sacraments would prove to be the more prudent course to follow. *Supra.* pp 104-105.

rations might well be included under the term *grave illness*. Frequently enough a sickness or crippling condition, even though it be not grave in itself, renders the afflicted one incapable of self-support. It appears, therefore, that the financial condition of the parties concerned again enters the picture. Fundamentally, however, grave illness can exist as a sufficient cause for the application of the brother-sister arrangement.

7. *Impossibility of Obtaining a Civil Divorce*

Ter Haar and others have pointed out that the brother-sister arrangement is permitted if the cohabitation and the proximate occasion of sin are truly necessary. They have also taught that this necessity is had if the parties have already entered a civil marriage which cannot be broken. Absolutely regarded, this condition is outside the pale of verification today in the United States. Any statistical account of our divorces will indicate that practically any reason or semblance of a reason can win a divorce if one has the requisite money and knows where to apply for it. Król speaks of a prominent judge, operating one of a number of the divorce courts in a large city, who boasted of his record of efficiency as a public servant. He had granted eighy-four divorces in less than two hours.[113]

In other countries, however, there are diriment matrimonial impediments recognized by the Church which are not recognized by the civil government. Coronata mentions that the civil codes of law of Belgium, France, Germany and Hungary do not recognize antecedent and perpetual impotence as an invalidating (diriment) impediment.[114]

In a relative sense, however, it is at times morally impossible for an individual couple to obtain a civil divorce in the United States. The obtaining of a divorce is sometimes quite expensive, so that the limited finances of the couple make it morally impossibe to acquire it. In some cases the obtaining of a divorce requires the establishment of residence in another state for six months, or possibly for a year. This proves to be a serious strain on limited finances. In this relative

---

[113]Król, in *The Jurist*, XI, (1951), 24.

[114]*De Sacramentis*, III, p. 374, n. 299; Cf. also Cappello, *De Matrimonio*, p. 388, n. 389; S. C. C., *Maurianen*, 15 dec. 1877—ASS, X, 504: S.C.S. Off., 8 mart. 1900—Coll. S. C. P. F., II, n. 2078; AAS, XXXII, 639-40.

sense, therefore, it is possible to present the cause in question as a reason for the brother-sister arrangement. It is evident, however, that this cause is seldom in itself sufficient in the United States.

The seven causes or reasons presented above as sufficing for the application of the brother-sister arrangement are the causes most frequently found to exist. These causes are quite generally listed by the authors, but it is indicated by them that there are also other causes which may prove sufficient to allow cohabitation on a brother-sister basis.

Article 5.   Proper Permission of Competent Authority

Since the brother-sister arrangement is an extraordinary remedy for invalid marriages, and since it is a *res plena periculis* which may easily threaten the spiritual welfare of the parties themselves as well as the people of the community, and, finally, since the conditions and requirements which must be verified and fulfilled are of a very delicate and involved nature, the proper permission of a competent ecclesiastical authority must be obtained for the licit use of the arrangement. Under normal conditions the brother-sister arrangement may be permitted by the ordinary, the pastor or the confessor. The competence of the one or the other of these three depends upon the circumstances and the nature of the individual case. Cases in the external forum which are exceedingly difficult to decide are referred to the Sacred Congregation of the Holy Office. Similiar cases in the internal forum may be referred to the Sacred Penitentiary. It will also be seen that all cases involving a priest as one of the parties are to be sent to the Sacred Penitentiary.[115]

Gasparri taught that, when the confessor and the pastor are in doubt, then the ordinary is to be consulted, and his instructions are to be followed.[116] Vlaming-Bender indicated that the granting of permission for the brother-sister arrangement rests within the prudent discretion of the confessor and the pastor, and also added that the counsel of the ordinary is to be sought in the more difficult cases. They then advanced a step in teaching that the ordinary is the proper authority

---

[115]*Infra*, pp. 130, 155.
[116]*De Matrimonio*, II, p. 249, n. 1181.

in the external forum regarding the granting of permission for the brother-sister arrangement, and that the confessor is the judge in the internal forum.[117]

De Smet allowed the use of the arrangement in a materially and formally public case provided there was a grave reason (v. g., serious illness) which prevented an immediate separation, and provided also that the parties were prepared to declare before two witnesses that they would separate as soon as possible. In this exceptional case, so De Smet maintained, the parties are to follow the instructions of the pastor. He did not here indicate that the ordinary's permission or consultation was necessary, and consequently he allowed one to conclude that the pastor may grant the permission in the external forum.[118]

Chrétien makes it clear that the pastor, in his care of souls, may suggest or permit the brother-sister arrangement in occult cases. No mention is made of the confessor as having the proper authority, but Chrétien later adds that the arrangement can be tolerated by the pastor with the consultation of the bishop. He makes no explicit reference to the distinction between the external and the internal forum with reference to the brother-sister arrangement.[119]

According to the authors, therefore, the licit use of the brother-sister arrangement requires the permission of a competent ecclesiastical authority. As indicated by the same authors, the confessor, pastor and ordinary are, under certain conditions, the authorities from whom the proper permission can be received. It is also evident that the granting of the permission for the brother-sister arrangement is not exclusively reserved either to the external or to the internal forum.

There is no doubt concerning the fundamental power of the confessor, the pastor and the ordinary to grant permission for the use of the brother-sister arrangement, but there has been some discussion whether and under what circumstances the confessor or the pastor may licitly and prudently approve cohabitation on a brother-sister basis

---

[117]*Praelectiones Iuris Matrimonii*, pp. 519-22.
[118] *Praxis*, p. 139, n. 88.
[119]*De Matrimonio*, p. 144.

without referring the matter to the ordinary. Since the authors are not very clear on this point, the writer has attempted, through a process of elimination, to point out the cases in which the confessor can grant the permission apart from all consultation with the ordinary. Although there is no positive universal law that expressly demands the consultation or the consent of the ordinary in this matter, it is reasonable to suggest that the safe and prudent solution of many cases on the basis of a brother-sister arrangement cannot be had without the consultation or possibly the consent of the ordinary.

1. *Public Cases*

It seems reasonable to assume that any case which is both materially and formally public must be referred to the ordinary. This is said, first of all, because the Code of Canon Law designates the bishop as having the right and the duty to govern the diocese in both spiritual and temporal affairs,[120] and specifically appoints him as the guardian of ecclesiastical discipline against abuses, especially in reference to the administration of the sacraments.[121] It is the bishop's duty, according to the same canon, to watch over the integrity of faith and morals within his diocese. It is his sacred duty to preserve sound doctrine, to protect right morals and to correct evils, to promote peace, piety, innocence and discipline among the people and the clergy, and otherwise to provide for the welfare of religion.[122]

In the case of public sinners the local ordinary may decree that the public sinner must first desist from his publicly scandalous way of living (e.g., from public concubinage) and make reparation for the scandal as prescribed by the Code before being admitted to Holy Communion.[123] Those who are regarded as *manifesto infames* are not to be admitted to the reception of Holy Communion until the three conditions of canon 855 are fulfilled. The sole judge of the cessation of the *infamia facti* is the ordinary. It is the ordinary's

---

[120]Can. 335.

[121]Can.336.

[122]"Ad sanam et orthodoxam doctrinam conservandam, bonos mores tuendos, pravos corrigendos, pacem, innocentiam pietatem et disciplinam in populo et clero promovendam ceteraque pro ratione adiunctorum ad bonum religionis constituenda . . . "—can. 343.

[123]Can. 855. Cf. Woywod, *Commentary*, I, p. 466, n. 753.

prerogative, upon consideration of all the circumstances and especially the prolonged amendment of the guilty party, prudently to judge whether the party has regained his good repute with righteous and serious-minded Catholics and has lost, thereby, the stain of infamy.[124]

For these reasons, coupled with the fact that most of the authors regard the ordinary as the proper authority in cases which arise in the external forum, it can be said that all cases involving an invalid marriage which is materially and formally public must be referred to the ordinary for the proper permission to use the brother-sister arrangement. A majority of the cases, however, are not both materially and formally public, and consequently are not absolutely reserved to the ordinary.[125]

If the case is materially public but formally occult, it seems that the pastor, independently of the ordinary's counsel or consent, could normally grant permission for the brother-sister arrangement. If the ordinary has reserved all public cases to himself, however, the ordinary must be consulted and a prudent affirmative decision can be made by the pastor only with the ordinary's consent. All public cases (either materially or formally public) are handled in the external forum. In some dioceses there is a regular form or questionnaire that must be submitted to the curia, along with the pastor's recommendations and personal observations.[126]

If the ordinary has not reserved to himself the cases which are only materially public, the pastor would nevertheless do well to consult the ordinary, although he is not strictly under obligation to do so. The simple confessor, however, should not handle any public

---

[124]Can. 2295.

[125]As previously explained, in order that an invalid marriage be materially and formally public it must be public in the sense that the marriage is known by the public to be invalid and also that the cause of the invalidity is known and recognized as irremovable. It should be added here that, even though actual knowledge is not as yet had, it is sufficient that the invalidity and its cause are prudently judged to become readily known. *Supra* pp. 97, 98, 101, 105.

[126]Cf. Król, in *The Jurist,* XI (1951), 31-32. (A few minor changes in the suggested form are recommended by the writer, *Infra,* p. 164-168).

case without the consultation and consent of the pastor or the ordinary.[127]

If the case is entirely occult, the confessor himself can grant permission for the brother-sister arrangement. It should be mentioned, however, that the confessor must be in a position whereby he can obtain certitude regarding the occult nature of the case. He must also have moral certitude concerning the meticulous conformity of the parties concerned with all the requirements and conditions of the arrangement. In order to be in this position, it seems that the confessor should be a priest who is more or less permanently attached to the parish in which the parties live.

It is most unlikely that a missionary or one who is merely helping out in a parish on a very limited basis (a few days or weeks) could ever be in a position whereby he could prudently grant permission for the arrangement without consulting the pastor or the ordinary. It is also most unlikely that a curate or assistant pastor will ever find himself in a position whereby he can prudently grant this permission to persons from another parish or from another diocese. Frequently enough the penitent may truly believe that the invalidity of his marriage is not publicly known, whereas in reality it may be (or soon will be) a subject of current gossip which is discreetly kept from his ears. The penitent may have been responsible for the breakup of a former marriage, and the granting of such permission to him would be regarded as the placing of a premium on his vice. Again, the confessor may be sure of the disposition of his penitent, but he has no easy method of ascertaining the willingness of the other party to forego all physical relations.

The assistant pastor or curate, however, is not only well qualified to judge the disposition of both parties in the internal forum, but he has easier access to the knowledge that a materially proximate occasion of sin is formally remote or factually non-existent in a particular case.[128] He is also better qualified to ascertain the occult nature of the case, and finds ready opportunity to handle the case

---

[127] I. e., the consent of the pastor in materially public cases, and the consent of the ordinary in a case which is materially and formally public.

[128] Vlaming, *Praelectiones Iuris Matrimonii*, II, n. 757.

in the extra-sacramental internal forum. Through use of the extra-sacramental internal forum the confessor is capable of ascertaining not only the perfect willingness of both parties to fulfill the conditions of the brother-sister arrangement, but also their mutual ability to fulfill the conditions.[129]

The assistant pastor or curate may, indeed, find repeated occasion for the application of the brother-sister arrangement, but he must consult the pastor or the ordinary if the case is materially or formally public. The confessor may grant permission for the arrangement on his own authority in those cases only which are both materially and formally occult.

2. *Doubtful and More Difficult Cases*

Authors generally concede that cases which are doubtful, or perhaps unusually difficult, should be referred to the ordinary. A case may be doubtful or difficult for various reasons. The doubt or unusual difficulty may exist in regard to the public or occult nature of the case, or perhaps it is linked with the cause or the reason proffered as being proportionate to the dangers involved. The latter may readily be the case when the persons requesting the permission are not advanced in age, or, though they be advanced in age, are still in excellent physical condition.

A confessor may find it difficult to decide whether the occasion of sin is proximate or remote. After deciding that the occasion is truly proximate, he has the added difficulty of deciding whether the proximate occasion is truly a necessary occasion. While many cases are certainly materially public, the pastor frequently finds it difficult to decide whether or not the invalid marriage is formally occult. It seems, therefore, that the general statement of the authors (i.e., that doubtful or unusually difficult cases must be referred to the ordinary) must be more specifically defined in order to be properly understood.

To say that all doubtful or difficult cases must be referred to the ordinary, regardless of the source or nature of the doubt or difficulty,

---

[129] Another advantage of using the extra-sacramental fourm is that the confessor is in a better position to defend the parties and to prevent scandal if the case accidently becomes public.

is entirely too broad a statement. Many doubts and difficulties can be overcome in various ways. Since, however, the ordinary is the proper authority in cases which are formally public, it seems that any reasonable doubt regarding the formal publicity of any case automatically reserves that case to the ordinary. Hence, if the pastor is certain that a case is materially public, but reasonably doubts whether it is or is not formally public, the case must be referred to the ordinary. When the confessor is in reasonable doubt concerning the material publicity of the case, he must refer the case to the pastor. If the doubt concerns the element of formal publicity, the confessor or the pastor must refer the case to the ordinary.

If, on the other hand, the doubt concerns an element other than the public or occult nature of the case (v.g., the proximate occasion of sin, a proportionate reason, etc.) the doubt can usually be removed without a referring of the case to the ordinary. Such doubts can be removed through further study or upon consultation with other priests. If, after consultation with other prudent priests and after an unsuccessful attempt to apply reflex principles, the doubt remains, then the confessor or the pastor should consult the ordinary.

In regard to unusually difficult cases which, according to the authors, are automatically reserved to the ordinary, it seems that emphasis should be placed on the term *unusually*. Every case has its difficulties, but the notion of an unusually difficult case, according to the writer's understanding, extends to only those cases in which the difficulty of arriving at a prudent decision cannot be overcome by the pastor or the confessor. In general, therefore, it can be said that a reasonable doubt about the public or the occult nature of the case automatically reserves the case to the ordinary. An *unusually* difficult case, i.e., one which the simple confessor or pastor finds morally impossible to decide, should also be referred to the ordinary.[180]

3. Reserved Cases

a) Reserved to the Sacred Penitentiary . . .

Absolution from the censure incurred by a priest who has attempted

---

[180]Cf. Gasparri, *De Matrimonio*, II, p. 249, n. 1181; Vlaming-Bender *Praelectiones Iuris Matrimonii*, pp. 519-22.

marriage, where separation is impossible, is reserved exclusively to the Sacred Penitentiary.[131]   Any doubts which were had regarding the nature of this reservation were permanently dissolved by a subsequent declaration of the Sacred Penitentiary.[132]   Outside of the danger of death (can. 2252) and notwithstanding any faculties granted by canon 2254, §1, all cases involving a priest must be submitted to the Sacred Penitentiary.   A special form of procedure and certain special safeguards and conditions are prescribed by the Sacred Penitentiary upon request of the permission.[133]

b) Reserved to the ordinary . . .

Through the legislation of the Code the ordinary has been granted the power to reserve cases to himself.[134]   In accord with that legislation, therfore, the ordinary can licitly reserve to himself all cases in which the brother-sister arrangement finds possible application.   Also in accord with that canonical legislation regarding diocesan reservations, the confessor and the pastor must refer brother-sister cases to the ordinary if the latter has in fact, reserved such cases to himself.[135]

A case which is materially and formally public seems, by its very nature, to be reserved to the ordinary. A case which is materially public but formally occult can be handled by the pastor alone unless the ordinary has reserved all brother-sister cases to himself. These two types of public cases reserved to the ordinary are to be handled in the external forum.   A case which is materially and formally occult can be handled by the confessor alone unless the ordinary has reserved all brother-sister cases to himself.   It seems rather unusual that cases which are entirely occult should be reserved to the ordinary.   If such cases are nevertheless reserved, the norms of the

---

[131]S. Poenit., 18 apr. 1936-*AAS*, XXVIII (1936), 242.

[132]S. Poenit., 4 maii 1937-*AAS* XXIX (1937), 283.

[133]Cf. Bouscaren, *Digest*, II, 579-581.

[134]Cans. 893, 895, 897, 898.

[135]Under canon 900 is found a list of circumstances in which reservations cease. Cf. also canons 899, 2252, 2254.

Code regarding the cessation of reservations should be kept clearly in mind.[186]

In relation to the latter case, i.e., the materially and formally occult case which is reserved to the ordinary, there is some question whether the ordinary can reserve the case in such a manner that even the most secret case is to be handled in the external forum. It seems that he cannot. If the parties of an entirely occult case are willing to present their case in the external forum and fill out the questionnaire, they may do so. There are some, however, who would find the exposition of their sinful life an unbearable burden.

In fact, such a demand seems to be a violation of a basic right to keep one's sins hidden. Undoubtedly, a demand of this nature would place an unmerited and unnecessary burden on those who had entered an invalid marriage through no fault of their own. Moreover, such a regulation would deter many, who are otherwise willing and worthy subjects, from applying for permission to live on a brother-sister basis.

It seems to the writer that their refusal to bring the case in the external forum cannot be interpreted as an indication of their unworthiness or unwillingness to fulfill all the necessary requirements of the brother-sister arrangement. The legislation of the Code itself points to the mind of the Church on this matter when it explicitly points out that regardless of the manner in which the case is reserved to the ordinary the reservation ceases whenever the faculty to absolve cannot be asked from the legitimate superior without great inconvenienec to the penitent, or without danger of violation of the sacramental seal.[187] It seems, therefore, that while the ordinary can reserve all brother-sister cases to himself, he cannot lawfully or prudently demand that all cases, even the most secret or occult, be handled in the external forum.

---

[186] A Titus-Bertha petition does not always sufficiently protect the secrecy. Cf. Gerald Kelly, S. J., "Notes on Moral Theology, 1951," *Theological Studies.* XIII (1952), 80-81; canons 900, 2252, 2254. If a Titius-Bertha petition can safely be submitted the suggested form (*infra.* pp. 164-168) can be readily adapted to the situation. The required information can be given while any and all identification of the parties can be omitted.

[187] Can. 900.

For the same reasons it also seems that, once the permission is granted in a given case, the parties should not be forced to reveal to the bishop any and all violations of their promise to abstain from marital relations. Król indicates that the parties must either separate completely or refer the matter of any violation of mutual continence to the ordinary. [138] A more practical and apparently an equally satisfying practice seems to be that, once the permission is granted by the proper authority, any future disposition of the case involving matters of the internal forum (v.g., occult sins of incontinence) should be left to the discretion of the confessor, as a confessor. Any or several violations of the promise to remain continent should be made known to the confessor in confession, and he in turn should excerise the principles of moral theology which apply to a person living in the proximate necessary occasion of sin. If there are several or repeated violations, the principles of moral theology regarding a recidivist or a habitual sinner may be applied. It should also be within the power of the confessor to decide whether or not complete separation must take place in the event of repeated sins of incontinence— and this, even though the permission was originally granted by the ordinary. In other words, the occult sins of the parties should remain matter for the internal forum and subject to the judical power of the confessor.

If the violation of the promise to remain continent is or becomes public (v.g., through the conception of a child), or if the promises which were made to protect the public welfare are violated in such a manner that scandal results,[139] then the matter should be handled by the ordinary in the external forum. In these cases of public violation of the promises the ordinary is to decide whether or not a complete separation must take place.

c) Cases involving a previous bond . . .

There is some question regarding the necessity of referring to the ordinary all cases which involve the impediment of a previous bond. While there is no positive law on this precise point, it may be in-

---

[138]Król, "*art. cit.*," *The Jurist* XI (1951), 32, PROMISE n. 5.

[139]V.g., by receiving the sacraments publicly when the parties are restricted to a private or secret reception only. Cf., *supra,* pp. 104-105.

directly argued that all or at least a vast majority of the cases involving a previous bond must be referred to the local ordinary. The fact that one or both of the parties who seek permission for the brothersister arrangement are bound by a previous marriage bond means that a separation from the spouse has taken place, and that the separation was either legitimately or illegitimately effected.

According to the Code, the parties of a valid marriage are obliged to preserve the community of conjugal life unless a just cause excuses them from this obligation.[140] Adultery on the part of one is listed as a just cause for the innocent party to enter into a complete and permanent separation. The innocent party may legitimately separate on his own authority. However, the innocent party loses the right of effecting a separation if he consented to the adultery, was the cause of it, expressly or tacitly condoned it, or, finally, committed the same crime. [141]

If the right of separation is lost by the innocent party in one or the other manner, the continued separation of the *coniuges* is illegitimate. The guilty party has no right to separate and is usually subject to being recalled by the innocent party.[142] An attempted marriage and the subsequent request for the brothersister arrangement by either the guilty or the innocent party call for adjudication on the part of the ordinary regarding the legitimacy of the separation from the valid spouse.

Other just causes for separation are listed,[143] but the legitimacy of the separation for these causes ordinarily presupposes and postulates the intervention of the ordinary. If the ordinary grants permission for the separation, it is done with the provision that the parties never remarry or never keep company during the lifetime of the other spouse. If the party violated this injunction by attempting the invalid marriage for which the brothersister arrangement is now sought, it seems that he or she should have to consult the ordinary. If the

---

[140]Can. 1128
[141]Can. 1129.
[142]Can. 1130.
[143]Can. 1131.

party separated in the previous marriage without the authority of the ordinary (which is usually the case), there is no canonist or moralist who excuses that party from the provisions of canon 1131, even when the party is involved in a subsequent invalid marriage.

It seems, therefore, that since the ordinary alone has the right and the duty (in most cases) to adjudicate the separation in the first marriage, at least on this score the petition for a brother-sister arrangement cannot be left to the sole discretion of the pastor or the confessor unless the ordinary delegates his authority to him.

Moreover, the reasons and circumstances surrounding the separation in the previous marriage will have pertinent bearing on the consideration of the brother-sister arrangement as a solution for the subsequent invalid marriage. The party guilty of causing the separation in the first marriage will not be granted the brother-sister arrangement as readily as will the innocent party. If the invalid marriage was entered in good faith, as may readily happen among some non-Catholics today who are firmly convinced that divorce and remarriage is permissible, the parties would receive more consideration than those who entered an invalid marriage in bad faith. Those who were in good faith have not been weakened by continuous sin and are more likely able to live together continently.

The confessor, therefore, who is more or less permanently attached to the parish in which the parties are living has the proper authority, independently of the pastor or the ordinary, prudently to grant the brother-sister arrangement in a case which is both materially and formally occult. This is stated, of course, with the proviso that the case is not reserved by law to the local ordinary or to the Holy See and does not involve a priest or a previous bond from which a legitimate separation was not granted, and with the proviso that the circumstances of the case have not given rise to any unusual doubts or difficulties.

At this point it seems appropriate to caution the confessor as well as the pastor that the brother-sister arrangement is a *res plena periculis* in both the internal and external forum . . . but especially in the internal forum. False charity or open laxity in such matters cannot be excused through an appeal to the dictum: "*sacramenta propter homines.*"[144] The confessor, in fulfilling his exalted position as a judge, as a doctor and as a father, must ever be conscious of the oft-repeated warning: "*ex magna absolvendi facilitate, magnam peccandi facilitatem oriri necessario debere.*"[145] He should not permit his spiritual patient and child anything that will prove to be a serious threat to salvation. Due consideration must be given to the preeminence of the spiritual good of the community.[146]

Being ever conscious of the dangers of this *res plena periculis* and realizing full well the weakened condition of the human nature with which he deals, the confessor cannot but use the utmost of caution in granting the brother-sister arrangement in those cases for which he himself has proper power to render judgment.

A final precaution which a confessor should employ when granting permission for the brother-sister arrangement in the internal forum is to instruct the parties that the authority he exercises as a confessor and upon which the permission rests is limited to the internal forum. If the case ever becomes public, the entire question is subject to a redisposition by the pastor or the ordinary, as the case may call for. The confessor might also instruct the parties that if the extra-sacramental internal forum is used in the granting of the permission, then the confessor is in a more advantageous position to prevent scandal and to aid the parties themselves if the case ever became public.

---

[144]Ter Haar, *De Occasionariis*, p. 413, n. 490.

[145]S. C. de Prop. Fide, instr. aug. 1827—*Fontes*, n. 4740; Benedictus XIV, ep. encycl. *Apostalica Constitutio*, 26 iun. 1749, § 22—*Fontes*, n. 400.

[146]Ter Haar, *op. cit.*, p. 424, n. 509.

CHAPTER V

DIRIMENT IMPEDIMENTS OCCASIONING THE

COHABITATION

Introduction

The purpose of this chapter is to indicate the nature of the diriment impediments which render an attempted marriage permanently invalid, and which, consequently, occasion the brother-sister arrangement on a permanent basis. As it was previously metioned,[1] there are five diriment impediments for which, under certain circumstances, the Church cannot or will not grant a dispensation. There are other diriment impediments of the same nature, but the five impediments under consideration are the ones which, perhaps more frequently, occasion the application of the brother-sister arrangement on a permanent basis.

The brother-sister arrangement cannot be used as a permanent solution for an invalid marriage which can be convalidated. As it was previously shown, the brother-sister arrangement is not a substitution for marriage, nor is it an optional matter, designed to obviate the difficulties involved in convalidating an attempted marriage.[2] While the arrangement can be considered as a temporary solution for all invalid marriages, it is available as a permanent solution for only those invalid marriages for which the remedies of convalidation, dissimulation or complete separation are impossible. The five diriment impediments which one might expect to occasion the arrangement on a permanent basis are: Prior Bond, Impotence, Consanguinity (also affinity), Holy Orders (Priesthood), and Specific Criminality (*Crimen*). Here, then, there are to be indicated the

---

[1]*Supra*, p. 85.
[2]*Supra*, pp. 55-56; also Chapter IV, art. 1.

conditions under which each of these impediments is unyielding to dispensation and accordingly becomes an occasion for the consideration of the brother-sister arrangement on a permanent basis.

Article 1. Prior Bond

A valid marriage ratified and consummated cannot be dissolved by any human power, or by any cause except death.[3] Canon 1118, more emphatically than others,[4] vindicates the absolute indissolubility of the ratified and consummated Christian marriage. It distinctly proclaims that no power on earth can dissolve the bond begotten by such a marriage, and that no cause except death can be instrumental in producing the same effect. Every resource which the Church has at its disposal witnesses the truth of this proposition.[5] The natural law endows marriage with a relative or intrinsic indissolubility[6] and this relative or intrinsic indissolubility becomes absolute or extrinsic if two Christians contract and consummate marriage, for thus the matrimonial bond that springs up between them receives its ultimate immutable seal.

Since the marriage bond described in canon 1118 cannot be dissolved and does not cease (except through the death of one of the parties), an attempted second marriage on the part of either party during the lifetime of the other is invalid and cannot possibly be convalidated the while both are alive. If a second marriage has been attempted, however, it is in this second and invalid marriage that the brother-sister arrangement may find a possible application on a permanent basis.[7]

---

[3]Can. 1118.

[4]Cans. 1013, § 2, and 1110.

[5]Conc. Trident., sess. XXIV, *doctrina de sacramento matrimonii*, and cans. 5, 8 and 9; Cappello, *De Matrimonio*, nn. 41-47; Noldin-Schmitt, *Summa*, III, pp. 523-532, nn. 517-525; Wernz-Vidal, *Ius Matrimoniale*, pp. 784-794, nn. 622-623; Mahon, *The Church and Divorce* (B. Herder Book Co.: St. Louis, 1926), pp. 1-69; can. 1118; F. J. Sheed *Nullity of Marriage* (London: Sheed and Ward, 1931), pp. 1-4.

[6]Cf. Petrovits, *The New Church Law on Matrimony*, pp. 19-20, n. 41; Cappello, *De Matrimonio*, p. 40, n. 45.

[7]The postulated requirements (*supra*, Chapter IV) must, of course, be verified.

While every prior marriage bond is by the divine law itself a diriment impediment to another marriage, not every prior bond is absolutely indissoluble. It is possible in some cases that a prior bond can be dissolved and a second marriage validly entered. If, therefore, there is reasonable hope in a particular case that the prior bond can be dissolved and the subsequently attempted marriage convalidated, the brother-sister arrangement cannot be adopted on a permanent basis as a solution for the attempted marriage.[8] Steps should be taken to have the prior bond dissolved and the second marriage convalidated. During the process of convalidation the brother-sister arrangement may find possible application, but only on a temporary basis.

A non-consummated marriage between baptized persons, or between a baptized and an unbaptized person, is dissolved automatically by law in consequence of a solemn religious profession made by one of the parties, and also by means of a dispensation from the Holy See, when such is granted for a good reason at the request of one or both parties.[9] A marriage between two unbaptized persons can be dissolved through the Pauline privilege, even though the marriage has been consummated.[10] A consummated marriage between a baptized person and an unbaptized person can also be dissolved by the Supreme Pontiff.[11] While the above-mentioned marriage contracts are intrinsically or relatively indissoluble, they do not have the absolute or extrinsic indissolubility of which Pius XII spoke. Therefore, when the subsequent invalid marriage is consequent upon a prior bond which lacks extrinsic or absolute indissolubility, the

----

[8] *Supra*, pp. 56, 83-85.

[9] Can. 1119. Cf. Wernz-Vidal, *Ius Matrimoniale*, pp. 794-809, nn. 624-628; Cappello, *De Matrimonio*, pp. 740-754, nn. 757-766; c. 2, 7, X, *de conversione coniugatorum*, III, 32; Esmein, *Le Mariage*, I, 124 ff.

[10] Cans. 1120-1127; Noldin-Schmitt, *Summa*, III, pp. 527-533, nn. 521-525; Wernz-Vidal, *Ius Matrimonale*, pp. 810-838, nn. 631-637; Petrovits, *The New Church Law on Matrimony*, pp. 395-416; Beste, *Introductio in Codicem*, pp. 551, 832; Bouscaren, *Digest (Suppl.)*, p. 173.

[11] Cf. Wernz-Vidal, *Ius Matrimoniale*, p. 838, nn. 637-638; S.C.S.Off., 5 nov. 1924—Bouscaren, *Digest*, I, 553; Cappello, *De Matrimonio*, pp. 783-790, nn. 789-792; Pius XII, *Allocutio*, 3 oct. 1941—AAS, XXXIII (1941,) 421; Bouscaren, *Digest*, II, 457; and *Suppl.* p. 174.

dissolution of the prior bond is to be sought, and a convalidation of the subsequent marriage is to take place in accordance with the law.

The temporary application of the brother-sister arrangement in marriages which are invalid by reason of a relatively indissoluble prior bond is governed by the same general rules and conditions as the permanent application of the arrangement in those cases in which the prior bond is absolutely indissoluble. The time consumed in the process of dissolving the prior bond and of convalidating the subsequent bond varies from case to case. Circumstances may necessitate an interval of a few weeks, or of a few months, or possibly even of several years. This time element does not affect the temporary status of the brother-sister arrangement in such cases.

If the prior marriage is absolutely indissoluable (a ratified and consummated marriage), or if there is no reasonable hope for the dissolution of the prior bond, or, finally, if the prior bond is adjudged indissoluble through a formal or informal judicial process, consideration can be given to the brother-sister arrangement as a permanent solution for the subsequent invalid marriage.

Care should be taken in the matter of suggesting or granting the brother-sister arrangement as a solution for marriages invalid by reason of prior bond. The principles of justice and the marital rights of the former spouse must not be laid open to transgression. It is normally demanded that a civil divorce be obtained before the arrangement can be prudently suggested or granted. Especially is this true if the petition or the subsequent granting of the permission is submitted in writing. If a civil divorce has not been acquired or is not at least in the process of being acquired, the priest and the second party of the invalid marriage could be subjected to the sanctions of the civil law regarding "alienation of affections," etc. In order to avoid a lengthy discussion regarding the Church's attitude and legislation relative to a Catholic person's obtaining a civil divorce, the writer simply suggests that, if the brother-sister arrangement is in fact the only solution for a particular case, the Catholic party has a sufficient cause for obtaining a civil divorce from his estranged spouse.[12]

---

[12]Keeping in mind the fact that the subsequent and invalid union or marriage (*supra*, pp. 57-59) has already been entered, cf. Kelly, "*Separation and Civil Divorce,*" *The Jurist*, VI (1946), 187-238.

Another question which merits separate consideration is that of presumed death. As it was previously indicated,[13] Reiffenstuel devoted considerable space to this question and he emphasized the importance of *mala vel bona fides* relative to the ultimate solution of the case. Modern legislation regarding cases of presumed death is essentially the same as that recorded and explained by Reiffenstuel. In either case, application of the brother-sister arrangement is definitely possible and sometimes demanded.

Gasparri wrote that in the case in which the presumed death of one of the parties of the first marriage became doubtful to both parties of the second marriage, neither party could ask for or render the marriage debt. He used a letter of Innocent III in support of this teaching. It is not clear whether Gasparri and Innocent III demanded complete separation *a cohabitatione,* but neither made any explicit provision for the brother-sister arrangement[14] Coronata, on the other hand, pointed out that there are those who teach that, if the doubt concerns not the validity of the former marriage, but only the continued life of the previous spouse, the use of matrimony is permitted after due inquiry has been made. But Coronata himself says that if both parties of a marriage contract their marriage *in mala vel dubia fide* concerning the death of the first husband or wife, or concerning the validity of a previous marriage, the common teaching is that neither party can use matrimony. However, he does not say that they must separate *a cohabitatione,* and thus it seems that one could validly conclude that the brother-sister arrangement is permissible.[15]

Cappello makes it very clear that, when the first marriage is

---

[13]Supra, pp. 43-49.

[14]Gasparri, *De Matrimonio,* I, p. 344, n. 559, and p. 349, n. 564; c. 4, X, *de bigamis non ordinandis,* I, 21; cans. 2356; 985, 3°; c. 44, X, *de sententia excommunicationis,* V, 39.

[15]Coronata, *De Sacramentis,* III, n. 338. Cf. Reiffenstuel, IV, 21, n. 25; Sanchez, *De Matrimonii Sacramento,* Lib. II, Disp. 42, n. 7. Gratian had written: "Accedit, quod, quamdiu ambo coniuges manent in dubio practico, an coniux prior adhuc vivat, consequenter an Matrimonium eorum mala fide contractum valeat, nec ne, hoc ipso debitum petere aut reddere non valeant, cum stante dubio practico operari non liceat, ut tenent communiter Theologi."- c. 5, C. XXXIV, q. 1.

not yet dissolved, then it would be illicit for the parties to use the second marriage if they entered it in bad faith. It would be illicit to use the latter marriage in the face of morally certain knowledge that the first marriage has not been dissolved, even though the latter union was contracted in good faith. If the parties entered the second marriage in bad faith, i.e., doubtful about the dissolution of the first marriage, then the newly contracted marriage would be forbidden them as long as the doubt remained.

Contrariwise, if they entered the marriage in good faith, and later there arose some doubt concerning the dissolution of the first marriage, then the use of the marriage would be forbidden them before and during the time of the investigation. If after a diligent inquiry the doubt remains, then they could use the prerogatives of matrimony. The brother-sister arrangement could possibly and perhaps should be used until the doubt is resolved in the case wherein the marriage was contracted in bad faith, and until diligent investigation has been made in the case wherein the marriage was contracted in good faith.[16] It should also be pointed out that as long as the doubt remains about the continuance of the earlier valid marriage, or about the validity of an earlier continuing union and consequently also about the second, neither may rush into another marriage, even though the case be such that in their second marriage the parties are not allowed to use the prerogatives of matrimony.[17]

According to Vlaming-Bender, if one has begun seriously to doubt the death of the prior spouse either before or after the second marriage was contracted, one may not indeed request the marriage debt, but one may render it when it is requested by the one who is still in good faith. If both parties are in doubt, neither can request or grant the exercise of the debt, and they must separate, unless they can live together as brother and sister without inviting the danger of incontinence.[18]

---

[16] Cappello, *De Matrimonio*, pp. 394-395, nn. 402-404.

[17] Cf. Cappello, *op. cit.*, n. 403, Also see the response of the Code Commission, June 26, 1947—AAS XXXIX, 374; Bouscaren, *Digest* (Suppl.), p. 149; S.C.S.Off., 22 mart. 1865 —Coll.S.C.P.F., I, n. 1272; Fontes, n. 982.

[18] *Praelectiones Iuris Matrimonii*, p. 202.

As a safeguard against the creating of a wrong impression it should be pointed out that the foregoing conclusions were reached only in and for the cases that involved some doubt. If the missing spouse actually did return after the second marriage had legitimately been entered, then the parties in the second marriage would be obliged to separate, and conjugal life should be restored between the two consorts of the original valid marriage. Doheny states that even if the re-establishment of conjugal life may not prove possible for one reason or another, the Church authorities must nevertheless insist on the separation of the parties of the subsequent marriage, except in extraordinary cases when the parties may be permitted to remain in good faith. The writer is convinced that Doheny is here speaking of a separation *a toro,* for all modern authors do make room for the broth-er-sister arrangement even in this case, although it should be only as a last resort.[19]

Article 2. Impotence

Most of the authors ascribe notable significance to the considera-tion of impotence and its effects upon marriage. For the purpose at hand, it suffices to consider that type of impotence which renders an attempted marriage permanently invalid, i.e., an antecedent and perpetual impotence which is either absolute or relative. There is no need to go into any lengthy consideration of precisely what constitutes impotence, or to seek a method for proving whether a person is or is not impotent. Any of the recognized authors furnish information on these points. In relation to the brother-sister arrangement, however, it is necessary to determine that the impotence is antecedent to the attempted marriage, and that it has the note of perpetuity. If the impotence is absolute or relative, but is actually antecedent and per-petual, the attempted marriage is invalid; convalidation is impossible; and the brother-sister arrangement can be considered as a possible solution on a permanent basis. Since most of the authors explicitly mention the brother-sister arrangement as a possible and sometimes re-

---

[19]Doheny, *Canonical Procedure in Matrimonial Cases,* II, 604.

quired solution for the case of antecedent and perpetual impotence, a somewhat detailed account of a few of these authors is in order.

Gasparri, in dealing with antecedent and prepetual impotence, stated that when it is undoubtedly present the marriage is null. He likewise stated that the parties (*coniuges*) could, if they wished, cohabit as brother and sister, as was granted in c. 5, X, *de frigidis et maleficiatis, et impotentia coeundi*, IV, 15, that is, in such a manner that no danger of incontinence be invited. But he also intimated that this danger is almost always present, and added that therefore the brother-sister arrangement seems not permitted unless the parties are far advanced in years,[20] or unless, when separated *a toro*, they manifest by special signs or guarantees that they will practice the virtue of chastity.[21]

Granted these conditions, the parties (*coniuges*) who after the marriage ceremony acquire certitude of their antecedent impotence must, according to Gasparri, separate *quoad torum* by their own authority, and they cannot indulge in those carnal actions which are licit for only the validly married. In other words, they must live as brother and sister. Further, if the case be accompanied with scandal, they must request a separation *a cohabitatione* from the legitimate ecclesiastical superior. But even the party who is not impotent may not enter a new marriage until, by due process of law, a declaration of nullity has been given by the ecclesiastical judge.[22] In support of this, Gasparri referred to a reply of the Sacred Congregation of the Council. It was asked what mode of action should be followed by bishops, pastors and confessors in regard to impotent persons who do not have a reason for a civil divorce in places where the civil law

---

[20]Chrétien seems to disagree, for he said that there is no danger of incontinence if the parties are impotent.—(*De Matrimonio*, p. 444). Evidently the presence or absence of this danger depends upon the nature of the impotence. Relative impotence does not remove the danger, whereas absolute impotence can remove the danger of incontinence in some cases. Cf. Cappello, *De Matrimonio*, p. 372, n. 368.

[21]Gasparri, *De Matrimonio*, I, p. 336, n. 549; Sanchez, *De Matrimonii Sacramento*, Lib. VII, Disp. 97, n. 5; St. Thomas, *Summa Theologica, suppl.*, q. 58, art. 1, *in fine*.

[22]Gasparri, *De Matrimonio*, I, p. 336, n. 549.

does not recognize the impediment of impotence. The answer was
that they are to live together as brother and sister. But if this cannot
be done apart from the danger of sin, then they are by all means
to separate.[23]

In the third edition of Gasparri's pre-Code *Tractatus Canonicus
de Matrimonio* a distinction was made between the one who posessed
and the one who lacked knowledge of the impediment before the marriage, with the result that the one who knew of the impotence was
obliged to adopt the brother-sister arrangement in the union. While
there is a like distinction in the *Nova editio* (a revision according to
the Code) between ignorance and knowledge of the impediment, there
is no mention that the one who has knowledge becomes obliged to live
with the other party in a brother-sister relationship. Rather, the
party concealing such knowledge from the other is held to be in-
excusable from grave sin.[24]

Another departure from the earlier law, as Gasparri pointed out,
is the non-granting of the three-year trial period formerly prescribed
by judges when the parties were in doubt about the existence of impotence. This experimental period is not mentioned in the Instruction
of the Holy Office of May 20, 1882, nor in the Code. Gasparri
taught that the possible use of this experimental period must be regarded as abolished in consequence of the norm now enacted in canon
6, 6°, of the Code, which abrogates, as long as it is not a divine law
or a law of the liturgy, any and every universal disciplinary law which
no longer receives at least an implicit mention in the Code.[25]

---

[23]S.C.C. *Maurianen.*, 15 dec. 1877: "Quaenam esse debeat agendi ratio
Episcopi, parochi et confessarii erga impotentes, qui ea ratione separari nequeunt, quod eorum separationi obsistat civilis Galliarum lex, quae im-
potentiae impedimentum non agnoscit?" . . . S.C.C. respondet, die 15 dec.
1877: "Vivant ut frater et soror: quod si id fieri non possit sine peccati periculo, separentur omnino, et ad mentem."—ASS, X, 504. A similar solution
was recommended in a reply given by the Holy Office on March 8, 1900.—
Coll. S.C.P.F., II, n. 2078.

[24]Gasparri, *Tractatus Canonicus de Matrimonio* (3. ed., 2 vols., Parisiis,
1904), Vol. 1, n. 600; also Gasparri, *De Matrimonio*, (nova ed.) I, p. 333,
n. 545.

[25]*De Matrimonio*, I, p. 331, n. 542.

For the confessor, Gasparri offered a practical rule. If the confessor finds the parties to be in good faith, inasmuch as they regard themselves as living in a legitimate marriage, or, though they recognize the impediment, they regard themselves as lawfully living together as brother and sister, and if at the same time he notes that the impotence is occult and that a separation is indeed morally impossible, he may leave them in good faith.[26] Cappello pointed out that if there is a rumor of the existing impediment, and a suspicion of incontinence between the parties, then a public scandal arises. In this case they must seek a separation and place the case before the ecclesiastical judge. When a public rumor exists, the matter is no longer simply one for the confessor in the internal forum, but it concerns the pastor in the external forum and possibly is to be decided by the ordinary. Since the impotence is perpetual and antecedent, the marriage is null, and no conjugal actions or relations are permitted in the putative marriage.[27]

In speaking of impotence as arising from *maleficium,* Cappello grants that God can certainly permit the devil to exercise some power over man, even in matrimonial matters. This seems acknowledged in the Scriptures (Tob., IV, 14 ff.; VII, 11 ff.), in the Councils, and in the Rituals, and by the theologians, canonists and Roman Pontiffs.[28]

If the antecedent impotence is certain and perpetual, then those who contract a union sin *"gravissime"* if they knew of the impotence. If only one party knew of it, he is guilty of grave injury to the other. In a case of antecedent and perpetual impotence there should be an immediate separation *quoad torum* executed indeed on the parties' own authority. An immediate separation *quoad cohabitationem* can also be undertaken on private authority, provided that no scandal is

---

[26]Gasparri, *De Matrimonio,* I, p. 336, n. 549, and II, pp. 250-251, nn. 1183-1184; Cappello, *De Matrimonio,* pp. 373, 369.

[27]Cappello, loc. cit.; *supra.* p. 61-62.

[28]Cappello, *De Matrimonio,* p. 371, n. 365; c. 4, C· XXXIII, q. 1; c. 2, X, IV, 15; Gregorius XV, const. *Omnipotentis Dei,* 20 mart. 1623 —*Fontes.* n. 202; St. Thomas, *Summa Theologica, Suppl.,* q. 58, art. 2; Sanchez, *De Matrimonii Sacramento,* Lib. VII, Disp. 94; Gasparri, *De Matrimonio,* I, p 334, n. 547.

occasioned through the separation. If for the parties there is danger of sin, then a separation from cohabitation must follow even though some scandal might arise.[29] If, however, there is no danger of sin (as explained in the preceding chapter) and scandal would result through a separation from cohabitation, then the parties may not separate from cohabitation on their own authority, but must wait for the intervention of ecclesiastical authority.[30]

Formerly it was permitted and even demanded that "married" couples, if they knew of the antecedent, perpetual impotence before the marriage ceremony, live together as brother and sister on a permanent basis. As was seen before (*supra*, pp. 40-42), Pope Sixtus V, by his Constitution *Cum frequenter*, on June 27, 1587, rejected this practice, and ruled that the parties mentioned by him had to separate. Cappello seems fully to agree, for he states that the danger of incontinence is normally always present.[31] But he immediately adds that, if it were morally impossible for the married couple to separate, then cohabitation by them as brother and sister would be permitted.

Cappello also points out that the practice of the Roman Church differed from the practice of the Church in France and Germany in impotence cases. The Roman Church customarily demanded that the parties live together as brother and sister.[32] In France and Germany, however, the Church in view of the usage existing there, demanded that they separate, and permitted the party who was not impotent to enter another marriage, or both of them if their impotence was of a purely relative character. This practice was not only tolerated, but was recognized as legitimate by the Roman Church through Alexander III. The practice of the Roman Church (the brother-sister arrangement) remained unchanged from Alexander

---

[29]Cf. *supra*, pp. 113-115.

[30]Obviously the brother-sister arrangement is here demanded as a solution on a temporary basis, and is permissible, in accord with the principles expressed (*supra*, Chapter IV), as a permanent solution. Cf. Cappello, *De Matrimonio*, p. 372, nn. 366-368.

[31]Cf. *supra*, p. 144,, footnote n. 20.

[32]C. 4, X, *de frigidis et maleficiatis, et impotentia coeundi*, IV, 15; Alexander III (1159-81) in c. 2, *de frigid.*, IV 16, in Comp. I; Clement III (1187-91) in c. 4, *de frigid.*, IV, 16, in Comp. I.

III.   When Sixtus V wrote his letter *Cum frequenter*, addressed to the Papal Nuncio to the Spanish kingdom, he clearly defined the doctrine of the nature and origin of the impediment of impotence regarding eunuchs and *spadones* who lacked both testicles, and at the same time decreed that parties of such unions were to be separated inasmuch as they were not married.   And this held true whether they had knowledge or were in ignorance of the impediment of impotence when they contracted their union. . . (*supra*, pp. 40-42). Benedict XIV in his Constitution *Dei miseratione* on November 3, 1741, accurately stated the form of procedure in impotence cases. Since then, various instructions of the Sacred Congregations have more specifically determined and explained the formalities to be observed in these cases.   But under the proper conditions, the brother-sister arrangement is still demanded in most cases as a temporary solution, and is permitted in some cases as a permanent solution.[33]

Coronata along with Cappello teaches that, if after the marriage an undoubtable impotence is discovered which is perpetual and antecedent, whether relative or absolute, the marriage must be declared invalid.[34]   The parties must consider the marriage as dissolved, and must immediately effect a separation *a toro*, and look for two conformable sentences of the tribunal for a separation *a cohabitatione et a mensa*.   Until that time, it is evident, they are to live together as brother and sister.   Both authors admit that it is not always possible for the parties to separate *a cohabitatione* and that, under proper conditions, the brother-sister arrangement can be permitted on a permanent basis.[35]

---

[33]S.C.S. Off., instr. a. 1858—*Fontes*, n. 946; instr. (ad Ep. Rituum Orient.) a. 1883—*Fontes*, n. 1076; instr. (Myssur.), 6 aug. 1890—*Fontes*, n. 1127; S.C.C., instr., 22 aug. 1840—*Fontes*, n. 4069; S.C. de Sacramentis, decr. 7 maii 1923—AAS, XV (1923), 389-436; 27 mart. 1929—AAS, XXI (1929), 490-493;S.C.S. Off., decr. 12 iun. 1942—AAS, XXXIV (1942), 200-202, cans. 1068, 1975-1981.

[34]Coronata, *De Sacramentis*, III, p. 418, n. 328; Cappello, *De Matrimonio*, p. 372, n. 368.

[35]Coronata, *De Sacramentis*, III, p. 374, n. 299; Cappello *De Matrimonio*, p. 388, n. 389.

As one of the three solutions upon the discovery of antecedent and perpetual impotence after the marriage has taken place. Chrétien lists the brother-sister arrangement. He adds a new note of leniency when he says that, if the other solutions (declaration of nullity and complete separation) are rejected, either because *of repugnance* to the parties or because of scandal, then the brother-sister arrangement can be used.[86]

While the Code does not advert to the brother-sister arrangement or to dissimulation as solutions in the event of marital unions affected with antecedent and permanent impotence (can. 1068), it does not prohibit them. From the authors and sources consulted it seems in summary, that the same five fundamental conditions (*supra,* pp.81-136), must be verified for a permissible application of the brother-sister arrangement on a permanent basis in the case of antecedent and perpetual (absolute or relative) impotence. In most of the cases the arrangement is demanded as a temporary solution, and in some of the cases (wherein complete separation is morally impossible) the arrangement is permissible as a permanent solution. The good or bad faith of the parties engenders no essential influence upon the ultimate solution of the case in the manner of the brother-sister arrangement.

Article 3. Consanguinity

The Code does not contain a definition of consanguinity but the traditional definition given by the authors is clear in itself.[87] Consanguinity denotes a relationship by blood between two persons in consequence of the descent of one from the other or of both from a common ancestor. It is a natural bond arising, as the etymology of the word implies, from a union of blood, and may result from law-

---

[86]"Vel, si ob putativorum coniugum repugnantiam aut ob scandalum istae solutiones sint reiiciendae, coniuges poterunt aut in bona fide relinqui aut, impedimenti non ignari, ut frater et soror cohabitare . . ." —Chrétien, *De Matrimonio,* p. 237, n. 149.

[87]"Vinculum personarum ab eodem stipite descendentium carnali propagatione contractum."—Hostiensis, *Summa,* Lib. IV, tit. 14, n. 1; also see St. Thomas, *Summa Theologia, Supplementum,* q. 54, art. 1; Sanchez, *De Matrimonii Sacramento,* Lib. VII, Disp. 50, n. 1.

ful wedlock or from illicit intercourse. The code indicates the relationship, its two lines (direct and collateral) and also the manner of computing the degree of relationship.[38]

The impediment of consanguinity is a legal barrier to a valid marriage between persons related within certain degrees of this relationship. The Code clearly states the degree of relationship within which a marriage is invalid.[39] The Code also clearly indicates the degree of relationship within which a marriage is not only invalid but impossible as well.[40] It is this indication of the Code which has direct bearing on any consideration of the brother-sister arrangement. In canon 1076, §3, the law states that, if there is any doubt whether the parties are related in any degree of the direct line or in the first degree of the collateral line, marriage between them cannot be permitted. The reason for this prohibition is that by the natural law marriage in the first degree of the direct line is *certainly* invalid and in other degrees of the direct line and in the first degree of the collateral line marriage is *probably* invalid, and the Church wishes to avoid any possibility of violating the natural law.[41]

It is generally admitted that the impediment of consanguinity is founded on the natural law and that the first degree of the direct line is an impediment of the natural law. Here, however, the unanimity of opinion ceases, and the further extent of the invalidating force of the natural law is the subject of considerable controversy among the authors.[42] This controversy has little effect on the consideration of the brother-sister arrangement for baptized persons. It is certain that the Church cannot dispense from the first degree of the direct line, and it is also certain that the Church *does* not dispense from other degrees of blood relationship in the direct line or from the first

---

[38]Can. 96.

[39]Can. 1076 § 1, § 2.

[40]Can. 1076 § 3: "Numquam matrimonium permittatur, si quod subsit dubium partes sint consanguineae in aliquo gradu linea rectae aut in primo gradu lineae collateralis."

[41]Cf. F.X. Wahl, *The Matrimonial Impediments of Consanguinity and Affinity.* The Catholic University of America Canon Law Studies, n. 90 (Washington, D.C.: The Catholic University of America, 1934), p. 28.

[42]Cf. Wahl, *op. cit.* pp. 29-40.

degree of the collateral line.[43]   The brother-sister arrangement is, therefore, a possible solution for the marriage which is invalid by reason of the blood relationship in any degree of the direct line or in the first degree of the collateral line.   This is true not only for those cases in which the relationship is certain, but also for those cases in which the relationship is doubtful.   In either case the Church does not dispense.[44]

With regard to the attempted marriages of the baptized in the controverted degrees,[45] the controversy has little importance, since these marriages are invalid by ecclesiastical law.   There is a practical importance, however, with regard to the marriage of unbaptized persons within the controverted degrees.   If while unbaptized, persons related within these degrees have contracted marriage and afterwards seek entrance into the Church, what is to be done about their marriage?

If there is a law of the civil authority or a legitimate custom invalidating such unions (v.g., between unbaptized brother and sister), the parties are invalidly married and are not permitted to live as husband and wife upon their conversion.[46] In this case, the brother-sister arrangement is clearly possible.   If, however, there is no such civil law or custom, it seems that the parties, upon their conversion, and with the consultation of the Holy See, may continue to live as husband and wife.[47]   In such cases, therefore, the brother-sister arrangement is not to be considered as a solution until after the Holy See has been consulted regarding the marital status of the parties.

In degrees other than the first degree of the collateral line the Church can and does dispense, and hence the brother-sister arrangement is not available as a permanent solution.

---

[43]Cf. Gasparri, *De Matrimonio,* pp. 434-435, n. 712; Payen,*De Matrimonio,* I, p. 1060, n. 1451; Cappello, *De Matrimonio,* p. 496, n. 525; S.C.C., Leodien., 14 dec., 1793—*Fontes,* n. 3888; S.C.S. Off., instr. (ad Ep. S. Alberti), 9 dec. 1874, n. 18, ad. 4 et 5—*Fontes,* n. 1036.

[44]Can. 1076, § 3.

[45]I.e., the first degree of the collateral line, and all degrees except the first degree of the direct line.

[46]Gasparri, *De Matrimonio,* pp. 146-160, nn. 240-256; Payen, *De Matrimonio,* I, pp. 1056-1058, n. 1448.

[47]Cf. Gasparri, *De Matrimonio,* pp. 433-434, n. 711; Wahl, *op. cit.,* pp. 39-40.

For any degree of the collateral line touching on the first, the Church dispenses only for grave and canonical reasons.[48] Since any application of the brother-sister arrangement also requires a grave or proportionate reason (*supra,* Chap. IV, art. 4), it is not likely that the brother-sister arrangement can be considered as a permanent solution for marriages invalid by reason of blood relationship of the first degree touching the second. If the reason proposed in the petition for a dispensation is not sufficent, it is unlikely but not impossible that the same reason would be sufficient for an application of the brother-sister arrangement on a permanent basis. The *modus agendi* in this case, however, is to apply for the dispensation. If the dispensation is refused because of an insufficient reason, then the case should be reconsidered on the basis of a possible brother-sister arrangement.

The impediment of affinity like that of consanguinity is an impediment *natura sua perpetua* and can be removed only by way of dispensation [49] Since the impediment of affinity is one of purely ecclesiastical law in every degree of either the direct or the collateral line, it is evident that the Church can dispense from affinity in any degree.[50] The impediment of affinity in any degree of the collateral line is usually amenable to dispensation by the Church. In the direct line, the Church will grant a dispensation for any degree, provided that the marriage from which the affinity arises is *unconsummated.* If the marriage was consummated, the Church, for a grave cause, will dispense in cases of affinity beyond the first degree,[51] but will not dispense from the first degree itself.[52]

The brother-sister arrangement, therefore, can be considered as a permanent solution for only that marriage which is invalid by reason of affinity in the first degree of the direct line, when the marriage which gives rise to the affinity has been consummated.

---

[48]S.C. de Sacramentis, instr., 1 aug. 1931—*AAS,* XXIII (1931), 413; cf. Beste, *Introductio in Codicem,* p. 548.

[49]Wernz-Vidal, *Ius Matrimoniale,* pp. 477-479, n. 369-370.

[50]Wahl, *op. cit.,* pp. 80-89; can. 80.

[51]Gasparri, *De Matrimonio,* n. 724; Payen, *De Matrimonio,* I, n. 1504.

[52]Chelodi, *Ius Matrimoniale,* n. 102; Cappello,*De Matrimonio,* p. 510, n. 539; can. 1043.

Article 4. Holy Orders

The impediment of Holy Orders is a circumstance bringing with it an inability disqualifying a cleric constituted in Sacred Orders from contracting a valid marriage,[53] or from continuing its licit use should the matrimonial bond have been contracted before his ordination in the Roman Rite. Among the major or sacred Orders are to be enumerated: The Episcopate, the Priesthood, the Diaconate, and the Subdiaconate.[54]

This impediment is of ecclesiastical origin,[55] and therefore it is within the power of the Church to dispense from it. Woywod (1880-1941) stated that the impediment of sacred Orders is one of those impediments from which the Holy See does not dispense. He then modifies this by saying that, if for special reasons a dispensation is granted, it is done secretly.[56] Actually there are several known cases in which a dispensation was granted in behalf of ecclesiastics below the Episcopate.[57] While the Church could dispense even in the case of a Bishop, history does not show that it has ever exercised such a right. Cappello pointed out that the Roman Pontiff has the faculty of dispensing, but that he rarely uses this faculty to dispense a subdeacon; he very rarely uses it to dispense a deacon; he most rarely dispenses a priest; and he never dispenses a Bishop.[58] A decree which the Sacred Penitentiary issued in 1936 stated that the law of celibacy for

---

[53]"Invalide matrimonium attentant clerici in sacris ordinibus constituti."—Can. 1072.

[54]Can. 949. Cf. Noldin-Schmitt, *Summa*, III, p. 585, n. 576; Gasparri, *De Matrimonio*, p. 367, n. 607; Conc. Trident., sess. XXIV *de matrimonio*, can. 9.

[55]Petrovits, *The New Church Law on Matrimony*, p. 193, n. 281; Noldin-Schmitt, *op. cit.*, p. 586, n. 576; Wernz, *Ius Decretalium*, IV, n. 392 ff; Sabetti-Barrett, *Compendium Theologiae Moralis*, p. 845, n. 879.

[56]Woywod, *A Commentary*, I, p. 719, n. 1059.

[57]Petrovits, *op. cit.*, pp. 193-194, n. 281; Cappello, *op. cit.*, p. 424, n. 442.

[58]"Dispensandi facultas competit R. Pontifici, qui *ea nunquam* utitur cum *Episcopis, rarissime* cum *presbyteris, rarius* cum *diaconis*, et *raro* cum *subdiaconis*.. Hodie dispensatio quoad diaconos et subdiaconos minore cum rigore quam in antiqua disciplina conceditur."—Cappello, *De Matrimonio*, p. 423, n. 442. Cf. also Augustine, *A Commentary on the New Code of Canon Law*, V, 187-188; Noldin-Schmitt, *op. cit.*, p. 586, n. 576; Gasparri, *De Matrimonio*, p. 373, n. 619.

the Latin clergy has always been and is now so treasured by the Church that, in the case of priests, dispensation from it, in past times, was hardly ever granted, and according to the present discipline is never given, not even in danger of death.[59]

The seriousness of the impediment and the severe relunctance with which a dispensation is granted to one having received the sacred Order of priesthood is indicated by the limitation placed on the extensive powers granted in virtue of canons 1043-1045. Under the conditions enumerated in these canons the ordinary, pastor and confessor receive the power in certain cases (i.e., *Urgente mortis periculo; casibus perplexis*) to dispense from all matrimonial impediments of ecclesiastical origin with two exceptions, one of which is the impediment that derives from the priesthood. Under the postulated conditions the ordinary, pastor or confessor can dispense a deacon or a subdeacon, but not a priest. Augustine, accordingly pointed out that, if such a case (v. g., a priest in danger of death) comes before a pastor or confessor, either of these can do no more than impart absolution, provided that the penitent is properly disposed and agrees to separate from the woman and repair the scandal he has given.[60] In other words, a dispensation from the impediment cannot be given in the case of a guilty priest in virtue of canons 1043-1045, but apparently it can be given in the case of a guilty deacon or subdeacon.

From this it is evident that the brother-sister arrangement is possible as a permanent solution in the case of a priest, since a dispensation from the impediment is never, or at best, most rarely given.[61] The arrangement is also possible in the case of a deacon or subdeacon, but since a dispensation is more readily given than in the case of a priest, the brother-sister arrangement is to be used only as a temporary solution until the petition for a dispensation has been made and the

---

[59] S. Poenit., 18 apr. 1936 —*AAS*, XXVIII (1936), 242; Bouscaren, *Digest*, II, p. 579.

[60] Augustine, *op. cit.*, V, 188. The writer wishes to interject that the brother-sister arrangement is certainly possible in such cases.

[61] Cappello, *De Matrimonio*, p. 423 ,note 39; Gasparri, *De Matrimonio*, p. 373, n. 619; Can. 214.

dispensation has been granted. If the dispensation is refused, then the arrangement can be considered as a possible permanent solution.

In the cases (*urgente mortis periculo; casibus perplexis*) and under the conditions as mentioned in canons 1043-1045 of the Code, a deacon or a subdeacon is to be dispensed, and the brother-sister arrangement is not to be considered as a solution. If for some reason the dispensation cannot be given, the brother-sister arrangement can surely be considered as a possible solution. In the same cases of canons 1043-1045 in which a priest is involved, however, the brother-sister arrangement is indeed a possible solution, since a dispensation and convalidation of the marriage cannot be had.

When there is question of granting permission for the brother-sister arrangement on a permanent basis in the case of a subdeacon or a deacon, then the general norms expressed in Chapter IV of the present work are to be followed. As was previously mentioned, however, the absolution from the censure incurred by a priest who has attempted marriage, even though in the present a separation is impossible, is reserved exclusively to the Sacred Penitentiary.[62] Cappello mentioned that the excommunication is considered as being reserved *specialissimo modo* to the Holy See. Therefore, if the case involves a priest, the brother-sister arrangement cannot be permitted by the ordinary or pastor or confessor, but is reserved exclusively to the Holy See. If the guilty priest is in danger of death, the brother-sister arrangement can be permitted by the same three, but there remains the obligation of having recourse to the Sacred Penitentiary as prescibed in canon 2252 for censures which are by law reserved most specially to the Holy See.[63]

In summary, then, the brother-sister arrangement is a possible solution for the invalid marriage of a priest, but the granting of the permission for the arrangement is reserved exclusively to the Sacred Penitentiary. In danger of death, the permission can be granted by the confessor, but recourse to the Sacred Penitentiary is necessary.

The brother-sister arrangement is also possible as a solution for

---

[62]*Supra*, p. 130-131.

[63]S. Poenit., 18 apr. 1936—AAS, XXVIII (1936), 242; S. Poenit., 4 maii, 1937—AAS, XXVIII (1937),283; Bouscaren, *Digest*, II, 579, 580.

the invalid marriage of a deacon or a subdeacon, but it is not to be granted on a permanent basis until it is certain that the Holy See will not permit convalidation of the marriage by way of dispensation. If the dispensation has been refused, the norms of Chapter IV of this work are applicable, and the ordinary or pastor or confessor can grant the permission in accord with those norms. In danger of death and in the more urgent cases, however, the deacon and subdeacon can be dispensed according to canons 1043-1045, and the marriage can be convalidated. In this case the brother-sister arrangement cannot be used.

Article 5. Specific Criminality

A marriage which is invalid by reason of the impediment of specific criminality (*crimen*) presents an involved question, but one in connection with which the brother-sister arrangement can be considered as a possible solution. There is something revolting and disgusting in the thought of accomplices in adultery seeking to enter a marriage upon the death of the spouse of the one or the other or of both; and something abhorrent in the thought of a murderer seeking marriage with the victim's erstwhile husband or wife. It is something repellent, not only in the moral code but also in the code of ethics set up by decent society.

The Catholic Church has, therefore, made specific legislation regarding this outrageous attempt to lower the morale of humankind. It has established this species of violation of the moral code as a diriment impediment to marriage. In prohibiting such marriages the Church considers the specific criminality (*crimen*) in all its phases. According to canon 1075, there are three types of specific criminality which nullify the subsequent attempted marriage between the partners in the criminal act:

1) If, during the continuation of the same lawful wedlock, persons commit adultery and as partners in this crime enter into a mutual promise to contract a later union, or attempt the very contracting of marriage itself, even by way of a mere civil ceremony;

2) If, during the continuation likewise of the same lawful wedlock,

persons commit adultery, and one of them kills the husband or
the wife of the accomplice in the adultery, or even his own wife
or her own husband.

3)   If, even apart from the committing of adultery, persons through
mutual help and co-operation, whether physical or moral, inflict
death upon the spouse marked by them as their victim.[64]

The Church, in establishing this impediment, does so with the
intention of protecting and preserving the conjugal faith of the wedded pair, and when it takes away the hope of marriage between the
accomplices in the adultery and in the murder of their victim it re-
moves the opportunity and principal reason for the commission of
these criminal acts.

By its nature the impediment of specific criminality (*crimen*) is
perpetual, and can therefore be taken away only by means of a dispensation. But since it is merely of ecclesiastical origin in regard to
each of its three species, the Church can certainly dispense, even when
it is a matter that involves the murder of one of the spouses, whether
the crime be occult or public.[65]

If the impediment arises through an act of adultery together with
a mutual promise to contract a later union, or together with an attempt
to contract marriage, the Holy See dispenses quite readily, e.g., if
a woman were to suffer the loss of her good name, or were constrained
to remain unmarried, or if a public scandal would arise, etc. The
reason for this readiness of the Holy See to grant a dispensation is
gathered from the words of canon 1042, 2, 5°, which state that an

---

[64]Can. 1075: "Valide contrahere nequeunt matrimonium:

1° Qui, perdurante eodem legitimo matrimonio, adulterium inter se consummarunt et fidem sibi mutuo dederunt de matrimonio ineundo vel ipsum
matrimonium, etiam per civilem tantum actum, attentarunt;

2° Qui, perdurante pariter eodem legitimo matrimonio adulterium inter se
consummarunt eorumque alter coniugicidium patravit;

3° Qui, mutua opera physica vel morali, etiam sine adulterio, mortem coniugi
intulerunt." Cf· c. 2, C. XXXI, q. 1; c. 6, X, *de eo qui duxit, etc.*, IV, 7.

[65]Cf. Cappello, *De Matrimonio*, p. 474, n. 504; J. F. Donohue, *The Impediment of Crime*, The Catholic University of America Canon Law Studies, n.
69 (Washington, D. C.: The Catholic University of America, 1931), p. 88.

impediment of this sort is of a minor degree only.[66] Obviously the brother-sister arrangement is not to be considered as a possible permanent solution for a marriage invalid by reason of this first type of specific criminality. The marriage is rather to be convalidated.

When the impediment is contracted on account of the other two causes, namely, adultery combined with the murder of the consort, or murder of the consort as the outcome of the plotting of the two accomplices, the Church does not dispense, nor is it inclined to dispense when the murder of the consort is a matter of public knowledge.[67] If the act of murder has remained occult,[68] the Sacred Penitentary though very rarely, in some instances does dispense, for the forum of conscience, namely, when it is not likely that the guilt of the parties in question will be divulged, and the cause is most urgent.[69] If the death of the consort has resulted from the administration of poison, Gasparri indicated that an additional difficulty is placed in the way of obtaining a dispensation.[70] Petrovits pointed out the rarity with which the dispensation is given when he said that, if the marriage is already contracted and a separation is not possible without the occasioning of grave scandal, and the danger of incontinence threatens, then the dispensation is granted, provided that the murder is secret.[71]

When there is an urgent danger of death none of the species of the impediment of specific criminality (*crimen*) is reserved. In accord with canons 1043-1044 the bishop, pastor and confessor can, under

---

[66] Cappello, *De Matrimonio*, p. 475, n. 504; Donohue, *op. cit.*, p. 89; Petrovits, *The New Church Law on Matrimony*, p. 219, n. 317.

[67] Cf. Cappello, *op. cit.*, p. 474, n. 504; Donohue, *op. cit.*, p. 89; Wernz, *Ius Decretalium*, IV, n. 534; Petrovits, *op. cit.*, p. 220.

[68] The terms *public* and *occult* as used in this instance are to be understood according to the definitions of the Code (canon 2195) as explained by the authors. They are not to be understood in the more restrictive sense adopted for the present work, *supra*, pp. 97-101.

[69] Cappello uses the phrase "*ex causa gravissima*"—*De Matrimonio*, p. 475, n. 504. Also see Gasparri, *De Matrimonio*, p. 415, n. 683; Payen, *De Matrimonio*, p. 1028, nn. 1410-1411 and p. 997, n. 1363; Wernz-Vidal, *Ius Matrimoniale*, p. 423, n. 339.

[70] *De Matrimonio*, p. 415, n. 683.

[71] *The New Church Law on Matrimony*, p. 220, n. 318.

varying conditions, dispense from the impediment, notwithstanding the fact that the murder of the consort was a public act. Similar is the power of the bishop over this impediment, whether the murder is public or secret, whenever the presence of conditions formerly referred to as the *causus perplexus* are verified.[72] The priest could in this case dispense only when the act of the murder is still occult and when at the same time a recourse to the bishop is difficult.

Since the brother-sister arrangement is a solution of last resort and cannot be granted on a permanent basis when the invalid marriage can be convalidated, the impediment of specific criminality affords only a limited use of this arrangement. The arrangement is never used when the impediment is of the first species of criminality, namely, when it arises through an act of adultery together with a mutual promise to contract a later union, or together with an attempt to contract marriage. In this case the Church readily grants a dispensation and the marriage can be convalidated.

The brother-sister arrangement is indeed applicable when the impediment is of the second or third species, namely, when the impediment involves adultery combined with the murder of the consort, or murder of the consort as the outcome of the plotting of the two accomplices. When the murder of the consort is public, the Church does not dispense, so that the brother-sister arrangement looms as a possible solution. When the murder is occult, the Church dispenses, but only *ex causa gravissima and rarissime*. It is the writer's opinion that in this case the Church would rather grant permission for the brother-sister arrangement than the dispensation. It is clear, however, that the Church does not always dispense even when the murder is occult, and in those cases the brother-sister arrangement can be considered as a possible solution.

In his consideration of the powers granted through canons 1043-1045 relative to the impediments of specific criminality (*crimen*) Cappello seems to have indicated that, when the murder of the spouse is a matter of public knowledge, then the powers granted to the bishop, pastor and confessor in cases of an urgent danger of death and in perplexing cases are of little practical value because of the scandal

---

[72] Can. 1045

that would arise.[73]   If this is actually the case, then the brother-sister arrangement can be considered as a possible solution in such cases of urgent necessity.

It should be mentioned that the impediment of specific criminality derives exclusively from the ecclesiastical law, and therefore the unbaptized are subject to it only indirectly. A decree of the Congregation for the Propagation of the Faith, on August 23, 1852, clarified this statement and also indicated to what extent the unbaptized person is subject to the impediment when he enters the Church, or when he wishes to marry a baptized person who has incurred the impediment. When the infidel is indirectly subject to the impediment, the norms for the possible application of the brother-sister arrangement remains the same as the norms expressed above.

S. C. de Prop. Fide, 23 Aug. 1852, ad 5) et 6) :

5)   *Vir infidelis qui ante baptismum copulam habuit cum infideli uxore alterius, cui, annuente muliere fidem de futuro matrimonio acceptante, mortem intulit, potestne post utriusque baptismum matrimonium inire cum dicta muliere?*

6)   *Possuntne hoc matrimonium contrahere si, quando patrarunt ista crimina, una pars fuerit christiana?*

Resp. (5) Affirmative.   (6) Negative.[74]

---

[73]"Facultas, de qua in cc· 1043-1045, respicit omnes species impedimenti criminis, *coniugicidio* etiam *publico* non excepto. Tamen dispensatio cum scandalo fidelium, ut patet, concedi nequit. Porro vix aut ne vix quidem abesset scandalum, si concederetur dispensatio in casu coniugicidii publici. Practice igitur huiusmodi dispensationi concedendae opportunitas et convenientia desunt."—(Cappello, *De Martimonio*, p. 475, n. 504, 6°.)

[74]Coll. *S.C.P.F.*, I, n. 1079. Cf., Donohue, *op. cit.*, pp. 83-87.

APPENDIX I

Article 1. May One Who Has Lived According To The Brother-Sister Arrangement be Granted Christian Burial?

If the invalid marriage in which the parties were living as brother and sister was materially and formally occult at the time of the death of one or the other party there is no difficulty. The party to be buried died in communion with the Church, and there would be no scandal through the Christian or ecclesiastical burial of such persons.

If the invalid marriage, however, is both materially and formally public (notorious) in the place where the burial is to take place, there may be some difficulty. On the one hand, the parties of the notoriously invalid marriage were lawfully but secretly reinstated in the Church (through the use of the brother-sister arrangement) and were receiving the sacraments privately or secretly for some time prior to death. On the other hand, the law of the Church demands that public and manifest sinners must be deprived of ecclesiastical burial, unless they gave some positive sign of repentance prior to death. Actually, the parties of the brother-sister arrangement did give very positive signs of repentance, but these signs are known only to the priest. The difficulty arises from the possible scandal that may be given if the Church grants public ecclesiastical burial to one who is commonly regarded as having been excommunicated or as a public and manifest sinner.

It is not considered prudent at present publicly to disclose the brother-sister arrangement as a possible solution for invalid marriages. It does not seem, therefore, that the pastor, in order to forestall in such a case the possible scandal attaching to the bestowal of Christian burial, should announce to the parish that the parties lived as brother and sister, and received the sacraments in private or in secret. Such a procedure could easily cause further scandal (especially if the parties were young), and would, indeed, render useless the practice of the private or secret reception of the sacraments by those who, through necessity, are living as brother and sister in a formally public invalid marriage.[1]

At the present time it seems to the writer that this case should be handled as any other death-bed conversion of a public sinner.[2] The pastor, if necessary, could announce to the parish that the party had repented of his sinful actions and received the sacraments of the Church. Having repented, the party is worthy of ecclesiastical burial.

Of course the degree of the possible scandal will vary in the different sections of the country. In smaller communities the possible emergence of scandal through the bestowal of Christian burial to such a person may be much more grave than in larger communities or cities. It may, then, be necessary for the pastor or the local ordinary to demand more than the public announcement of repentance. The elimination of pomp and ceremony at the funeral could serve to reduce the possibility of scandal. At least it will sufficiently mark the distinction between a Catholic who has publicly and faithfully observed all his religious duties, and one who, for a time, was publicly unworthy of the benefits of the Church.

It should be remembered that the parties of the formally public invalid marriage have something in their favor in that they publicly observed all the other religious duties (i.e., attended Mass, devotions, etc.) and that only the reception of the sacraments was done in private or secret. Hence they should be given more consideration than the public sinner who was completely separated from the Church up to the last minute prior to death.

Then, too, the parties who were culpably involved in a formally public invalid marriage should be cautioned when they receive permission for the brother-sister arrangement that they may possibly have to forego the pomp and ceremony which attends the normal Catholic funeral or ecclesiastical burial.

The ordinary should be consulted regarding the procedure to

---

[1] Cf. *supra*, pp. 104-105.

[2] Cf. Chas. Kerin, *The Privation of Christian Burial*, The Catholic University of America Canon Law Studies, n. 136 (Washington, D.C.: The Catholic University of America Press, 1941).

be followed in the burial of those who lived as brother and sister in
a formally public invalid marriage.

Article 2. Age Limit

It does not seem that the brother-sister arrangement as a possible
solution for invalid marriages can be absolutely restricted to those
persons who are in extreme old age. Granted, the older a person
is the less likely he is to fall into any externalized sin of incontinence.
However, the internal sin of incontinence (through thought or desire)
as well as the externalized sin must of necessity be avoided by anyone
living in the brother-sister arrangement. The writer has no direct
information on the point, but it seems quite possible that the old and
and the young are or can be equally susceptible to the danger of grave,
internal sins of incontinence.

While the arrangement will be more readily granted to an
older couple, it should not be refused to a younger couple simply
because they are not of an advanced age. If a young couple is
capable of fulfilling the required conditions (Chapter IV) the case
should be given consideration. It is known that the brother-sister
arrangement has been granted in cases in which the parties were
perhaps no more than thirty years of age.

Article 3. A Remedy of Transient Duration

It should be mentioned that the present work was written primarily in view of the possible use of the arrangement on a permanent
basis. The arrangement, however, is certainly not limited to those
cases which call for its permanent use. The brother-sister arrangement is equally and perhaps even more readily applied in those cases
which require only a temporary or transient use of the arrangement,
v.g., in the case of attempted marriages which are in the process of
being convalidated or adjudicated in the matrimonial tribunal. The
transient or temporary application of the arrangement gives rise to
far less likelihood of the dangers of incontinence and scandal. It
should be metioned, however, that the same general conditions must

be verified for any use of the arrangement, whether it be of a transient or indeed of a permanent character.

APPENDIX   II.

The following suggested form is, for the most part, the same
as the form presented by Bishop Król in *The Jurist* (Vol. XI, 1951,
31-32) A comparison of the two forms, however, indicates that the
writer has suggested a few changes.   For example, it is not demanded
that the parties requesting the permission be in old age or gravely ill,
but simply that a proportionate reason be in evidence; it is not
demanded that the parties take an oath that they will remain faithful
to the promises made; occult violations of the arrangement are referred
to the confessor, and violations which are or become public are referred to the ordinary (*supra,* p. 133).   When the seal of the confession is in force regarding a case which is completely occult, but
reserved to the ordinary, the following form can usually be adopted
to a "Titus-Bertha" case.

Form n. 1.

DIOCESE OF————————————————— Number—————————

NAME—————————————————

PETITION FOR PERMISSION TO LIVE AS BROTHER AND SISTER

N. B. This petition may be used if (1) there is no other possible
solution, (2) there is no danger of grave scandal through the
use of the arrangement, (3), any proximate occasion of sin is a
necessary one and the attendant likely danger is efficaciously
forestalled, (4) there is a proportionately grave reason for the
arrangement, (5) the case is formally or materially public, or
presented to the priest in the external forum.   (Parties are inter-
viewed separately and alone.)

Most Reverend Bishop:

We, the undersigned, realizing that our marriage is invalid in
the sight of God and that we have no marriage rights whatsoever,
finding it extremely difficult to separate, humbly request permission
to live together as brother and sister, and to be readmitted to communion with the Church.

QUESTIONNAIRE FOR THE MAN

1. Name and address _______________________________
2. Date and place of birth _________________________________
3. Religion ______________ (If Catholic) When did you last
    receive the secraments _________________________. (If Non-
    Catholic) Do you want to become a Catholic?_______________
4. Have you ever applied for such permission before?___________
    When? ___________ Where? ___________ Granted? _______
5. When, where, and before whom did you attempt your present
    marriage? ____
6. About how many people knew at that time that the marriage was
    invalid? _________ Did you know that it was invalid? _________
    How? ____
7. Give the names and ages of children born of your present union.

    ____

8.. How long have you lived in this general locality? _________
    Do any of your neighbors or friends know that your marriage
    is invalid?_________ Do they know why it is invalid?_________
    How many know these things? (Give Number) _________
9. How many Catholics (relatives and friends included) know that
    your marriage is invalid? _________ How many of these know
    that it cannot be convalidated? (Give Number) _________
10. Why is it impossible to separate? (i.e., morally impossible)_____

    ____

11. (If ill) Nature of your illness?_________________________
    (If wife is ill) Nature of wife's illness? _________________
12. How many times were you previously married? _____________
13. Give date and place of former wife's death? _____________
14. If former wife is still living give the following data:
    a. Name of spouse (maiden name) _________________
       Religion? ___________ Is she a practicing Catholic?_______
    b. When, where, and before whom were you married? _______

       ____

    c. Number of children by this marriage?_________ Ages?_______
       Where do they live now? _________________________
    d. Cause of separation and divorce? _________________
    e. When, where, and by whom was the divorce secured? _____

    f. Present name and address of your former wife? _____________

    g. Has she remarried?_________ When?_________ Where?_________

    (If there was more than one previous marriage, Question 14 should be answered for each marriage on an attached note.)

15. Are you convinced that you can keep your promise to live as a brother with a sister?_________ Why do you say so?_____________

16. Have you tried to live in such manner?_________ How long?_____

17. Could you support your present consort if she were separated from you?_________ (A negative answer requires verification by way of information about the petitioner's income and assets.)

18. Is it morally possible for you and your wife to move to a place in which your marital status is completely unknown?

QUESTIONNAIRE FOR THE WOMAN

(To be interrogated separately and alone.)

1. Maiden Name and address?_______________________________

2. Date and place of birth? _________________________________

3. Religion?_________________ (If Catholic) When did you last receive the sacraments? _____________________ (If Non-Catholic) Do you want to become a Catholic?_____________

4. Have you ever applied for such a permission before?_________ When?_____________ Where?_____________ Granted?_________

5. When, where, and before whom did you attempt your present marriage? ____

6. About how many people knew at that time that the marriage was invalid? _________ Did you know that it was invalid?_________ How? ____

7. Give names and ages of the children born of your present union.
____

8. How long have you lived in this general locality?_____________ Do any of your friends or neighbors know that your marriage is invalid?_________ Do they know why it is invalid?_________ How many know these things? _____________________

9. How many Catholics (relatives and friends included) know that your marriage is invalid?_____________ How many of these know

that it cannot be convalidated? _______________

10. Why is it impossible to separate? (i. e., morally impossible)_____

11. (If ill) Nature of illness?_____________________
    (If husband is ill) Nature of illness?_____________

12. How many times were you previously married? _________

13. Give date and place of former husband's death?_________

14. If former husband is still living give the following data:

    a. Name and present address?_________________

    b. When, where, and before whom were you married?_______

    c. Number of children by this marriage?_______ Ages?_______
       Where do they live now? _________________

    d. Cause of separation and divorce? _______________

    e. When, where, and by whom was the divorce secured?_______

    f. Has your former husband remarried?_______ When, where,
       and with whom? _____________________

    g. Is your former husband a Catholic?_______ Since when?_____

    h. Was his present spouse free to marry?_________ Was she
       a Catholic?_______________________

    (If there was more than one previous marriage, Question 14
    should be answered for each marriage on an attached note.)

15. Are you convinced that you can keep your promise to live as
    a sister with a brother?_______ Why do you say so?_________

16. Have you tried to live is such manner?_____ For how long?_____

17. Could your husband provide for your support, or could you
    support yourself if you were separated from him?_________
    If not, please explain.
    PROMISES . . . . (To be made separately by each party in the
    presence of the other party.)

With complete sincerity and realizing my obligation before God,
I solemnly promise:

    1. that under no circumstance will I attempt to live as a husband
       (wife) with my present consort;

    2. that if I violate this promise, I will report such violation to
       the proper authority (confessor or ordinary) and will follow
       his directions;

    3. that I will remove any and all unnecessary, proximate oc-

casion of sin;

4. that I will receive the Sacrament of Holy Communion only in such churches and under such conditions wherein scandal will not be given . . . according to the judgment of my confessor or pastor;

5. that I will take all precaution to preclude scandal from the use of the brother-sister arrangement for which I herewith petition, and will immediately report any substantial change in the public or occult nature of my case;

6. that I will reveal or conceal the true nature of my marital status according to the judgment and explicit directions of my ordinary;

7. that the marriage will be validated as soon as this becomes possible.

Signed (Man) _______________________________

Signed (Woman) _______________________________

S E A L

Priest ____

Date ____

Place ____

N.B. If the case is either materially or materially and formally public, or otherwise reserved to the ordinary, kindly return this petition to the Chancery Office. The ordinary will render a decision and inform you of the procedure to be followed. This petition should be accompanied with a letter from the priest giving further information in whatever measure may prove necessary, and giving his own opinion regarding the prudent disposition of the case. This form may be used after the fashion of a Titus-Bertha case if the case is completely occult and the parties refuse to have their names revealed. This form may never be used in a fashion which may jeopardize the *sigillum sacramentale*.

* * * *

Form n. 2.

The following forms are suggested for the granting of the permission. Neither of these forms should be used if a previous civil marriage bond from which a divorce has not been obtained is still in existence.

No.________________

Date________________________________

To whom it may concern:

In view of the petition submitted and the solemn promises made,

N. N. ____________________ and N. N.____________________ are hereby granted permission to live together according to the broth-er-sister arrangement as long as the requirements and conditions of that arrangement are fulfilled. The same persons are permitted to receive the sacraments in a place and manner which, according to the judgment of the priest, will not give rise to scandal.

This permission is subject to immediate revocation at the discre-tion of the confessor, pastor or ordinary.

The grantees are hereby admonished that the circumstances and conditions which attend the burial of either party are, without ques-tion, to be determined by the ordinary. It is also within the discre-tionary power of the local ordinary to reveal, if necessary, the true marital status of the above mentioned parties.

Faculties are hereby granted for the absolution of censures possibly incurred..

Signed ___________________________________

SEAL   *Ordinary*

Date ___________________________________

Form n. 3

No.________________

Date____________________________

Permission for N. N.__________ and N. N.________ (nee) ________ to live together as brother and sister is hereby granted under the following conditions:

1. that the Sacraments of Penance and Holy Communion be re-ceived in a place or manner which, according to the judgment of the priest, will not give rise to scandal;

2.   that there be no scandal given or received as a result of this brother-sister arrangement;
3.   that the proximate occasion of sin be removed by:
     a) maintaining separate bedrooms;
     b) avoiding all signs or acts of endearment or affection
         that may be a danger to perfect purity;
4.   that a complete separation be immediately effected if, in the
future, this privilege is revoked for any reason by the bishop;
5.   that any violation of this arrangement be reported immediately
to your regular confessor, and his directions be followed; that
if the violation is or becomes public, a report be made to the
bishop;
6.   that the revelation or concealment of your true marital status
depends solely on the explicit direction of the bishop;
7.   that the marriage be validated as soon as this becomes possible;
8.   that the circumstances of the burial of either party depend solely
on the judgment of the bishop.

____

Ordinary

S E A L

N.B. This copy is to be kept in the parish files.

CONCLUSIONS

1. The brother-sister arrangement was officially presented by the Church as a possible solution for invalid marriages as early as the 13th century. (pp. 20-21; 28-29).
2. The Code of Canon Law contains no direct reference to the brother-sister arrangement.
3. The brother-sister arrangement is not a substitute for marriage nor is it an optional matter. It is a solution of last resort. (pp. 56, 81-87).
4. Permission for the brother-sister arrangement is juridically distinct from a dispensation or a privilege in the strict sense. (p. 69).
5. The brother-sister arrangement is a practical solution for invalid marriages and should be regarded as such in diocesan legislation and practice. (p. 79).
6. For any application of the arrangement it is postulated that the parties have actually attempted marriage or at least have established a union which has the appearance of marriage. (p.59).
7. It is absolutely demanded that the parties use separate beds. They must, if possible, use separate rooms for sleeping. (p. 64).
8. There is no innate prohibition against extended family outings or vacations. (p. 64).
9. The common social courtesies or amenities are to be observed by a couple living as brother and sister. (p. 65).
10. The brother-sister arrangement is unanimously regarded as a *res plena periculis*, especially because of possible scandal and the danger of incontinence. (p. 72).
11. There are five essential requirements which must be verified for the licit use of the brother-sister arrangement. (p. 53-Chapter IV)
12. The brother-sister arrangement can be used on a permanent basis in those "marriages" only which are invalid by reason of a diriment impediment which does not cease, or one which cannot or usually does not yield to dispensation. (p. 84).
13. The public or occult nature of both the invalid marriage and

the impediment causing the invalidity must be known for the proper and licit granting of the permission. (p. 92).

14. The term "public" must be understood in the sense of canon 2197, 1°. (pp. 100-101).

15. The brother-sister arrangement is not usually permissible in a case which is both materially and formally public.[1] (pp. 89, 101).

16. The public reception of the Sacraments is always inadmissible in formally public cases. (p. 103).

17. The private or secret reception of the sacraments is permissible only if it is morally impossible to remove the scandal of continued cohabitation. (p. 105).

18. The brother-sister arrangement and subsequent public reception of the sacraments are usually possible in a case which is materially public but formally occult. (pp. 105-106).

19. From the viewpoint of scandal, the brother-sister arrangement and the public reception of the sacraments are always possible in a case which is materially and formally occult. (p. 109).

20. The proper permission of a competent ecclesiastical authority must be obtained for the licit use of the brother-sister arrangement. (p. 124).

21. There is no doubt concerning the fundamental power of the confessor, the pastor and the ordinary lawfully to grant permission for the brother-sister arrangement. (p. 125).

22. A case which is both materially and formally public (cf. footnote n. 1) must be referred to the ordinary. (p. 126).

23. Most cases involving a previous bond must be referred to the ordinary. (pp. 133-134).

24. The ordinary can, in accord with canons 893-899, reserve all brother-sister cases to himself, but he cannot lawfully demand that all cases (even the most secret) be handled in the external forum. (p. 132)

---

[1] In order rightly to understand conclusions 15-19 it is necessary to have a proper understanding of the terms public and occult, formal and informal, Cf. *supra* pp. 100-101.

25. A case which is doubtful as to its formal publicity must be referred to the ordinary. (p. 130).

26. A case which is unusually difficult must be referred to the ordinary. (p. 130).

27. A case which is materially public but formally occult (cf. footnote n. 1) can be handled by the pastor unless the case is reserved to a higher authority. (p. 127).

28. A case which is materially and formally occult (cf. footnote n. 1) can be handled by the confessor, but only in the internal forum. This is said with the provision that the case is not reserved. (pp. 128, 135).

29. After the permission has been granted, the confessor is the judge in the internal forum regarding occult violations of the arrangement (i.e. acts of incontinence), and the possible continuation or cessation of the arrangement. (p. 133).

30. The ordinary is the judge in the external forum regarding the continuation or cessation of the arrangement in the event of the public violation of the arrangement by the parties. (p. 133).

BIBLIOGRAPHY

SOURCES

Acta Apostolicae Sedis, Commentarium Officiale, Romae, 1909-1929;
Civitate Vaticana, 1929-

Acta Santae Sedis, 41 vols., Romae, 1865-1908.

Bouscaren, T. Lincoln, *The Canon Law Digest* 3 vols. Milwaukee,
Wisc.: The Bruce Publishing Co., 1934-1943-1949-1953.

*Codex Iuris Canonici Pii X Pontificis Maximi iussu digestus, Bene-
dicti Papae XV auctoritate promulgatus, Praefatione, Fontium
Annotatione et Indice Analytico-Alphabetico ab Emô Petro Card.
Gasparri Auctus*, Romae, Typis Polyglottis Vaticanis, 1917;
reimpressio, 1934.

Codicis Iuris Canonici Fontes, cura Emï Petri Card. Gasparri editi,
9 vols., Romae (postea Civitate Vaticana): Typis Polyglottis
Vaticanis, 1923-1939. (Vols., VII-IX, ed. cura et studio Emï
Iustiniani Card. Serédi).

Collectanea S. Congregationis de Propaganda Fide, 2 vols., Romae:
Typographia Polyglotta S. C. de Propaganda Fide, 1907.

Corpus Iuris Canonici, ed. Lipsiensis secunda, post Aemilii Richteri
curas . . . instruxit Aemilius Friedberg, 2 vols., Lipsiae, 1879-1881.

Corpus Iuris Civilis, 3 vols., Berolini, 1928-1929. *Codex Iustinianus*,
quem recognovit et retractavit P. Krueger, ed. stereotypa 10.,
1929; *Novellae*, quas recognovit R. Schoell, et absolvit G. Kroll,
ed. stereotypa 5., 1928.

*Decretales D. Gregorii Papae IX, suae integritati una cum glossis
restitutae, cum privilegio Gregorii XIII, Pont. Max., et Aliorum
Principum*, Romae, 1582.

*Decretum Gratiani emendatum et notationibus illustratum cum glossis,
Gregorii XIII, Pont. Max., iussu editum*, 2 vols., Romae, 1582.

Denzinger, Heinrich—Bannwart, Clemens—Umberg, Johannes—

Rahner, Carolus, *Enchiridion Symbolorum Definitionum et Declarationum de Rebus Fidei et Morum*, ed. 28 augmentata, Friburgi Brisgoviae: Herder 1952.

Jaffé, Philippus, *Regesta Pontificum Romanorum ab condita Ecclesia ad annum post Christum natum MCXCVIII*, ed. 2 correctam et auctam auspiciis Gulielmi Wattenbach curaverunt S. Loewenfeld, F. Kaltenbrunner, P. Ewald, 2 vols., Lipsiae, 1885-1888.

Mansi, Joannes, *Sacrorum Conciliorum Nova et Amplissima Collectio*. 53 vols. in 60, Parisiis, 1901-1927.

Migne, J. P., *Patrologiae Cursus Completus, Series Graeca*, 161 vols., Parisiis, 1857-1866.

——*Patrologiae Cursus Completus, Series Latina*, 221 vols., Parisiis, Parisiis, 1844-1855.

Schroeder, H. J., *Canons and Decrees of the Council of Trent*, St. Louis: Herder, 1941.

REFERENCE WORKS

Aertnys, J.-Damen, C. A., *Theologia Moralis secundum doctrinam S. Alfonsi de Liguori*, 14 ed., 2 vols., Taurini: Marietti, 1944.

Aquinas, St. Thomas, *Summa Theologica (Supplementum)*, 4. ed., 10 vols., Parisiis, 1939.

Augustine, Chas., *A Commentary on the New Code of Canon Law*, 8 vols., St. Louis: Herder, 1925-1938. Vol. VIII, 3. ed., 1931.

Berardi, C. S., *Gratiani Canones Genuini ab Aprocryphis Discreti, Corrupti ad Emendatiorum Codicem Fidem Exacti, Difficiliores Commoda Interpretatione Illustrati*, 4 vols., in 3 tomes, Venetiis, 1777.

Beste, Udalricus, *Introductio in Codicem*, Editio altera, Collegeville, Minn., St. John's Abbey Press, 1944.

Bouscaren, T. L. Ellis, A. C., *Canon Law, A Text and Commentary*, Milwaukee: Bruce Co., 1946; Reprint 1948.

Cappello, Felix, *Tractatus Canonico-Moralis de Sacramentis*, 5 vols., Vol. V, De Matrimonio, 5. ed., Romae: Marietti, 1947.

——*Summa Iuris Canonici*, 3 vols., Vol. I, 5. ed., 1951; Vol. II, 4. ed., 1945; Vol. III, 3. ed., 1948, Romae: Apud Aedes Universitatis Gregorianae.

Chelodi, *Ius Canonicum de Matrimonio*, 5 ed., Vicenza: Società Anonima Tipografica Editrice, 1947.

———, *Ius Matrimoniale iuxta Codicem Iuris Canonici*, 4. ed. recognita et aucta a Vigilio Dalpiaz, Tridenti: Liberia Moderna Editrice A. Ardesi, 1937.

Chrétien, P., *De Matrimonio*, 2. ed., Metis: "Le Lorrain," apud J. Hocquard, 1937.

Cicognani, Amleto, *Canon Law*, 2. ed., Revised, English version by J. O'Hara and F. Brennan, Westminster, Maryland: Newman Press, 1949, Reprint of 2. ed., Philadelphia: The Dolphin Press, 1935.

Coronata Matthaeus Conte a, *Institutiones Iuris Canonici, De Sacramentis, Tractatus Canonicus*, Vol. III, *De Matrimonio*, Taurini: Romae, 1946.

D'Annibale, J., *Summula Theologiae Moralis*, 4. ed., 3 vols., Romae, 1896-1897.

D'Avack, P. A., *Cause di Nullita e di Divorzio nel Diritto Matrimoniale Canonico*. Vol. I, Firenze: Casa Editr. C. Cya, 1952.

Davis, Henry, *Moral and Pastoral Theology*, 4. ed., 4 vols., London: Sheed & Ward, 1943.

DeBecker, Julius, *De Sponsalibus et Matrimonio*, 2. ed., Lovanii, 1903-1913.

De Smet, A., *De Sponsalibus et Matrimonio*, 4, ed., Brugis, 1927.

———*Praxis Matrimonialis ad Usum Parochi et Confessarii*, 2. ed., Brugis: C. Beyaert, 1939.

Doheny, Wm. J., *Canonical Procedure in Matrimonial Cases*, 2 vols., Vol. II, *Informal Procedure*, Milwaukee: Bruce, 1944.

Donohue, J. F., *The Impediment of Crime*, The Catholic University of America Canon Law Studies, No. 69, Washington, D. C.: The Catholic University of America, 1931.

Durantis (Durandus), G., *Speculum Iuris*, 2 vols., Venetiis, 1577.

Esmein, A., *Le Mariage en Droit Canonique*, 2 ed., 2 tomes, par R. Gènèstal et Jean Dauvillier, Paris: Recueil-Sirey, 1929-1935.

Ferraris, Lucius, *Prompta Bibliotheca Canonica, Iuridica, Moralis, Theologica, nec non Ascetica, Polemica, Rubristica, Historica*, ed. novissima, 9 vols., Romae, 1885-1899.

Freisen, Joseph, *Geschichte des canonischen Eherechts*, Paderborn, 1893.

Gasparri, Petrus, *Tractatus Canonicus de Matrimonio*, 3. ed., 2 vols., Parisiis, 1904.

______*Tractatus Canonicus de Matrimonio*, ed. nova ad mentem *Codicis Iuris Canonici*, 2 vols., in 1, Romae: Typis Polyglottis Vaticanis, 1932.

Hostiensis, Cardinalis, *Summa Aurea*, Lugduni, 1568.

Jone, H—Adelman, U., *Moral Theology* 3. ed., Westminster, Maryland: Newman Bookshop, 1947.

Joyce, H., *Christian Marriage*, 2. ed., London: Sheed & Ward, 1948.

Kerin, Chas. A., *The Privation of Christian Burial*, The Catholic University of America Canon Law Studies, No. 136, Washington, D. C.: The Catholic University of America Press, 1941.

Lega, Michael, *De Delictis et Poenis*, 2. ed., Romae, 1910.

Mahon, Thomas, *The Church and Divorce*, St. Louis: B. Herder, 1926.

Merkelbach, B., *Summa Theologiae Moralis*, 3. ed., 3 vols., Parisiis: Desclee, de Brouwer et Soc., 1938-1939.

Mueller, Jos., *The Fatherhood of St. Joseph*, St. Louis: B. Herder, 1952.

Nau, Louis J., *Marriage Laws of the Code of Canon Law*, New York: Pustet, 1933.

Noldin, H.—Schmitt, A., *Summa Theologiae Moralis, iuxta Codicem Iuris Canonici*, 3 vols., 26. ed., Oeniponte-Lipsiae: Feliciani Rauch, 1940-1941.

Panormitanus, Abbas (Nicholaus de Tudeschis), *Commentaria in Quinque Libros Decretalium*, 5 vols. in 7, Venetiis, 1588.

Payen, G., *De Matrimonio in Missionibus ac Potissimum in Sinis Tractatus Practicus et Causus*, 2. ed., 3 vols., Zi-ka-wei: In Typographia T'ou-se-we, 1935-1936.

Petrovits, Joseph, J. C., *The New Church Law on Matrimony*, Philadelphia: J. J. McVey, 1921.

Prümmer, Dominicus M., *Manuale Theologiae Moralis*, 3. ed., 3 vols., Friburgi Brisgoviae: Herder, 1936.

Raymundus de Pennafort, Sanctus, *Summa S. Raymondi de Pennafort*.

Barcinonensis de Paenitentia et Matrimonio, 3 vols., Veronae 1744.

Reiffenstuel, A., *Ius Canonicum Universum*, 5 vols. in 6, Romae, 1831-1834.

Sabetti, A.,—Barrett, T., *Compendium Theologiae Moralis*, 22. ed., Cincinnati: Frederick Pustet & Co., 1915.

Sanchez, Thomas, *Disputationum de Sancto Matrimonii Sacramento Tomi Tres*, Antverpie, 1626.

Santamaria, F., *Commentarios al Código Canónico*, 6 vols., Madrid, 1919-1922.

Schroeder, H. J., *Disciplinary Decrees of the General Councils*, St. Louis: Herder, 1937.

Sheed, F. J., *Nullity of Marriage*, London: Sheed & Ward, 1931.

Ter Haar, *Casus Conscientiae*, 3, ed., 2 vols., Taurini: Marietti, 1944.
——*De Occasionariis et Recidivis*, ed. altera, Taurini: Marietti, 1939.

Van Hove, Alphonsus, *Commentarium Lovaniense in Codicem Iuris Canonici*, 1 vol. in 5 tomes, Tom. I, *Prolegomena*, 2. ed., Mechliniae-Romae: H. Dessain, 1945.

Vermeersch, A.—Creusen, J., *Epitome Iuris Canonici cum Commentariis ad Scholas et ad Usum Privatum*, 6. ed., 3 vols., Mechliniae, Romae: Dessain, 1937-1946.

Vlaming, Th., *Praelectiones Iuris Matrimonii ad Normam Codicis Iuris Canonici*, 3. ed., Bussum in Hollandia, 1919-1921.

Vlaming, Th.—Bender, L. *Praelectiones Iuris Matrimonii*, 4. ed., Bussum in Hollandia: Brand, 1950.

Wahl, F. X., *The Matrimonial Impediments of Consanguinity and Affinity*, The Catholic University of America Canon Law Studies, No. 90, Washington, D. C., The Catholic University of America, 1934.

Wernz, Franciscus X., *Ius Decretalium*, 6 vols., Romae, 1898-1914.

Wernz, Franciscus-Vidal, Petrus, *Ius Canonicum ad Codicis Normam Exactum*, 7 vols. in 8, Vol. V, *Ius Matrimoniale*, 3. ed., Romae: Apud Aedes Universitatis Gregorianae, 1946.

Woywod, Stanislaus, *A Practical Commentary on the Code of Canon Law*, revised by Callistus Smith, revised and enlarged edition, 2 vols., New York: J. F. Wagner, Inc., 1948.

ARTICLES

Kelly, Gerald, "Notes on Moral Theology, 1951," *Theological Studies*, XIII (1952), 59-100; in particular, 80-81.

Król, John, "Permission to Parties Invalidly Married to Live as Brother and Sister," The Jurist, XI (1951) 7-32.

UNPUBLISHED MATERIAL

Harrington, Paul, *Impotence The Notion and Impediment, A Historical Synopsis,* Typewritten licentiate dissertation, School of Canon Law, The Catholic University of America: Washington, D. C., 1950.

Wrzaszczak, C. F., *The Betrothal Contract in the Code of Canon Law, A Historical Synopsis,* Typewritten licentiate dissertation, School of Canon Law, The Catholic University of America, Washington, D. C., 1950.

ABBREVIATIONS

AAS—*Acta Apostolicae Sedis*
ASS—*Acta Sanctae Sedis*
Coll. S.C.P.F.—*Collectanea S. Congregationis de Propaganda Fide.*
Fontes—*Codicis Iuris Canonici Fontes*
Jaffé—*Regesta Pontificum Romanorum*
    JE—Jaffé, *Regesta Pontificum Romanorum*, ed. curavit P. Ewald (590-882)
    JK—Jaffé, *Regesta Pontificum Romanorum*, ed. curavit F. Kaltenbrunner (ad annum 590)
    JL—Jaffé, *Regesta Pontificum Romanorum*, ed. curavit S. Loewenfeld (882-1198)
Mansi—*Sacrorum Conciliorum Nova et Amplissima Collectio*
MPG—*Migne, Patrologia Graeca*
MPL—*Migne, Patrologia Latina*

BIOGRAPHICAL NOTE

Bernard Owens Sullivan was born of William and Mary Sullivan September 28, 1924, in East Saint Louis, Illinois. He there attended Holy Angels Parochial School and Central Catholic High. In September of 1941 he entered Saint Henry's Preparatory Seminary, Belleville, Illinois. He later entered Saint Louis Preparatory Seminary, and finally Kenrick Seminary, where he pursued his studies in philosophy and theology. Having been ordained to the Holy Priesthood on May 28, 1950, by His Excellency, the Most Reverend Albert R. Zuroweste, D. D., Bishop of Belleville, he was engaged in parochial work until the fall of 1951. He then entered the School of Canon Law of the Catholic University of America, Washington, D. C., from which he received the degree of Baccalaureate in Canon Law in June, 1952, and the degree of Licentiate in Canon Law in June, 1953.

CANON LAW STUDIES

349. Bottoms, Rev. Archibald M., J.C.L., The discretionary authority of the ecclesiastical judge in matrimonial trials of the first instance.
350. Kekumano, Rev. Charles A., A.B., J.C.L., The secret archives of the diocesan curia.
351. McGrath, Rev. Robert Eamon, O.M.I., J.C.L., The local superior in non-exempt clercial congregations.
352. McManus, Rev. Frederick Richard, A.B., J.C.L., The Congregation of Sacred Rites.
353. Rodimer, Rev. Frank J., A.B., S.T.L., J.C.L., The canonical effects of infamy of fact.
354. Rouillard, Rev. Jacques, A.B., Ph.B., J.C.L., Une étude comparée du droit canonique et du droit civil paroissal de la Province de Québec dans l'administration des biens paroissaux.
355. Ryan, Rev. Thomas C., J.C.L., The juridical effects of the *sanatio in radice*.
356. Sullivan, Rev. Bernard Owens, J.C.L., Legislation and requirements for permissible cohabitation in invalid marriages.
357. Tatarczuk, Rev. Vincent Anthony, A.B., S.T.L., J.C.L., Infamy of law.

For a complete list of the available numbers of this series apply to the Catholic University of America Press, 620 Michigan Ave., N.E., Washington 17, D. C., for a general catalogue.

CPSIA information can be obtained at www.ICGtesting.com
Printed in the USA
BVOW07*1140191214

379714BV00001B/4/P